Witchcraft and Colonial Rule in Kenya, 1900–1955

Focusing on colonial Kenya, this book shows how conflicts between state authorities and Africans over witchcraft-related crimes provided an important space in which the meanings of justice, law, and order in the empire were debated. Katherine Luongo discusses the emergence of imperial networks of knowledge about witchcraft. She then demonstrates how colonial concerns about witchcraft produced an elaborate body of jurisprudence about capital crimes. The book analyzes the legal wrangling that produced the Witchcraft Ordinances in the 1910s, the birth of an anthro-administrative complex surrounding witchcraft in the 1920s, the hotly contested Wakamba Witch Trials of the 1930s, the explosive growth of legal opinion on witch-murder in the 1940s, and the unprecedented state-sponsored cleansings of witches and Mau Mau adherents during the 1950s. A work of anthropological history, this book develops an ethnography of Kamba witchcraft or *uoi*.

Katherine Luongo received her Ph.D. from the University of Michigan, Ann Arbor. In 2003–2004, she held a Fulbright-Hays Fellowship to conduct archival and ethnographic research in Kenya and was a research associate at the Institut Français de Recherche en Afrique in Nairobi. Currently, she is an assistant professor of history at Northeastern University in Boston. Luongo's articles have appeared in *History in Africa*, *African Affairs*, the *Journal of Eastern African Studies*, and the *Cahiers d'études africaines*. Her research and teaching interests include the occult, legal systems, and anthropological history.

AFRICAN STUDIES

The African Studies series, founded in 1968, is a prestigious series of monographs, general surveys, and textbooks on Africa covering history, political science, anthropology, economics, and ecological and environmental issues. The series seeks to publish work by senior scholars as well as the best new research.

EDITORIAL BOARD

David Anderson, *University of Oxford*
Catherine Boone, *University of Texas at Austin*
Carolyn Brown, *Rutgers University*
Christopher Clapham, *University of Cambridge*
Michael Gomez, *New York University*
Nancy J. Jacobs, *Brown University*
Richard Roberts, *Stanford University*
David Robinson, *Michigan State University*
Leonardo A. Villalón, *University of Florida*

A list of books in this series will be found at the end of this volume.

Witchcraft and Colonial Rule in Kenya, 1900–1955

KATHERINE LUONGO
Northeastern University

CAMBRIDGE
UNIVERSITY PRESS

32 Avenue of the Americas, New York NY 10013-2473, USA

Cambridge University Press is part of the University of Cambridge.

It furthers the University's mission by disseminating knowledge in the pursuit of education, learning and research at the highest international levels of excellence.

www.cambridge.org
Information on this title: www.cambridge.org/9781107529847

© Katherine Luongo 2011

This publication is in copyright. Subject to statutory exception and to the provisions of relevant collective licensing agreements, no reproduction of any part may take place without the written permission of Cambridge University Press.

First published 2011
First paperback edition 2015

A catalogue record for this publication is available from the British Library

Library of Congress Cataloguing in Publication data
Luongo, Katherine, 1975–
Witchcraft and colonial rule in Kenya, 1900–1955 / Katherine Luongo.
   p. cm.
Includes bibliographical references and index.
ISBN 978-1-107-01218-9 (hardback)
1. Witchcraft – Kenya – History – 20th century.   2. Witchcraft – Political aspects – Kenya – History – 20th century.   3. Kamba (African people) – History – 20th century.   4. British – Kenya – History – 20th century.
5. Colonial administrators – Kenya – History – 20th century.
6. Trials (Witchcraft) – Kenya – History – 20th century.
7. Witchcraft – Law and legislation – Kenya – History – 20th century.
8. Kenya – Colonial influence.   9. Kenya – Politics and government –
To 1963.   10. Kenya – Social life and customs – 20th century.   I. Title.
BF1584.K4L86   2012
133.4′30967620904–dc22   2011015310

ISBN 978-1-107-01218-9 Hardback
ISBN 978-1-107-52984-7 Paperback

Cambridge University Press has no responsibility for the persistence or accuracy of URLs for external or third-party internet websites referred to in this publication, and does not guarantee that any content on such websites is, or will remain, accurate or appropriate.

For My Parents

Contents

List of Photographs		*page* x
Acknowledgments		xi
1.	Introduction	1
2.	Clans and Councils, Caravans and Conquest, Cosmology and Colonialism: Ukambani in the Late Nineteenth and Early Twentieth Centuries	29
3.	Understanding *Uoi*, *Uwe*, and *Kithitu* in Ukambani	45
4.	The "Cosmology" of the Colonial State	71
5.	The Wakamba Witch Trials: A Witch-Murder in 1930s Kenya	98
6.	Witchcraft, Murder, and Death Sentences after *Rex v. Kumwaka*	129
7.	The World of Oathing and Witchcraft in Mau Mau–era Machakos	158
8.	Cleansing Ukambani Witches	183
9.	Epilogue	207
Glossary		219
Bibliography		221
Index		237

Photographs

1. A street in Machakos Town named after the Kamba prophet who is reputed to have predicted the arrival of the British in Kenya — *page* 31
2. A Kamba diviner in her Kibera home and place of business — 60
3. British and Kamba authorities at a Machakos witch-cleansing, circa 1955 — 189
4. Burning Witchcraft in Mau Mau–era Machakos — 194

Acknowledgments

A project such as this is only possible with the support of numerous individuals and institutions. I could not have imagined a better mentor than David William Cohen, whose thoughtfulness as a scholar, a teacher, and a person demonstrates the best "way-of-being-in-the-world." Frederick Cooper has always seriously considered my questions and ideas without telling me *what* to think. His scholarship has been a consistent source of intellectual excitement and his judicious advice about how to sharpen my perceptions and prose was never far from my mind in writing this book. Mamadou Diouf has directed me in how to delve deeply into context and in how to find the joy in the process of writing. Ann Laura Stoler's work has provided important "aha!" moments. I am also grateful to the following professors: Jane Burbank, Fernando Coronil, Nancy Rose Hunt, and Sonya Rose. I was lucky to have the following people as classmates and friends at the University of Michigan: Grace Davie, Andrew Ivaska, Caroline Jeannerat, Molly Michelmore, Vanessa Noble, Grace Okrah, Monica Patterson, and Katharine Worboys Izsak.

At the University of Iowa Jim Giblin and Paul Greenough introduced me to the worlds of "peasant intellectuals" and subalterns who might, or might not, be able to speak. During my undergraduate days at Vanderbilt, Michael Bess's careful comments on my writing laid a solid foundation for all my subsequent work with words. I also benefited greatly from the teachings of Joyce Chaplin, James Epstein, and Frank Wcislo.

Numerous gifted scholars have inspired and assisted me. Adam Ashforth, Florence Bernault, Diane Ciekawy, Peter Geschiere, and Harry West each shaped my work on witchcraft in important ways. Richard

Waller has proved an invaluable guide in navigating the supernatural state of twentieth-century Kenya. Each chapter of this book bears the mark of his unfailing generosity and astute criticism. I first "met" Richard Roberts through his work on law in Africa, which sparked my interest in using legal sources to do social history. In recent years, Richard has provided me with constructive criticism and with opportunities to present and to publish, all of which have greatly facilitated my scholarly development. His encouragement and guidance were central to the completion of the manuscript.

I also owe intellectual and personal debts to several scholars of Kenya. David Anderson has been central to the success of this project on many levels. His work helped shape my thinking on the sociolegal history of Kenya. Dave also offered important advice on the practicalities of research in the Kenya National Archives and the Public Record Office, introduced me to his Ph.D. students, and fielded my endless questions about all things Kenyan. His constructive critiques over the last eight years have undoubtedly made my work better.

The work of Bruce Berman and John Lonsdale continues to be highly instructive as does that of Derek Peterson. Timothy Parsons's and Myles Osborne's research offered fresh avenues through which to approach Kamba history. Before I met them, Brett Shadle and Lynn Thomas inspired me through their creative scholarship on law in East Africa. I am happy to be able to count them now as friends.

The young scholars of Africa with whom I've worked and played over the last decade have been essential not simply to the realization of this book, but to my professional development overall. During fieldwork in Kenya and subsequently, Daniel Branch, Elizabeth Campbell, Jolene and Matthew Carotenuto, Nic Cheeseman, Miatta Fahnbulleh, Gabrielle Lynch, Gerard McCann, and Harsha Thirumurthy have proved the best of companions and collaborators. I also appreciate Stacey Hynd and François Grignon for generously sharing their respective research on the death penalty in East Africa and Kamba oathing.

I am grateful to the British Institute in Eastern Africa (BIEA) and the Institut Français de Recherche en Afrique (IFRA) for welcoming me during 2004. At the BIEA, Andrew Burton and Justin Willis kindly shared their expertise in the histories of Kenya and of criminality. As director of IFRA, Bernard Charlery de la Masselière did me the invaluable favors of providing me a place to write and including me in an intellectual community that was "good to think with" – although my efforts to think in French continue to fall short. Hélène Charton-Bigot and Judi-Lyn Rabar reinforced IFRA's *accueil chaleureux*. Thanks also go to the University of Nairobi Department of History and Milcah Achola for granting me an affiliation. The Office of the President, Government of Kenya, provided research clearance.

Staff at the Kenya National Archives made research an enjoyable and fruitful undertaking. I am especially grateful to Peterson Githuka for doggedly hunting down even the most obscure file and for introducing me to John Nottingham who generously spoke with me at length about his experiences in Kenya's colonial administration. In Machakos, the hospitality of Cyprian Kavivya and his family made my first foray into anthropological fieldwork a wholly positive experience. I also thank Cyprian for sharing his own research on Kamba witchcraft and for recommending Josephat Mbithi wa Mutunga as a research assistant. Mutunga's initiative in organizing interviews as well as the energy and care he brought to the intense labor of simultaneous translation were essential to the success of this project. His unfailing good nature in enduring the long hikes, the even longer country bus trips, and the countless plates of *ugali* and *sukuma* interspersed among our interview appointments was much appreciated.

During various sojourns in Africa, Europe, and the United States over the last decade, the following people offered indispensable companionship, hospitality, and support: Cedric Barnes, Jasmin Bhanji, Jim Brennan, Anne-Sophie Brouillot, Fred Chilcott, Anne-Lyse Coutin, Marie-Ange Goux, Jean Huchon, Sloan Mahone, Matthieu Miralles, and Dmitri van den Bersselaar.

Hervé Maupeu has been an unstinting supporter of this project since my first tentative efforts to present my findings on Kamba witchcraft at the BIEA-IFRA conference on criminality in 2002. Since then he has become a dear friend. I am especially grateful for everything he did to facilitate my research during the year that we overlapped in Nairobi. His generous invitation to spend part of the autumn of 2008 in residence at the Centre de Recherche et d'Etude sur les Pays d'Afrique Orientale in Pau gave me the literal and figurative space to write.

Raja Adal, Timothy Brown, and Ilham Khuri-Makdisi provided critical advice and materials and even more essential friendship and encouragement during the later stages of writing. Friends who kindly listened to me explain the intricacies of the Kenya Penal Code and who sweetly insisted that I needed to get out more also deserve heartfelt thanks: Ned Bertz, Nahomi Ichino, David Lenter, Amanda Moniz, Barbara Soukup, Lane Summers, Charissa Threat, and Karin Vélez.

At Northeastern University, Bill Fowler and Laura Frader provided helpful advice. Students in my graduate seminars in Anthro-History and in African History, especially during 2009–2010, renewed my excitement about African history at critical junctures in the revision process. Ethan Hawkley, Andrew Jarboe, Andrew Kuech, and Joshua Sooter contributed invaluable assistance in proofreading the manuscript.

I would also like to express my deep gratitude to the anonymous readers who applied careful, considered attention to the manuscript's shortcomings and strengths. Their judicious critiques greatly enhanced the manuscript. Many thanks also go to Eric Crahan at Cambridge University Press for his enthusiasm for the project and for his forbearance throughout the revision process.

Support during coursework, research, and writing was generously provided by a Ford Foundation Crossing Borders Fellowship, a Fulbright-Hays Fellowship, United States Department of Education FLAS and FLEP Fellowships, and an American Historical Association Bernadotte Schmitt Grant, as well as fellowships and grants provided by the University of Michigan Center for Afro-American and African Studies, the University of Michigan History Department, the University of Michigan International Institute, the University of Michigan Rackham Graduate School, and Northeastern University. The publishers of the *Cahiers d'études africaines*, *History in Africa*, and the *Journal of Eastern African Studies* graciously provided permission to reproduce materials published in those journals in Chapters 6 and 8 and in the epilogue. All faults and failings that remain are my responsibility alone.

My greatest debt is of course to my parents, Angelo and Catherine, whose love and support have made everything possible. This book is as much theirs as it is mine.

Boston 2011

I

Introduction

"FICTIVE NARRATIVES" IN COLONIAL EAST AFRICA

Before embarking on her well-known series of autobiographical novels, the white Kenyan writer Elspeth Huxley was the author of a cycle of crime novels set in Chania, a fictional East African colony modeled on interwar-era Kenya. In her 1937 mystery, *Murder at Government House*, the plot of which centered on the strangling of Chania's governor, Huxley included a lengthy, elaborate anecdote about another high-profile murder case in the colony, the "Wabenda witchcraft case."[1] Chania's secretary for Native Affairs recounted the local narrative of the "Wabenda witchcraft case" to the detective in charge of investigating the governor's murder:

> The Wabenda, among whom witchcraft was more strongly entrenched than among most Chania tribes, had put to death an old woman, who, they alleged, was a witch. The woman had stood trial before the elders and the chiefs of the tribe, had been subjected to a poison ordeal, and found guilty of causing the death of one of the head chief's wives and the deformity of two of his children. Then, following the custom of the tribe, she had been executed, in a slow and painful manner.... It was a horrible death, but meted out after due trial, and for the most anti-social crime in the Wabenda calendar.[2]

After outlining the circumstances surrounding the witch-killing, the secretary for Native Affairs turned to how Wabenda and British

---

[1] Elspeth Huxley, *Murder at Government House* (1937. Reprint, London: J. M. Dent and Sons, 1987), 56.
[2] Ibid.

conceptions and processes of justice collided in the context of the case. He elaborated,

> The chiefs and elders were put on trial for the murder of the old witch. Forty-five of them appeared in the dock – a special dock built for the occasion. They did not deny that the witch had died under their instructions. They claimed that in ordering her death they were protecting the tribe from sorcery, in accordance with their obligations and traditions. They were found guilty and condemned to death. There was no alternative under British law; the judges who pronounced sentence did so with reluctance and disquiet.[3]

But as the secretary for Native Affairs noted, the "Wabenda witchcraft case" was not easily resolved by the sentencing of the forty-five Wabenda in the British courts. He noted,

> The Government was in an awkward position. It could not, obviously, execute forty-five respectable old men, many of them appointed to authority and trusted by the Government, who had acted in good faith and according to the customs of their fathers. In the end it had compromised. Thirty-four of the elders had been reprieved and pardoned. Ten had been reprieved and sentenced to terms of imprisonment. In one case, that of the senior chief who had supervised the execution, the death sentence had been allowed to stand.[4]

Finally, the secretary for Native Affairs addressed some of the ways in which the case was figured in additional "judicial settings"; in the Supreme Court of Chania, in the governor's Privy Council, and in the equally salient "courts of opinion" of various metropolitan and Chanian publics.[5] He explained,

> The case was not yet over. The sentenced chief, M'bola, had appealed to the Supreme Court, lost, and finally appealed to the Privy Council. Feeling in native areas ran high. Agitators had seized upon the case as an example of the tyranny and brutality of British rule. Administrators feared serious troubles should it be carried out.[6]

The detective to whom the story of the case had been addressed nodded in assent to the secretary's explanations, noting that the events were "familiar" to him as well as to "every European in the colony."[7]

---

[3] Ibid.
[4] Ibid.
[5] David William Cohen and E. S. Atieno Odhiambo, *Burying SM: The Politics of Knowledge and the Sociology of Power in Africa* (Portsmouth, NH: Heinemann, 1992), 11.
[6] Huxley, *Murder*, 57.
[7] Ibid.

At first glance, the description of a witch-killing and the administrative-judicial dilemmas it invited may seem to be something of a literary non sequitur in a novel otherwise in keeping with the general conventions of genre and period. Within the strict context of *Murder at Government House*, the story of the "Wabenda witchcraft case" operates loosely as a plot device to forward the metanarrative of the simmering unrest that serves as the backdrop to the governor's strangling. Nonetheless, the inclusion of such an elaborate anecdote invites questions about the "culturally reasonable conjecture" that Huxley would have been able to ascribe to her readers.[8] What sort of knowledge would British readers in Kenya and the metropole have brought to bear on their readings of these events in Chania? Why would a story of witchcraft, law, and the colonies have resonated with British reading publics at home and abroad?

As was the case with the secretary for Native Affairs and the detective, the events of the "Wabenda witchcraft case" would likely have seemed familiar to Huxley's audience because the fictional events mirrored the terms of the most high-profile witch-killing case of the colonial era, the "Wakamba Witch Trials," which had taken place in Kenya fewer than six years before the publication of Huxley's novel. The Wakamba case, in turn, formed part of a long-standing, circuitous, imperial story of African witchcraft beliefs and practices challenging the ability of colonial states to achieve law and order in the British African Empire.

In the course of the 1931–1932 Wakamba Witch Trials, sixty Wakamba men were sentenced to death in Kenya's highest court for killing a neighbor woman whom they believed to have been a "witch." Like the fictional Wabenda, Kamba people carried (from the perspectives of black Kenyans and white colonials alike) a reputation as being steeped in witchcraft and, although the Wakamba Witch Trials did not necessitate the construction of a special dock, the number of participants exceeded the capacity of the Supreme Court and proceedings were played out in the theater of Nairobi's Railway Social Institute.[9] Like their fictional counterparts, defendants in the Wakamba Witch Trials asserted that they had done nothing wrong in killing the alleged witch but, instead, had been carrying out *king'ole*, the Kamba institution of justice directed against social malefactors like recidivist witches and thieves.

---

[8] Ann Laura Stoler, "'In Cold Blood': Hierarchies of Credibility and the Politics of Colonial Narratives," *Representations* 37 (1992): 53.
[9] "A Strange Setting for a Murder Trial," *East African Standard (EAS)*, 2 February 1932.

However, under the 1930 Kenya Penal Code, the justices had no other recourse than to sentence the sixty Kamba men to death. Like the Wabenda chief, M'bola, the Kamba men appealed their case, but the Court of Appeal for Eastern Africa struck down the appeal while recommending clemency to the Governor-in-Council who ultimately overturned the death sentences, substituting varying terms of hard labor. Although neither oral nor written sources offer a record of Kamba people's reactions to the Wakamba Witch Trials, a range of documents reveals that the Wakamba Witch Trials formed the nucleus of widespread, virulent debates in Kenya and the metropole over what constituted justice, law, and order in the African Empire.

As events in Chania were tied into a wider context of witchcraft-related unrest, so did the Wakamba Witch Trials form the center of a broader situation of witchcraft-driven disorder in Kenya. While the Wakamba Witch Trials stood out because of the unprecedented number of defendants and the resultant international attention that the court proceedings garnered, the basic circumstances surrounding the case were by no means unique or even atypical in the bureaucratic annals of colonial Kenya. Indeed, from the beginning of the colonial period to the eve of independence, colonial documents are replete with discussions of witchcraft beliefs and practices and their relationship to disorder. Taking the Wakamba Witch Trials as a starting point, this book demonstrates the ways in which an anthrohistorical analysis of witchcraft "in a small part of Africa" can tell us broad stories about the messy intersections of culture and crime, violence and law, the state and the supernatural.[10]

Despite the furor they produced during the 1930s and their lasting impact on Kenyan jurisprudence, the Wakamba Witch Trials have been generally neglected in historiography. Yet this neglect is largely unsurprising for a variety of reasons. First, witchcraft in Africa, formerly the domain of anthropologists, has only recently emerged as an area of inquiry for historians, particularly those concerned with the development of colonial states. Second, witchcraft in areas outside the Kenyan coast has been of little interest to social scientists working on Kenya. And third, historiography on Kenya has overlooked Kamba people, places, and things as scholars have focused on the more politically powerful Kikuyu, Luo, and Kalenjin groups.

---

[10] Richard Rathbone, *Murder and Politics in Colonial Ghana* (New Haven: Yale University Press, 1993), 1.

In contrast, this book breaks with such historiographical trends by treating contests over crimes related to witchcraft among the Kamba as a central, critical means by which to investigate and understand the construction of state power in Kenya. It argues that the continuous problem of violence related to witchcraft has consistently posed practical and epistemological challenges to the state's authority from the early twentieth century to the present day. This book traces the development and refinement of anti-witchcraft law and anthro-administrative practice in the opening decades of colonial rule, examines the local and empire-wide ramifications of the Wakamba Witch Trials, analyzes case law and sentencing protocols in World War II-era cases of witch-killing, details how and why colonial authorities ultimately broke with the long-standing policy of *not* officially engaging witchcraft-related methods and actors to combat witchcraft-driven challenges to state authority during the Mau Mau era, and traces the contemporary reach and resonance of witchcraft.

Accordingly, the following core questions frame this study: What sorts of practices and beliefs has witchcraft encompassed? How has witchcraft operated as a category of understanding for state officials and Africans? How has the state developed and brought to bear anthro-administrative knowledge of witchcraft? How were witchcraft-related criminal cases used by the state to define violence and to designate those who could employ it legitimately?

THE LEXICOGRAPHY OF WITCHCRAFT, *UOI*, AND *UWE*

Writing on reproduction in the Congo, Nancy Rose Hunt traces the development of a "colonial lexicon," a compilation of the vocabularies and vernaculars tied up in the shifting ways that Congolese women have negotiated state interventions into pregnancy, parturiency, and parenthood during the twentieth century.[11] The colonial lexicon, Hunt writes, offers "a vocabulary list open to abstract, bodily, and spiritual [phenomena]," words that were "alive as speech in a context of language and colonial power, a context of complex hierarchies and differential translations."[12] In Hunt's analysis, colonial and Congolese vocabularies pertaining to reproduction reflected not only how birth rituals were changing but also how the terms of debate surrounding reproduction shaped outcomes.

---

[11] Nancy Rose Hunt, *A Colonial Lexicon of Birth Ritual, Medicalization, and Mobility in the Congo* (Durham: Duke University Press, 1999), 12.

[12] Ibid.

Accordingly, this book attends to the significance of the *terms* through which colonial and Kamba actors struggled over witchcraft. While dead and damaged bodies produced by competing forms of juridical violence offered the primary focal points of colonial and Kamba contests about witchcraft, these contests hinged on living, lexical words. Each side had its own vocabularies for talking about invisible malevolence (and its remedies): the "supernatural," "magic," and "witchcraft" in English, and *uoi* and *uwe* in Kikamba. Both regarded witchcraft as wrapped up in discursive violence. Colonial authorities read the witchcraft accusation as violent. Kamba people regarded the thought and spoken words necessary to mobilize *uoi* as violent. As the following chapters demonstrate, these competing perspectives and their corresponding articulations emerged in especially high relief in the space of the courts as British authorities developed vocabularies to entrap and contain the complexities of witchcraft in flattened administrative and legal discourse while Kamba people, in turn, wrestled to translate the perilous experiences "of living in a world with witches" from their own nuanced lexicon into a language that had insufficient words.[13]

The terms through which Kamba people have understood and discussed the people, powers, and objects glossed as the "supernatural," "magic," and "witchcraft" in the colonial lexicon have been significant to the sociopolitics of twentieth-century Kenya. Kamba discourse has readily employed *uoi* and *uwe*, Kikamba words loosely translatable as "witchcraft-for-harm" and "witchcraft-for-healing."[14] Eschewing the sharp binaries drawn by "black magic" versus "white magic," each Kikamba term carries the implicit understanding that neither can ever be completely severed from the other.[15]

Further, *uoi* and *uwe* entail subtleties collapsed by the catchall "witchcraft" or the blanketing "supernatural." Colonial-era documents and contemporary ethnography concur that *uoi* has existed in two basic varieties, embodied and "bought," and that while embodied *uoi* has been

---

[13] Adam Ashforth, "On Living in a World with Witches: Everyday Epistemology and Spiritual Insecurity in a Modern African City (Soweto)," in *Magical Interpretations, Material Realities: Modernity, Witchcraft, and the Occult in Postcolonial Africa*, ed. Henrietta L. Moore and Todd Sanders (London: Routledge, 2001), 206.

[14] This book employs the terms *uoi* and *uwe* in discussing Kamba attitudes, actions, and objects; it uses the "supernatural," "magic," and "witchcraft" in discussing colonial ones. In doing so, it consistently underscores the contested, contingent character of colonial terms and engages the subtleties of Kamba ones.

[15] Harry G. West, *Kupilikula: Governance and the Invisible Realm in Mozambique* (Chicago: University of Chicago Press, 2005), 7.

practiced primarily by post-pubescent women who have mobilized an inborn capacity, the bought variety, requiring paraphernalia, has been used by adults of both sexes.

In contrast to the undefined "witchcraft," *uoi* has entailed a complex nomenclature corresponding to how *uoi* has affected its victim. For example, the sort of *uoi* alleged in the course of the Wakamba Witch Trials to have been deployed by the deceased is called *ndia* in Kikamba. The practitioner's envy has been typically regarded as driving the exercise of all varieties of *uoi*.

Uwe, in turn, has carried more complexity than "witchcraft" or even "white magic." *Uwe* has been conceptualized as a vocation requiring inborn power, external paraphernalia, and a significant period of apprenticeship in how to use both. The primary work of *uwe*, carried out by male and female specialists, has been identifying the origins of *uoi* and treating its ill effects.

For Kamba people, *uoi* and *uwe* have been both lived realities and ways of making order out of disorder. Writing on "witchcraft," or *uwavi*, in postcolonial Mozambique, Harry West explains that *uwavi* is a "discursive genre" through which the Muedan people have "comprehended and – even if euphemistically – commented upon the workings of power in their midst."[16] In Ukambani, *uoi* and *uwe* have worked similarly as a discursive genre, *uoi* situating and naming particular kinds of "badness" and *uwe* (sometimes) proffering remedies.[17]

West rightly cautions that to overstate the discursive aspect of witchcraft risks eliding the lived realities of witchcraft.[18] Among Kamba people, *uoi* and *uwe* discourse has lent coherency, shape, and voice to the fraught *experiences* brought about by "living in a world with witches."[19] Experience and expression have been enmeshed with belief and knowledge.

In the Kamba context, what mobilizes a knowledge of *uoi* and *uwe* – whether it be the knowledge that *uoi* or *uwe* resides in one's own body or in the instructions accompanying the paraphernalia one has obtained – is

---

[16] Harry G. West, *Ethnographic Sorcery* (Chicago: University of Chicago Press, 2007), 11. For an analysis of how Maragoli widows have made sense of and interacted with power through the sentimental discourse of *kehenda mwoyo* during the twentieth century, see, Kenda Mutongi, *Worries of the Heart: Widows, Family, and Community in Kenya* (Chicago: University of Chicago Press, 2007).

[17] James Howard Smith, *Bewitching Development: Witchcraft and the Reinvention of Development in Neoliberal Kenya* (Chicago: University of Chicago Press, 2008), 5.

[18] West, *Ethnographic Sorcery*, 24.

[19] Ashforth, "On Living," 206.

belief in the efficacy of *uoi* and *uwe*. Further, many people who claim to have no direct knowledge of *uoi* and *uwe* themselves readily believe that others do and that each variety works. Overall, completing the cycle of efficacy is Kamba people's belief in the "knowledge" that they share their environment with malevolent actors who can and do deploy invisible powers against ordinary people and with benevolent actors who harness invisible powers to undo *uoi*. Thus, as Adam Ashforth cogently explains in writing on witchcraft in twentieth-century South Africa, "The point is not *that* they believe, but what they believe, how they believe it, and with what consequences for the conduct of their lives."[20]

Throughout the first half of the twentieth century, "witchcraft," the "supernatural," and "magic" were key terms in the lexicon that colonial actors employed in describing and analyzing sociopolitical situations in Kenya and across the British African Empire more generally. "Supernatural," widely conceptualized as unseen power, offered colonial authorities a broad rubric under which to lump a range of "local" attitudes, actions, and actors that they could not otherwise effectively manage or efficiently explain away. And within the African imperial context, colonial characterizations of someone or something "supernatural" did dismissive work as well, distinguishing the supernatural person, practice, or object from the nexus of the normal/natural/visible valorized by a colonial power-knowledge complex centered on "reason" and "science."[21]

Colonial actors also frequently employed the term "magic" when describing and analyzing local beliefs and practices or when characterizing local people whom they had difficulty disciplining and whose powers they aimed to ultimately deny. In colonial discourse, magic stood for the wielding of power attributable to supernatural forces or to the use of means imbued with such power. Further, magic was typically modified as "black," that is, "harmful," or more infrequently as "white," that is, "healing." In either instance, the term "magic," like "supernatural," did

---

[20] Adam Ashforth, *Witchcraft, Violence and Democracy in South Africa* (Chicago: University of Chicago Press, 2005), 122.
[21] See Georges Canguillhem, *The Normal and the Pathological* (New York: Zone Books, 1991), 125. In a discussion of "the normal" he writes, "(1) normal is that which is such that it ought to be; (2) normal, in the most usual sense of the word, is that which is met with in the majority of cases of a determined kind, or that which constitutes either the average or standard of a measurable characteristic. In the discussion of these meanings it has been pointed out how ambiguous this term is since it designates at once a fact and 'a value attributed to this fact by the person speaking, by virtue of an evaluative judgment for which he takes responsibility'."

evaluative work, distancing magical people, practices, and objects from the "disenchantment" of modernity.[22]

In colonial parlance, "witchcraft" denoted an embodied capacity, an object, or a practice that mobilized an invisible, malevolent power in order to harm the person, psyche, property, or kin of another. Less often, colonial actors used "witchcraft" to mark the abilities, modes, and means used to counter the effects of malevolent "witchcraft" as described. "Witchcraft" was mobilized in much the same way as "supernatural" and "magic," marking people and practices as irrational and atavistic. It also bore another layer of meaning, indicating the violence that witchcraft ineluctably wrought or remedied.

Overall, witchcraft was a discursive genre for colonial authorities too. While these officials discounted the ability of witches to actually do magic, they recognized the power of the *beliefs* in the efficacy of supernatural practitioners and their concomitant powers to challenge the authority of the state. Witchcraft thus offered intelligibility, form, and articulation to what might be termed "official misfortune" – the inability to establish order and implement policy – occasioned by "living in a world with witches."[23] This book's anthro-historical analyses of witchcraft as a matrix of discourse, experience, knowledge, and belief for black Kenyans *and* for colonial authorities alike constitutes one of its primary interventions into the literatures on witchcraft and on governance in Africa.

HISTORIC AND HISTORIOGRAPHIC CONTEXTS

This book originates from a question posed by a Labour member of Parliament (MP) to the secretary of state for the Colonies in the House of Commons in 1932, asking about the fate of sixty Wakamba men sentenced to death for the murder of an alleged witch in Kenya.[24] Tracing the circumstances surrounding this passing question led to an ever-widening web of evidence about the prevalence and significance of witchcraft-driven

---

[22] Michael D. Bailey, "The Disenchantment of Magic: Spells, Charms, and Superstition in Early European Witchcraft Literature," *American Historical Review* 111.2 (April 2006): 383. In his historical analysis of the Weberian thesis of Western "disenchantment," Bailey writes, "Magic and cultural perceptions of the magical occupy a critical place particularly in sociological and anthropological conceptions of modernity, and issues of 'magical thought' and 'superstition' in opposition to 'scientific rationalism' frame discussions not only of the modern West but of instances in which Western modernity confronts the traditional beliefs and practices of other world cultures."

[23] Ashforth, "On Living," 206.

[24] House of Commons Debates. 10 February 1932. Volume 261. 857–858.

challenges to state authority in the British African Empire. Using conflicts over witchcraft as a lens, this book makes important contributions to and interventions in scholarship on administrative policy and practice, law and order, and the constitution and deployment of anthropological knowledge spanning Kenya and across British Africa more generally. It is also the first monograph-length treatment of Kamba history in more than thirty-five years and offers a rare historical treatment of witchcraft, a subject most often the domain of anthropologists.[25]

Scholarship on colonial governmentality in Africa and elsewhere has demonstrated that far from being hegemonic, administrative control was often contradictory, tenuous, and ad hoc.[26] The objects, technologies, applications, effects, and appropriateness of administrative control were sites of struggle.[27] This was certainly the case in the British African Empire where the Lugardian model of Indirect Rule – a system in which British rule was to be effected through African institutions and African intermediaries overseen by British officials – ultimately tasked colonial officials with instituting, in Sara Berry's famous phrase, "hegemony on a shoestring."[28]

In Kenya, a settler colony, the multifarious sociopolitical "fissures" existing around "race, class, and clan" further complicated the colonial situation.[29] As Bruce Berman and John Lonsdale have ably demonstrated,

[25] J. Forbes Munro, *Colonial Rule and the Kamba: Social Change in the Kenya Highlands, 1889–1939* (London: Oxford University Press, 1975). On "witchcraft," see John Middleton and E. H. Winter, eds., *Witchcraft and Sorcery in East Africa* (London: Routledge and Kegan Paul, 1963).

[26] Ann Laura Stoler and Frederick Cooper, "Beyond Metropole and Colony: Rethinking a Research Agenda," in *Tensions of Empire: Colonial Cultures in a Bourgeois World*, ed. Ann Laura Stoler and Frederick Cooper (Berkeley: University of California Press, 1997), 1–57. See also, Nicholas Dirks, ed., *Colonialism and Culture* (Ann Arbor: University of Michigan Press, 2004).

[27] David Scott, "Colonial Governmentality," *Social Text* 43 (1995): 191–219; Peter Pels, "The Anthropology of Colonialism: Culture, History, and the Emergence of Western Governmentality," *Annual Review of Anthropology* 26 (1997): 168–183. Clifton Crais, ed., *The Culture of Power in Southern Africa: Essays on State Formation and Political Imagination* (Portsmouth, NH: Heinemann, 2003).

[28] Sara Berry, "Hegemony on a Shoestring: Indirect Rule and Access to Agricultural Land," *Africa* 62.3 (1992): 327–355. See also, Frederick Lugard, *The Dual Mandate in British Tropical Africa* (London: W. Blackwood and Sons, 1922).

[29] Bruce Berman and John Lonsdale, *Unhappy Valley, Conflict in Kenya and Africa, Book One: State and Class* (Oxford: James Currey, 1992), 2. See also, Bruce Berman, *Control and Crisis in Colonial Kenya: The Dialectic of Domination* (Nairobi: East African Educational Publishers, 1990), 67–69. M. Georges Balandier, "The Colonial Situation: A Theoretical Approach," in *Africa: Social Problems of Change and Conflict*, ed. Pierre L. Van den Berghe (San Francisco: Chandler, 1965), 34–61.

the broad, formalized forces of "state-building" and the "anonymous," individuated forces of "state-formation" collided in Kenya and in turn precipitated a model of governance that aimed to negotiate "the imperatives of accumulation and control, metropolitan and indigenous interests, exploitation and material rewards, coercion and collaboration."[30] This book demonstrates that witchcraft was a key locus of struggles over authority among and between black and white populations both in Kenya and across the British African Empire more generally, conflicts that in turn extended to metropole. Witchcraft in Kenya was closely imbricated in state-building, as the colonial administration endeavored through the development of a power-knowledge complex rooted in anthropology and via the elaboration of law, to extend its coercive capacities over local cultural and juridical forms related to witchcraft. At the same moment, witchcraft was a central arena of state-formation as the achievement of the goals of governance was challenged by the witchcraft beliefs, knowledge, and practices of countless, often anonymous, black Kenyans.

As Berman notes, "The key elements of bureaucratic 'work' consist largely of the collection and analysis of information leading to the selection and implementation of programmes of action or 'policies.'"[31] The collection of knowledge about witchcraft in Kenya reflected the bureaucratizing impetus common to colonial administrations in Africa and beyond.[32] In the Kenyan context, this work sometimes increased steadily, occurred at other times in fits and starts, but proceeded apace in the World War II period as the exigencies of the era conspired to move colonial governance toward welfare and development. As Frederick Cooper writes of colonial mentalities at this juncture, "Colonial regimes – in exceptionally frank moments of introspection during and after the war – admitted to themselves that their less interventionist approach to economic change had resulted in woefully inadequate infrastructure, poor educational facilities, inadequate colonial contributions to imperial economies, and anger and discontent among colonial populations."[33] The move toward welfare and development resulted not only in the expansion of the ranks

---

[30] Berman and Lonsdale, *Unhappy Valley I*, 15,163.
[31] Berman, *Crisis and Control*, 88.
[32] On India, see Bernard Cohn, *Colonialism and Its Forms of Knowledge* (Princeton: Princeton University Press, 1996). See also, on Southeast Asia, Ann Laura Stoler, *Along the Archival Grain: Epistemic Anxieties and Colonial Common Sense* (Princeton: Princeton University Press, 2010).
[33] Frederick Cooper, *Decolonization and African Society: The Labor Question in French and British Africa* (Cambridge: Cambridge University Press, 1996), 384.

of colonial administrators but also in the engagement of new cadres of technical experts.[34]

Many of these technical experts, attached to departments like Labour or Agriculture, dealt with the practicalities of "development" – for instance, imagining and implementing projects concerned with things like soil conservation. But the technocratic ranks also included specialists whose valuable expertise resided not in the soil but in the social – government anthropologists and government sociologists. These anthropologists and sociologists were the most highly trained group with the most clearly focused research interests in African societies. The information that they produced broke new ground but also sharpened and augmented the knowledge collected by earlier generations of colonial officers, many of whom acted as amateur "anthro-administrators," cataloguing and working through knowledge about "their" people. These new cadres of technical experts also supplemented and refined the knowledge generated by academic anthropologists who had preceded them in Africa and who had worked in collaboration with but not necessarily under the employ of colonial administrations, or who had studied "colonial" problems like the effects of "detribalization" on African communities.[35]

By tracing the birth and burgeoning of colonial anthropological knowledge and expertise concerning witchcraft in Kenya, this book makes important interventions into the history of colonial knowledge production in Kenya and across the British African Empire. First, it illustrates the progressive synergy of anthropology and administration around the problem of witchcraft in Kenya through six decades of British rule, analyzing how "pioneer" anthro-administrators like C. W. Hobley wrestled with "Bantu beliefs and magic" and how academic anthropologists like Bronislaw Malinowski concerned themselves with witchcraft as a problem of colonial governmentality in Kenya.[36] This book shows how this

---

[34] For a detailed analysis of colonial welfare and development policy and implementation in Kenya, see Joanna Lewis, *Empire and State-building: War and Welfare in Kenya, 1925–1952* (Oxford: James Currey, 2000). For how colonial welfare and development policies contributed to discontents driving Mau Mau, see David Throup, *Economic and Social Origins of Mau Mau, 1945–1953* (Athens: Ohio University Press, 1988). Also, D. A. Low and John M. Lonsdale, "Introduction: Towards the New Order, 1945–1963," in *History of East Africa, Volume III*, ed. D. A. Low and Alison Smith (Oxford: Clarendon Press, 1976), 1–63.

[35] Lyn Schumaker, *Africanizing Anthropology: Fieldwork, Networks, and the Making of Cultural Knowledge in Central Africa* (Durham: Duke University Press, 2001).

[36] C. W. Hobley, *Bantu Beliefs and Magic* (London: Frank Cass, 1922). See also, Chapter 4, this volume.

synergy reached its apex in Ukambani in the mid-1950s as the government sociologist and the local district officer joined forces to imagine and institute a witch-cleansing program targeted to break collaborative ties between Kamba witches and Mau Mau rebels.[37]

Further, this book's critical attention to witchcraft offers insights not only into how and by whom anthro-administrative knowledge was collected but also to the scope and scale of colonial "circuits" of knowledge.[38] Writing on anthro-administrative knowledge in Kenya, Berman highlights the parochial quality of this knowledge and the ad hoc nature of its dissemination.[39] However, by tracing the ways colonial authorities sought to generate "usable" knowledge about witchcraft through the development of an anthro-administrative complex that communicated across British Africa and extended to the metropole, this book brings to the fore the workings of *empire*-wide networks of colonial knowledge. It shows how the circulation of anthro-administrative knowledge about witchcraft policy and practice transpired among administrators across districts, provinces, and colonies as well as between the colonies and the metropole. Overall, it shows how witchcraft was a critical node through which various debates about effective governance in the British African Empire passed.

The issue of what made British justice in an imperial setting was a central strand in these debates. Literature on law and legal systems in Africa has tended to focus on "customary" law. The early compendiums of customary law assembled by anthro-administrators treated customary law as a closed and static system. Subsequent work, undertaken largely by academics in the course of their own research or under the auspices of think tanks or as part of governmental inquiries, pointed in a different direction. This research showed how the new "social situations" of colonialism rendered customary law dating from the precolonial era open to change but did not assign the state an active role in rearticulating and implementing it. In contrast, recent literature has foregrounded the state's role in constituting "customary" law. Martin Chanock has famously argued that customary law was constructed by British officials and "tribal" elders who manipulated each other's understandings of

---

[37] Katherine Luongo, "If You Can't Beat Them, Join Them: Government Cleansings of Witches and Mau Mau in 1950s Kenya," *History in Africa* 33.1 (2006): 451–471. The cleansings are discussed in detail in Chapter 8.
[38] Stoler and Cooper, "Beyond Metropole," 28.
[39] Berman, *Crisis and Control*, 93.

"custom" in order to produce inflexible customary laws that served their respective interests.[40]

Scholarship on Kenya has complicated Chanock's stark formulation. Brett Shadle's work on colonial officials' opposition to codifying customary law demonstrates that such law comprised a flexible body of rules and norms, which predated colonialism, changed according to circumstance, and continued to do so throughout the colonial era.[41] Further, Lynn Thomas's study of sociolegal controversies over female circumcision in Meru and Shadle's analysis of the intertwined social and legal crises over marriage in Gusiiland demonstrate the willingness of colonial officials and Africans – both authorities and ordinary people – to *negotiate* customary law, creating fresh, fluid rules and norms.[42] This book joins such literature through its investigations of the ways in which witchcraft was one of the key arenas where "colonialism changed African law – its rules, institutions, procedures, and meanings" and "affected as well the way African peoples perceived and understood law."[43]

At the same moment, by focusing strongly on *criminal law*, this book departs from the bulk of scholarship on law both in Kenya and across the British African Empire more broadly. Tracing the ways state and local legal systems collided forcefully and frequently around witchcraft-driven crimes, particularly the murders of alleged witches, it breaks with Mahmood Mamdani's contention that "custom" constituted one half of a "bipolar" colonial legal system in which "customary" law and "native" courts governed African affairs while civil law and "metropolitan-style" courts regulated non-natives. Rather, such conflicts around witchcraft

---

[40] Martin Chanock, *Law, Custom and Social Order: The Colonial Experience in Malawi and Zimbabwe* (Portsmouth, NH: Heinemann, 1985). See also, Sally Falk Moore, "Treating Law as Knowledge: Telling Colonial Officers What to Say to Africans about Running 'Their Own' Native Courts," *Journal of History and Society* 26.2 (1992): 11–46.

[41] Brett L. Shadle, "'Changing Traditions to Meet Current Altering Conditions': Customary Law, African Courts and the Rejection of Codification in Kenya, 1930–60," *Journal of African History* 40.3 (1999): 389–411. For a trenchant analysis of the continued salience and malleability of "customary" law in postcolonial Kenyan legal settings, see especially Cohen and Odhiambo, *Burying SM*.

[42] Lynn M. Thomas, *Politics of the Womb: Women, Reproduction, and the State in Kenya* (Berkeley: University of California Press, 2003). Brett L. Shadle, *"Girl Cases": Marriage and Colonialism in Gusiiland, Kenya, 1890–1970* (Portsmouth, NH: Heinemann, 2006). See also, Fiona D. Mackenzie, *Land, Ecology, and Resistance in Kenya, 1880–1952* (Portsmouth, NH: Heinemann, 1998).

[43] Kristin Mann and Richard Roberts, "Law in Colonial Africa," in *Law in Colonial Africa*, ed. Kristin Mann and Richard Roberts (Portsmouth, NH: Heinemann, 1991), 5.

demonstrate how criminal law, its cases fought out in East Africa's highest courts, constituted a central space for governing African affairs.[44]

"Witchcraft" was the "outstanding problem of the lawgiver" in colonial Kenya.[45] This was indeed true whether the "lawgiver" was a British justice sitting on East Africa's highest courts or an elder occupying a slot on a juridical council such as the Kamba *king'ole*. This book illustrates that colonial and local authorities concurred in regarding witchcraft as a serious criminal matter and shows how they differed significantly over the ways witchcraft-driven crimes should be managed. The colonial legal system in Kenya "created new crimes" by criminalizing both the witchcraft accusation, like that put forward by the men tried in the Wakamba Witch Trials, and the often-lethal anti-witchcraft actions of local juridical bodies, like those undertaken by the Kamba *king'ole*, or by individuals claiming to act in the name of local justice.[46] Even if the colonial administration was "decidedly nonhegemonic" and willing to negotiate customary law pertaining to civil matters like marriage, initiation, and land ownership, a careful analysis of colonial jurisprudence surrounding witchcraft-driven crimes shows that colonial officials were decidedly unwilling to cede the state's monopoly over juridical violence.[47]

In adjudicating witchcraft-driven crimes, the colonial state simultaneously retrenched its power through the exercise of "lawfare" and engaged the problem of the mens rea of its "backward" colonial subjects.[48] Through close readings of colonial case law and documents and transcripts from East Africa's highest courts, this book demonstrates that jurisprudence pertaining to witchcraft-driven crimes was a key space in which fundamental legal principles – for instance, "grave and sudden

---

[44] Mahmood Mamdani, *Citizen and Subject: Contemporary Africa and the Legacy of Late Colonialism* (Princeton: Princeton University Press, 1996), 16–23.

[45] Richard Waller, "Witchcraft and the Law in Colonial Kenya," *Past and Present Society* 180.1 (October 2003): 241.

[46] David Killingray, "The Maintenance of Law and Order in British Colonial Africa," *African Affairs* 80 (1986): 413.

[47] Stoler and Cooper, "Beyond Metropole," 22.

[48] John L. and Jean Comaroff explain "lawfare" as a state's "use of its own rules – of its duly enacted penal codes, its administrative law, its states of emergency, its charters and mandates and warrants, its norms of engagement – to impose a sense of order upon its subordinates by means of violence rendered legible, legal, and legitimate by its own sovereign word." John L. and Jean Comaroff, "Law and Disorder in the Postcolony: An Introduction," in *Law and Disorder in the Postcolony*, ed. John L. and Jean Comaroff (Chicago: University of Chicago Press, 2006), 30. See also, Robert B. Seidman, "Mens Rea and the Reasonable African: The Pre-Scientific Worldview and the Mistake of Fact," *International and Comparative Law Quarterly* 15 (1965): 1135–1164.

provocation" and "reasonableness" – were elaborated for application in imperial settings.[49]

The sorts of scenarios articulated above emerged in high relief in Ukambani, the region southeast of Nairobi that today comprises the districts of Machakos and Kitui.[50] The region, sometimes referred to as Kambaland, was one of the first places in Kenya to experience a sustained British presence, beginning in the mid-1880s. Nonetheless, the more arid hills and plains of Ukambani never underwent the same concentrated degree of white settlement as did neighboring Kikuyu areas. Less numerous than their Kikuyu neighbors and largely disinterested in mission education, for the most part the cattle-rich Kamba eschewed both the colonial labor market and anti-colonial politics.[51]

Accordingly, the rather limited anthropological and historical literature on Kamba people, places, and things has tended to focus on either a central moment or a key modality of engagement with the colonial state. First, scholars have addressed the "destocking controversy" of 1938 during which Kamba people launched an ultimately successful campaign, including a protest march to, and organized sit-ins in, Nairobi, protesting the government's order that the "overpopulated" Kamba reserve be "destocked" to prevent soil erosion.[52] Second, literature has also attended to the stereotype of the Kamba as "martial race," and, in a related vein, to Kamba people's employment in the colonial police and military.[53]

---

[49] Katherine Luongo, "Motive Rather than Means: Legal Genealogies of Witch-Killing Cases," *Cahiers d' études africaines* 189–190 (2008): 35–57.

[50] Munro notes, "From 1895 to 1902 the Machakos area was part of an ill-defined Athi district, which also included Kitui; in 1902 the two Kamba Districts separated, the western one becoming Ulu district. In 1920 Ulu district changed its name to the modern form, Machakos district…. Machakos District was part of Ukamba Province (which included Kitui and Kiambu) until 1933, when Ukamba Province amalgamated with Kikuyu Province to form Central Province." Munro, *Colonial Rule*, 54.

[51] Robert L. Tignor, *The Colonial Transformation of Kenya: The Kamba, Kikuyu, and Maasai from 1900–1930* (Princeton: Princeton University Press, 1976).

[52] Robert Tignor, "Kamba Political Protest: The Destocking Controversy of 1938," *International Journal of African Historical Studies* 4.2 (1971): 237–251. Also Fay Gadsen, "Further Notes on the Kamba Destocking Controversy," *International Journal of African Historical Studies* 7.4 (1974): 681–687.

[53] Timothy Parsons argues that the colonial stereotype of the Kamba as a "martial race" was not rooted in "specific pre-colonial military traditions," but was rather "an index in the changing political economy of recruitment." See Timothy Parsons, "'Wakamba Warriors Are Soldiers of the Queen': The Evolution of the Kamba as a Martial Race, 1890–1970," *Ethnohistory* 46.4 (1998): 671. Myles Osbourne takes the opposite position. See Myles Osborne, "Changing Kamba, Making Kenya, 1880–1964" (PhD diss., Harvard University, 2008).

However, despite Kamba people's long-standing, widespread reputation as Kenya's most virulent and efficacious witches and the myriad colonial documents concerned with the supernatural state of Ukambani, both anthropological and historical scholarship have largely overlooked Kamba witchcraft.[54] This book, in contrast, fills those lacunae, offering both a historical ethnography of Kamba *uoi* and *uwe* and a detailed analysis of the interpenetration of witchcraft and governmentality in Kenya. In doing so it also provides important insights into the most widely discussed event in Kenyan history, the anti-colonial Mau Mau rebellion of the 1950s.

Literature on Mau Mau has focused overwhelmingly on Kikuyu people, the principal participants in the rebellion.[55] This anti-colonial insurgency was stoked by black Kenyans' decades of social, political, and economic marginalization under colonial rule and was undertaken by primarily by Kikuyu guerrilla fighters in the forests around Mount Kenya and in Nairobi and its environs.[56] Numerous Kikuyu "loyalists" actively and passively supported the colonial regime, which won the Mau Mau war but ultimately lost the battle to keep Kenya a British colony.[57] Nonetheless, numerous documentary and ethnographic sources indicate that neither Kamba participation in the rebellion nor colonial officials' anxiety about it was negligible or localized.[58]

This book offers an extensive treatment of Mau Mau in Ukambani and breaks new ground by reading Mau Mau among the Kamba as an ineluctably "supernatural" situation. It argues that in the Kamba

---

[54] Work on the Kamba "supernatural" has tended to focus on possession and prophecy movements rather than on Kamba "witchcraft." For example, see Sloan Mahone's engaging analysis of how colonial authorities read Kamba possession and prophecy through the paradigm of "madness." Sloan Mahone, "The Psychology of Rebellion: Colonial Medical Responses to Dissent in British East Africa," *Journal of African History* 47 (2006): 241–258.

[55] F. D. Corfield, *Historical Survey of the Origins and Growth of Mau Mau* (London: Her Majesty's Stationery Office [H.M.S.O.], 1960). See also, David M. Anderson, *Histories of the Hanged: The Dirty War in Kenya and the End of Empire* (New York: W.W. Norton, 2005). Caroline Elkins, *Imperial Reckoning: The Untold Story of Britain's Gulag in Kenya* (New York: Henry Holt, 2005).

[56] Tabitha Kanogo, *Squatters and the Roots of Mau Mau, 1905–63* (Nairobi: East African Educational Publishers, 1987). Also Throup, *Economic and Social Origins*.

[57] Daniel Branch, *Defeating Mau Mau, Creating Kenya* (Cambridge: Cambridge University Press, 2009).

[58] Myles Osbourne's recent article on Mau Mau in Ukambani attends to how loyal Kamba chiefs drew upon such fears in order to accrue political power. Myles Osbourne, "The Kamba and Mau Mau: Ethnicity, Development, and Chieftainship, 1952–1960," *International Journal of African Historical Studies* 43.1 (2010): 63–87.

context, the rebellion was not simply a military and political conflict but also a strongly supernatural contest that pitted a Kamba cosmology centered on *uoi* against a colonial worldview rooted in bureaucratic control. The supernatural nature of the conflict was encapsulated in the colonial administration's cleansing programs, instituted at the behest of loyal Kamba chiefs, to purge the intertwined scourges of Mau Mau and *uoi*.

In analyzing the interpenetration of witchcraft and politics in Kenya, this book, a work of anthropological history, is indebted to key anthropological texts on witchcraft and the state in Africa. First, Peter Geschiere's foundational work on the "modernity" of witchcraft in Cameroon demonstrates how witchcraft is not a cultural artifact but is instead squarely situated in the "here-and-now" of Cameroonian society and politics.[59] Writing on witchcraft in post-apartheid South Africa, Adam Ashforth frames the experiences of "living in a world with witches" as a matter not only of personal distress but also of political dislocation, a concern not just of ordinary Sowetans but also of the South African state.[60] And Harry West delineates witchcraft as a significant medium through which state power has been experienced and articulated by the people of Mozambique's Mueda Plateau. Further, his work traces how ethnography and "witchcraft" each entail imaginative, interpretive, transformative labors.[61] Engaging these ways of thinking about witchcraft, this book shows that in colonial Kenya witchcraft, or *uoi*, involved perceptions and experiences of dislocation and disruption, of the unsaid and the unthinkable, as frequently for state officials as it did for Africans.[62]

Anthropological and historical literature on witchcraft in East Africa is considerably more limited than that on West and Southern Africa. In the Kenyan context, scholarship on witchcraft has tended to be either squarely ethnographic or solidly archival. Anthropologists have examined the witchcraft practices and beliefs of specific ethnic groups in the late twentieth and early twenty-first centuries.[63] Historical studies of witchcraft – developing oral histories of witchcraft or examining

---

[59] Peter Geschiere, *The Modernity of Witchcraft: Politics and the Occult in Postcolonial Africa* (Charlottesville: University of Virginia Press, 1995).
[60] Ashforth, "On Living" and *Witchcraft*.
[61] West, *Kupilikula* and *Ethnographic Sorcery*.
[62] Michel-Rolph Trouillot, *Silencing the Past: Power and the Production of History* (Boston: Beacon Press, 1995).
[63] Smith, *Bewitching*. See also, Justus M. Ogembo, *Contemporary Witch-Hunting in Gusii, Southwestern Kenya* (Lewiston, NY: Edwin Mellen Press, 2006).

witchcraft as part of larger histories of legal administration – are more rare.[64] Chief among these works are Diane Ciekawy's ethnography of Mijikenda witchcraft and Richard Waller's foundational article on the history of witchcraft and colonialism in Kenya. Ciekawy offers a useful rubric for witchcraft – "magical harm" – and a nuanced reading of the affective registers of witchcraft in contemporary Kenya.[65] Engaged by Ciekawy's emphasis on affect, this book argues that "magical harm" was a category of the colonizer, not simply of the colonized. It examines how "magical harm" was a space of potent dramas and discontents from the perspectives of British officials and black Kenyans alike.

In addressing "why legislation against witchcraft was deemed necessary, how it was shaped and applied, and what administrative and legal interests and 'moral worlds' were involved," Waller skillfully argues for the centrality of witchcraft to issues of British justice and demonstrates the incredible utility of legal records as an historical source for studying witchcraft.[66] Inspired by Waller's analyses, this book deepens and expands the study of the supernatural state of twentieth-century Kenya. It marries history and ethnography in examining witchcraft and state relations in Kenya. Delving deep into the colonial archives, it traces the history of colonial governmentality in Kenya and historicizes Kamba *uoi* and *uwe*. Engaging anthropological fieldwork and anthropology in the archives, it offers intertwined ethnographies of the Kamba supernatural and of colonial statecraft.

SOURCES AND SITES

Knowledge of witches and bureaucrats, of the supernatural state of twentieth-century Kenya, resides in densely layered colonial archives and in the deep stratum of Kamba people's recollections. Following Ann Laura Stoler, I endeavored to "treat 'the archives' as something between

---

[64] For example, David M. Anderson, "Black Mischief: Crime, Protest, and Resistance in Colonial Kenya," *Historical Journal* 36 (1993): 851–877. Also Jeffrey Fadiman, *When We Began There Were Witchmen: An Oral History from Mount Kenya* (Berkeley: University of California Press, 1993).

[65] Diane Ciekawy, "Witchcraft in Statecraft: Five Technologies of Power in Coastal Kenya," *African Studies Review* 41.3 (1998): 119–142. See also, George Clement Bond and Diane Ciekawy, "Introduction: Contested Domains in the Dialogues of 'Witchcraft,'" in *Witchcraft Dialogues: Anthropological and Philosophical Exchanges*, ed. George Clement Bond and Diane Ciekawy (Athens: Ohio University Center for International Studies, 2003), 1–38.

[66] Waller, "Witchcraft," 242.

a set of documents, their institutions, and a repository of memory – both a place and a cultural space that encompass official documents but are not confined to them."[67] I began my experiment in the "archaeology of knowledge," which ultimately produced this book, in the collection of the Kenya National Archives (KNA) in Nairobi.[68]

Colonial officers were officially tasked with completing reams of paperwork, which was organized according to different bureaucratic genres. Reports were compiled in district and provincial record books at annual, semi-annual, and quarterly junctures. These reports, loosely organized under broad headings, contained narrative about and statistics on the social, economic, and political "conditions" of African populations, and by extension on the "progress" (or lack thereof) of the colonial administration. They often contained anthropological asides, or even special appendices about points of anthropological interest, such as spirit possession rituals or "customs" pertaining to death. Information about witchcraft typically appeared under headings about "crime," the "social condition of African peoples," or sometimes simply and pointedly under "witchcraft."

District and provincial officials also assembled "intelligence" reports on the political conditions of their areas of responsibility and reported on the *safari* or tours, they took throughout these areas, the *baraza* or town meetings they held along the way, and the *shauri* or conflicts that they mediated in between declaiming government business (in Kiswahili) and literally flying the flag.[69] These documents were subject to consumption by multiple audiences: fellow officers and administrative higher-ups, technocrats and legislators in the capital, Colonial Office bureaucrats in London, and even metropolitan governmental officials. Their contents were discussed in reams of correspondence that moved in hierarchically organized government networks from district to province to colonial capital to the metropole and back again.

I began my research by reading all the administrative reports available in the KNA on Machakos and Kitui Districts and on Ukamba Province. This survey revealed the contours of colonial administration in Kamba areas and the scale of challenges that witchcraft posed to administrative

---

[67] Stoler, *Archival Grain*, 49.
[68] Michel Foucault, *The Archaeology of Knowledge* (New York: Pantheon, 1982).
[69] Jan-Georg Deutsch, "Celebrating Power in Everyday Life: The Administration of the Law and the Public Sphere in Colonial Tanzania, 1890–1914," *Journal of African Cultural Studies* 21 (2002): 95–100.

"progress." It revealed the degree of colonial authorities' knowledge of, and frustration with, Kamba witchcraft.

The next phase of research in the KNA entailed reading all the administrative dossiers indexed under an array of categories pertaining to the occult, for instance, "witchcraft," "witchdoctors," "magic," "medicine," "possession," "prophets," and "supernatural." This survey demonstrated that witchcraft, and the administrative anxieties it provoked, were particularly pronounced and concentrated in Ukambani. It also showed that witchcraft and related issues of governance were not confined to Kamba areas but were present in varying degrees across the colony. Like the information contained in the bureaucratic genres discussed earlier, knowledge about witchcraft flowed through imperial circuits. Colonial documents bear out James Howard Smith's conclusion regarding postcolonial Kenya that "witchcraft discourse constitutes a field of knowledge that has been central to the work of governance in Kenya."[70]

I approached these sources with the following questions in mind: How did the literary conventions of colonial reports shape what was said and what was *not* said in discussions of witchcraft?[71] To what extent did discussions of witchcraft contain "fictive" elements that transformed accounts of witchcraft from isolated or serialized events into narratives that were broadly intelligible to British officials?[72] In what ways can ethnological/anthropological documents be read as historically produced even if they are written in an ethnographic present?[73]

But this book, initiated by a question about the fate of sixty Kamba men in East Africa's highest courts, is also story of law. Accordingly, I examined a range of legal documents and texts held in the KNA, in the University of Nairobi Law School, and the library of the School for Oriental and African Studies (SOAS) in London. The Ministry of Legal Affairs dossiers held in the KNA contain files of capital cases heard and appealed in East Africa's highest courts. These files vary considerably in the completeness of their contents, some housing a scant sheet of paper, others including all the trial transcripts pertaining to a case, the lower court proceedings, the reports of various experts like the medical examiner, witness affidavits,

---

[70] Smith, *Bewitching*, 20.
[71] George Bornstein, "How to Read a Page: Modernism and Material Textuality," *Studies in the Literary Imagination* 32.1 (1999): 29–58.
[72] Natalie Zemon Davis, *Fiction in the Archives: Pardon Tales and Their Tellers in Sixteenth Century France* (Stanford: Stanford University Press, 1987), 2–4.
[73] Nicholas Dirks, "The Policing of Tradition: Colonialism and Anthropology in History," *Comparative Studies in Society and History* (1997): 182–212.

supporting evidence, and other documents. These files are indexed only by the case name and date – there is no indication of the circumstances surrounding the crime. A fire in the Secretariat in 1939 destroyed case files predating the late 1930s. I surveyed 100 of these dossiers chronologically and ordered twenty more dossiers on files with multiple defendants. This survey revealed that nearly 15 percent of the cases were murders of alleged witches and that the defense regularly put forward the alleged witchcraft of the deceased as a mitigating circumstance. These documents were valuable not simply for what they revealed about judicial protocols and practices but also because they are one of the rare spaces in which African voices are present, albeit in highly mediated forms. As Kristin Mann and Richard Roberts write, "Work with little-used legal records, a necessary part of much legal research, generated data of unparalleled richness and detail about the daily lives of ordinary Africans, a subject about which historical data is hard to find."[74]

In the KNA, I also surveyed the attorney general files, reading not only for information about witchcraft, but also to glean how the state legal apparatus engaged customary law and African legal systems. I am especially grateful to Richard Waller for generously sharing with me his notes and photocopies pertaining to the elusive AG 1/610, the attorney general's file on witchcraft now lost in the KNA's prodigious depths.

In Nairobi and London, I read through all available digests of the Supreme and High Courts of Kenya, Tanganyika, and Uganda, and of the High Court of Appeal for Eastern Africa, compiling my own thick dossier of reports on cases in which the defense or appellant(s) posed the alleged witchcraft of the deceased as mitigation. I also delved into contemporary published sources on the problem of witchcraft and law in the British African Empire. Reading all of these documents and texts in conversation enabled me to develop a clear analysis of the complex jurisprudence surrounding witchcraft. These sources also underscored how witchcraft was considered a serious impediment to British justice, both in Kenya and across the British African Empire more generally, and revealed the networks through which both knowledge and angst traveled. I engaged these sources with the following questions at hand: What kind of violence – epistemic, archival, or both – was produced when British law aimed to recondition African codes about witchcraft?[75]

---

[74] Mann and Roberts, "Introduction," 5.
[75] Sandhya Shetty and Elizabeth J. Bellamy, "Postcolonialism's Archive Fever," *Diacritics* 30.1 (2002) 28–45.

Were laws and other official discourses about witchcraft "reality-based fictions?"[76] At which moments and for what reasons did British authorities and other writers employ "languages of affect" in writing about witchcraft and crime?[77]

I also researched the records of the Colonial Office and the Foreign Office held in the Public Record Office in Kew Gardens. I examined an array of files on East Africa and on issues of law and administration in the African Empire. Starting with the Colonial Office file on the Wakamba Witch Trials, I was able to use the original Colonial Office indexing system to trace the routes that files on witchcraft traveled throughout the Colonial Office and various African colonies.

The metropole was also an important site of academic and popular debate about witchcraft in Kenya and in British Africa. I examined Bronislaw Malinowski's and Isaac Schapera's papers at the London School of Economics (LSE). I also researched the *Journal of African Administration*, a journal dealing with administrative best practice, and *East Africa*, a newspaper produced for white Kenyans and white Kenyan expatriates, both sources held in the SOAS library. At Rhodes House Library, Oxford, I investigated the papers of the Anti-Slavery and Aborigines Protection Society, a key voice in the debates about the Wakamba Witch Trials, as well as the papers of anthro-administrators working in Kenya and documents on Oxford's "summer schools" for colonial officers. I also traced discussions of witchcraft in the *Times of London* and the *Manchester Guardian* and in the *East African Standard*, Kenya's major daily. These sources offered insights into how both the intelligentsia and the reading public in Britain considered witchcraft a central concern of colonial governance. I approached these sources with the following questions in mind: In what ways was legal, anthropological, anecdotal, and other evidence about witchcraft an effect of colonial power/knowledge rather than a mark of "prior realities"?[78] In what ways did instructions and recommendations for dealing with witchcraft and related crimes belong to a genre of best practices that held more value for the "experts" who produced them than for the administrators

---

[76] Mark Dressman, "Theory *into* Practice? Reading against the Grain of Good Practice Narratives," *Language Arts* 78.1 (2002): 50–58.

[77] Ann Laura Stoler, *Carnal Knowledge and Imperial Power: Race and the Intimate in Colonial Rule* (Berkeley: University of California Press, 2002).

[78] Premesh Lalu, "The Grammar of Domination and the Subjection of Agency: Colonial Texts and Modes of Evidence," *History and Theory*, Theme Issue 39 (December 2002): 45–68.

meant to apply them?[79] In what ways did public reportage and commentaries become "constitutive features" of witchcraft court cases?[80]

In drawing upon such sources and approaches, this book offers a thorough anthropology of the colonial archive but only a partial story of the supernatural state of twentieth-century Kenya. A purely archival approach largely leaves wanting Kamba people's perspectives on and recollections of witchcraft and the colonial state's involvement with it. Accordingly, this book also relies strongly on oral sources.

At a series of pre-fieldwork meetings in Nairobi, I provided my research assistant, J. Mbithi wa Mutunga, with a detailed synopsis of my project, a basic "oral script" of interview questions and themes, a list of locations in Machakos gleaned from archival material, and a list of individuals, also culled from archival materials. Using these resources and Mutunga's contacts in his native Machakos, we developed an informant pool of elderly Kamba men and women born between 1898 and 1939 who shared their knowledge, memories, and *chai* over the course of thirty sittings in Nairobi and Ukambani.

These old Kamba patiently answered my questions about the content and contours of *uoi* and *uwe*, in almost all cases volunteering anecdotes, information, and narratives that far exceeded the scope of my questions. In addition, archival research had led me to consider whether colonial legislation and prosecution of witchcraft had created *lieux de mémoire* in Ukambani.[81] Kamba people frankly discussed their memories and knowledge of the moments at which colonialism collided with *uoi* and *uwe*, stating freely when an event or initiative over which colonial actors had spilled much ink was unfamiliar to them. Experiences in Ukambani and Nairobi recalled for me what E. E. Evans-Pritchard wrote of his fieldwork in early twentieth-century Sudan: "I had no difficulty in discovering what Azande think about witchcraft, nor in observing what they do to combat it. These ideas and actions are on the surface of their life and are accessible to anyone who lives for a few weeks in their homesteads."[82]

Most elderly Kamba speak no English and limited Swahili, and prefer to discuss matters pertaining to *uoi* and *uwe* in Kikamba. As I speak

---

[79] Dressman, "Theory."
[80] Cohen and Odhiambo, *Burying SM*, 50–52.
[81] Pierre Nora, "Between Memory and History: Les Lieux de Mémoire," *Representations* 26 (Spring 1989): 7–24.
[82] E. E. Evans-Pritchard, *Witchcraft Oracles, Magic among the Azande* (Oxford: Clarendon Press, 1937), 1.

no Kikamba, Mutunga offered invaluable research assistance, providing running translation during interviews, which generally lasted between two and three hours. He also transcribed and translated interview tapes, which we later discussed, comparing them with my fieldnotes from our sessions. Mutunga also transcribed and translated a published Kikamba ethnography, *Mukamba wa Wo*, as well as a Kikamba audiocassette, "Frederick Muule," about the contemporary supernatural.[83]

This book also draws upon conversations in Nairobi with J. C. Nottingham, who as a young district officer co-organized the witch-cleansings in Mau Mau-era Ukambani and authored an article about them for the *Journal of African Administration*.[84] Over multiple cups of tea, he graciously answered my logistical and narrative queries about the cleansings. He generously volunteered anecdotes about the totality of his experiences in dealing with witchcraft and Mau Mau and the exigencies of colonial administration more generally.

"CRITICAL EVENTS" IN THE COLONIAL COMPENDIUM

This study is framed by a focus on a series of "critical events" pertaining to witchcraft that spanned the six decades of British rule in Kenya. In her history of female circumcision in Meru, Thomas explains that "critical events are those that rework 'traditional categories', prompting 'new modes of action' to come into being." These events, Thomas adds, "leave their mark on a variety of institutions, including 'family, community, bureaucracy, courts of law, the medical profession, the state and multi-national corporations.'"[85] From this perspective, "critical events" could be extrapolated further as "key moments" that precipitate flux, produce controversies, and prompt redefinitions and which can also promote change *or* entrenchment among a broad array of organizations and actors.

In examining the supernatural state of twentieth-century Kenya, training a scholarly lens on "critical events" works as a structuring tool and as an analytic tool. An attention to "critical events" yields a sturdy temporal framework, foregrounding significant moments of witchcraft-related challenge to state authority and following related shifts in discourse,

---

[83] David N. Kimilu, *Mukamba wa Wo* (Kampala: East Africa Literature Bureau, 1962).
[84] J. C. Nottingham, "Sorcery among the Akamba of Kenya," *Journal of African Administration* 11.1 (January 1959): 2–14.
[85] Thomas, *Politics*, 6–7.

policy, and practice across several decades. A focus on "critical events" also enables analysis, tracing witchcraft mentions through a spectrum of sources and marking the junctures at which accumulations of witchcraft-related disorder spilled over into the sort of witchcraft-driven disobedience that the state could not ignore. The following chapters analyze the "critical events" that produced evolutions and entrenchments of policy and practice concerning witchcraft in twentieth-century Kenya.

Chapter 2 addresses Kamba history from the late 1800s through the establishment of British administration in the opening decades of the twentieth century, a fraught period in which a previous prosperity was offset both by far-reaching famines and violent colonial conquest. It provides an overview of some of the central institutions of Kamba social and political life – for instance, clans and councils – and important elements of Kamba economic life such as caravans and cattle raising. The chapter also sketches out the different categories of Kamba supernatural actors, focusing on the ways in which they operated in the institutions noted earlier and engaged the advent of colonial rule.

Chapter 3 offers a deep ethnographic context to the "critical events" analyzed throughout this book. It explains Kamba cosmology, attending strongly to beliefs, practices, knowledge, and actors concerned with *uoi*, *uwe*, and the most significant Kamba oath, *kithitu*. It also focuses on the significance of *uoi*, *uwe*, and *kithitu* to perceptions about Kamba ways-of-being-in-world.[86]

Chapter 4 elucidates the broad structure of the colonial state and traces the contours of colonial bureaucratic practices in Kenya. It details the history of state legal and policy efforts to deal with witchcraft in Ukambani, focusing particularly on the development of the Kenya Witchcraft Ordinances and the burgeoning of Kamba witchcraft as an area of anthro-administrative investigation. The chapter traces the ways witchcraft became an issue of widespread preoccupation for colonial authorities in the metropole and abroad. It analyzes how concerns about witchcraft contributed strongly to the formalization of anthropology as an arm of colonial administration.

Chapter 5 traces the development and outcomes of the Wakamba Witch Trials. The case exemplifies the ways in which witchcraft-related criminal cases reveal the broader circumstances of clashes over justice,

---

[86] A focus on Kamba "supernatural beliefs and practices" is not intended to suggest that the author or informants regard such as static or unitary. The exigencies of anthro-historical approaches to Kamba cosmology are discussed in Chapter 3.

law, and order in Africa. The chapter also addresses the absence of the trials from Kamba collective memory.

Chapter 6 examines murder cases from East Africa's highest courts in which defendants and appellants argued that the witchcraft of the deceased had provoked them to kill. Close readings of these cases demonstrate the degree to which state authorities' often competing understandings of witchcraft exerted a tacit influence on jurisprudence concerning capital murder, working alternately to reinforce and revise key concepts such as "reasonableness" and "provocation."

Chapter 7 examines Kamba people's engagement in the anti-colonial Mau Mau revolt of the 1950s and colonial authorities' perceptions of this engagement. It analyzes the development of a specifically Kamba variety of Mau Mau oath, situating this new oath within the deeper anthropology and history of Kamba oathing more generally. The chapter also interrogates the "de-oathing" campaign developed by the colonial state in an effort to cleanse known and alleged Kamba adherents to the Mau Mau movement. It addresses Kamba people's memories of the oathing and of Mau Mau overall.

Chapter 8 delves even deeper into Kamba people's engagement with Mau Mau, focusing strongly on the intersection of *uoi* and Mau Mau. It investigates the impetus and rationale underpinning the colonial administration's organization of a series of public and openly sponsored witch-cleansings targeted to neutralize known or suspected Kamba witches who were alleged by black members of Kenya's colonial administration to be aiding Mau Mau fighters. The chapter also shows how the cleansings constituted a radical break with the colonial state's avowed policy of *not* officially employing witchcraft methods and means to combat witchcraft. It illustrates how the imagining and execution of the cleansings composed the ultimate exponent of the synergy between anthropology and administration in colonial Kenya. It addresses Kamba people's memories of this aspect of Mau Mau as well.

The book concludes by examining the attitudes of contemporary Kamba people about consistency and change in *uoi* and *uwe* beliefs and practices. It also analyzes the remarkable continuity in postcolonial Kenyan jurisprudence concerning witchcraft-related violence. It addresses how *contemporary* anthro-administrative networks of knowledge about witchcraft are emerging as African asylum seekers increasingly make claims before the United Nations High Commissioner for Refugees (UNHCR) and immigration courts in the global North that witchcraft-driven violence should constitute grounds for asylum.

Overall, the following chapters demonstrate the ways that witchcraft has constituted an important space in which larger questions of power have been contested. Witchcraft has existed not as an anthropological curiosity but as a popularly and practically recognized source of violent disorder. Until witchcraft is really recognized as such, the problems it has consistently produced will persist.

2

Clans and Councils, Caravans and Conquest, Cosmology and Colonialism

Ukambani in the Late Nineteenth and Early Twentieth Centuries

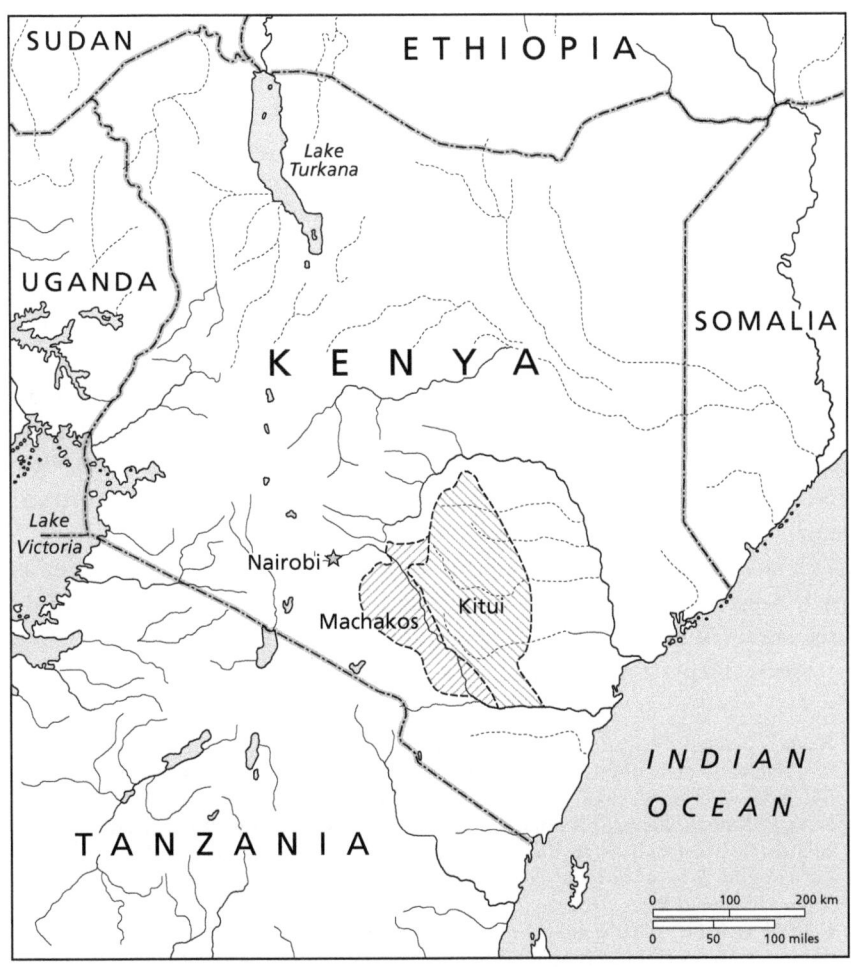

Machakos District, Kitui District, and Nairobi.

Competing myths, traditions, and memories propose various points of origin for the Kamba people. For example, different narrations of how the Kamba came to reside in Ukambani alternately pose Nzaui as a sort of Kamba "Eden" – that is, the place where the creator god put down the first man and first woman – as the location where Kamba "rain-followers" established the clan structure for which the Kamba people are well known, and as the spot where Kamba populations settled after migrating from Kilimanjaro.[1] Other traditions assert that the Kamba people originated in locations as diverse as Shungwaya and Egypt.[2] These competing sources concur that since the seventeenth century Kamba people have inhabited the highlands and plains in the area southeast of what was to become Nairobi.[3]

The scanty documentary record before the late nineteenth century consists of the observations of the few Victorian explorers and those of the even less numerous, but even more intrepid, European missionaries who had preceded them by decades, traversing Ukambani, often in pairs or sometimes solo. Missionaries' maps dating back to the early 1850s indicate that there were people calling themselves "Kamba" in the southeastern part of central Kenya and that these Bantu-language speakers called this area "Ukambani."[4]

With the arrival of the Imperial British East Africa Company (IBEAC) in the late 1880s, the documentary record treating Ukambani increased significantly. Many of the "company" men went on to join the first British colonial administrative corps. In Ukambani, C. W. Hobley, K. R. Dundas, and John Ainsworth had published ethnographic articles and made reports to metropolitan geographic and anthropological associations, and as colonial "anthro-administrators" they continued in their efforts to make local cultures "knowable."

Oral sources offer an important avenue into Ukambani's histories as well. Nuggets of information about Kamba "ways-of-being-in-the-world" are contained in oral histories and oral traditions, in songs and stories, in proverbs and performances. Further, scholars like J. Forbes Munro, Robert

---

[1] Kennell Jackson, "An Ethnohistorical Study of the Oral Traditions of the Kamba" (PhD diss., University of California, Los Angeles, 1972), 46–47. *Nzaui*, often spelled *Nzawi*, in Machakos District was the site of the first inland Africa Inland Mission (AIM) station in 1895 and the location from which the men tried in the Wakamba Witch Trials hailed.

[2] Munro, *Colonial Rule*, 7–10; Gerhard Lindblom, *The Akamba in British East Africa: An Ethnological Monograph* (Uppsala: Appelbergs Boktryckeri Aktiebolag, 1920), 9–21.

[3] Munro, *Colonial Rule*, 7–10.

[4] Kennell Jackson, "The Family Entity and Famine among the Nineteenth-Century of Akamba of Kenya: Social Responses to Environmental Stress," *Journal of Family History* 1.2 (1976): 196.

Clans and Councils, Caravans and Conquest

PHOTOGRAPH 1. A street in Machakos Town named after the Kamba prophet who is reputed to have predicted the arrival of the British in Kenya.

Tignor, Kennell Jackson, Hitoshi Ueda, and Jeremy Newman, working in Ukambani in the 1960s and 1970s, were able to interview elderly Kamba people who had lived through the coming of colonialism and its aftermath. This composite of documentary and oral sources stretching from the mid-nineteenth century through the dawn of the twentieth century tells us about clans and councils, caravans and conquest, cosmology and colonialism. Documentary and oral sources alike all underscore the centrality of the Kamba supernatural to the sociopolitics of Ukambani.

Prophets or seers, called *athani* in Kikamba, highly regarded ritual specialists who could foretell the future, were entangled in the region's earliest colonial histories.[5] The most renowned Kamba prophet, Syokimau, is widely credited with having foretold during the late nineteenth century that "a long narrow snake would move from the coast toward the setting sun"[6] bringing an influx of people "with skins like raw meat" who spoke

---

[5] Jackson, "Ethnohistorical Study," 332–333.
[6] Charles Ambler "What Is the World Going to Come To? Prophecy and Colonization in Colonial Kenya," in *Revealing Prophets: Prophecy in Eastern African History*, ed. David M. Anderson and Douglas H. Johnson (Athens: University of Ohio Press, 1999), 222.

"like birds."[7] More literally, as one elderly Kamba man explained to me in 2004, "She predicted about the railroad line and the white people."[8] The historical reputation of Syokimau remains such that a main road in Machakos Town, the provincial seat of Ukambani, is named for her. "Machakos," in turn, is the British corruption of the name of one of Syokimau's contemporaries, Masuku wa Musya, a *muthani* known for his ability to predict rainfall who lived near the site of what became the initial, major British administrative center in upcountry Kenya.[9]

Kamba rainmakers like Masuku were highly regarded ritual specialists in Ukambani because of the exigencies of the province's drought-prone ecology, and thus by extension, famine-prone, environment. As Paul Kavyu notes in his study of Kamba rain-making, the preponderance of drought conditions in Ukambani "made the people involved in the search for rain (*Athanima mbua*) whether by magic or by means of prophecy more respected and famous than others."[10] The district divisions of Machakos and Kitui correspond broadly to ecological divisions in the province. The hill country of Machakos, taking in the western and northern part of the province, has been favorable both to the cultivation of an array of crops – "maize, millet, peas, beans, sweet potatoes, bananas, yams, tobacco, sugar cane" – and to pastoralism.[11] By 1750, the Machakos hills supported thickly settled agricultural communities.[12] The arid plateaus of Kitui, covering the eastern part of the province, have been more hospitable to pastoralism. Kitui was settled by Kamba migrants from Machakos attracted by the area's expansive grazing lands.[13]

While Kitui, with its dry, burnt orange earth, has been historically prone to droughts, the comparatively verdant rose gold soils of Ukambani have been periodically parched as well. These droughts have produced a series of devastating famines, called *mayua* in Kikamba. *Mayua* have been recalled through Kamba oral traditions and histories dating from

---

[7] Munro, *Colonial Rule*, 27.
[8] K. K. Kilungu, August 2004.
[9] Munro, *Colonial Rule*, 32.
[10] Paul Kavyu, "Rain Making and Prophecy in Kamba People," Seminar Paper No. 54, Institute of African Studies, University of Nairobi, December 1973, University of Nairobi Library, 1.
[11] John Ainsworth, "A Description of the Ukamba Province, East Africa Protectorate, and Its Progress under British Administration," *Journal of the Manchester Geographic Society* 16 (1900): 192.
[12] Jackson, "Family Entity," 196.
[13] H. E. Lambert, "Land Tenure among the Kamba," *African Studies* 6.3 (September 1947): 141–142.

the mid-nineteenth century onward. *Mayua* were also noted in the books and articles produced by the European explorers and travelers who traversed Ukambani throughout the Victorian era. For example, in the early 1880s, Scottish explorer Joseph Thompson contrasted the hills of Machakos, which he described as "densely inhabited, fertile, and well cultivated, with cattle in great numbers," with Kitui where the "people were dying of famine," making it impossible for his own hungry expedition to acquire any food.[14] The famine that Thompson described is called *Nzana* in Kamba oral histories, signifying that the population was reduced to eating monitor lizard.[15] About a decade later, H. R. Tate described how famine devastated both districts of Ukambani, noting that "both Kitui and Ulu suffered terribly from the famine of 1898 and 1899, when fifty percent of the Akamba are estimated to have died."[16] The severity and cyclical nature of the famines dogging Ukambani was reiterated ten years later by Charles Dundas who noted that "all Akamba can tell of seven famines, some of many more," and emphasized that "famines have in the past harassed the Akamba more than any other adversity."[17]

Kamba people coped with these famines, which Kennell Jackson has poignantly characterized as "threat and actuality, future possibility and past history," through a variety of means.[18] Kamba migrated to join kinsmen in less affected areas, some going as far as Rabai on the coast where a Kamba population had developed through the long-distance trade between the Swahili Coast and the East African interior.[19] Kamba people also migrated to neighboring Central Province, trading with the Kikuyu and pawning their family members. As Tate noted, in the aftermath of the famine of 1888–1889, "many Akamba migrated to Kikuyu country,

---

[14] Joseph Thompson, *Through Masai Land, a Journey of Exploration among the Snowclad Volcanic Mountains and Strange Tribes of Eastern Equatorial Africa* (London: Sampson, Low, Marston, Searle, and Rivington, 1885), 339.

[15] Jackson, "Family Entity," 196.

[16] H. R. Tate, "Notes on the Kikuyu and Kamba Tribes of British East Africa," *Journal of the Royal Geographic Society of Great Britain and Ireland* 34 (January–June 1904): 135. The devastation of the famines of the later 1800s were compounded by the rinderpest epidemics of 1890–1891 and 1898 which decimated cattle populations across East Africa, including those of the Kamba.

[17] Charles Dundas, "History of Kitui," *Journal of the Royal Anthropological Institute of Great Britain and Ireland*, 43 (July–December, 1913): 480.

[18] Jackson, "Family Entity," 212.

[19] Ibid., 200. Dundas, "History of Kitui," 485; Isaria N. Kimambo, "The Economic History of the Kamba," in *Hadith 2: Proceedings of the 1968 Conference for the Historical Association of Kenya*, ed. Bethwell A. Ogot (Nairobi: East African Publishing House, 1970), 80.

where they stayed until 1900, selling cattle, and leaving their children in payment of food, to be afterwards redeemed when better days came round."[20] This history of Kamba-Kikuyu trade and temporary transference in times of ecological crisis was deeply situated enough that a Mau Mau-era Colonial Office official mused that Jomo Kenyatta was a closet Kamba, "one of the many children placed by Mkamba parents with Kikuyu in times of pestilence, etc. – Kamba country is very barren, stock deseases [sic] are rife and the adjoining Kikuyu country is fertile and well-watered."[21]

Kamba people also mobilized supernatural means, approaching rainmakers like Masuku to bring or to find water. For example, in 1911, the Swedish anthropologist Gerhard Lindblom recorded a Kamba women's song offered to a rainmaker which underscored how famine impinged directly upon social reproduction. The women sang, "Ea eeh/We come to get rain so that we can get food for our husbands/Who cannot accomplish their sexual duties, if they are weak from hunger."[22] Through song, the women expressed anxiety, not simply over their own capacities to bear children in a time of hunger, but also over the continuation of lineages more generally.[23]

Kamba familial organization has occurred at levels both larger and smaller than the lineage. The clan, or *mbai*, in Kikamba has been the broadest unit through which families have been organized. An *mbai* was composed of multiple lineages, which in turn comprised numerous extended families.[24] Clan membership has been traced through generations, via the patrilineal line. A 1909 Machakos District administrative report noted twenty-one clans scattered through Ukambani.[25] Each clan was known by a name, often pertaining to a cosmological or geographical element, and was invested with a recognized character or "communal image."[26] Certain clans were known to produce members with inheritable supernatural capacities. Oral sources indicate that

---

[20] Tate, "Notes," 135.
[21] PRO CO 822/780, *Infiltration of Mau Mau into Tribes other than the Kikuyu in Kenya, 1954–1955*. Comment; signature illegible. No date.
[22] Lindblom, *The Akamba*, 276.
[23] Jackson, "Family Entity," 193–194; G. Beresford-Stooke, "An Akamba Ceremony Used in Times of Drought," *Man* 28 (August 1928): 139–140.
[24] Lambert, "Land Tenure," 132–133.
[25] Jackson, "Ethnohistorical Study," 61. Munro identified twenty-five clans in the course of his fieldwork in the mid-1960s. Munro, *Colonial Rule*, 11; Kennell Jackson, "Gerhard Lindblom and the First Treatment of the Akamba Clans," in *Hadith* 2 (1970): 42–59.
[26] Jackson, "Ethnohistorical Study," 66.

particular clans were known to produce rainmakers or prophets while others, such as the Amutei clan of Machakos and the Atangwa clan of Kitui, were cited as being "witchcraft clans" whose female members passed down embodied *uoi*.[27]

Although clans were numerous, far-ranging, and recognized as having particular characters, they were not corporate actors in Kamba society.[28] Political and economic activity occurred at the village, or *utoi*, level among the several large lineages making up the community.[29] Jackson identifies these large lineages, called *mbaa* in Kikamba, as the "basic units of Akamba society," while Munro similarly cites the *mbaa* as the "effective unit of kinship" among Kamba people.[30] *Mbaa* were composed of three or four "localized extended family groups," while the extended family itself was a multi-generational, patrilocal unit headed by a senior man and including his wives and minor children and his adult sons their wives and children.[31] In the bounds of the *utoi* were assembled several extended families of up to sixty members each who belonged to different lineages and to a variety of clans. Unity of purpose in such a diversely constituted grouping was wrought supernaturally through oathing, a primary building block of Kamba cosmology.[32] Acting in concert, *utoi* members labored together, defended each other's property, and effected marriages among different *mbaa* and *mbai*.[33]

Kamba social life was patterned not simply along family lines but also through life stages. Circumcision, practiced on both males and females, occurred in two phases, the first in early childhood, the second in adolescence. The second circumcision, and its concomitant initiation ceremonies, marked an important turning point from adolescence to

---

[27] K. N. Nzawi, September 2004. Masuku is typically counted among the *Atangwa* clan. Jackson, "Ethnohistorical Study," 66. This informant's citation of *Atangwa* as a "witchcraft clan" points to the discursive and practical gray areas between the use of "supernatural" power for harm and its use for benevolent purposes. It is not clear from documentary or oral sources how a clan's characterization as a "witchcraft clan" affected (or not) the marriage prospects of the women belonging to it.

[28] Jackson, "Ethnohistorical Study," 70.

[29] Ibid., 71. Several neighboring *utoi*, in turn, could be grouped together to form an *ivalo*, a town-like organization overseen by a body of elders; Munro, *Colonial Rule*; Lambert, "Land Tenure," 139–140.

[30] Jackson, "Ethnohistorical Study," 60; Munro, *Colonial Rule*, 14.

[31] Jackson, "Ethnohistorical Study," 60.

[32] Munro, *Colonial Rule*, 14. Munro states that *utoi* were united through the *ndundu* oath. However, Kamba informants consulted in Machakos in 2004 stipulated that *ndundu* was an oath to cleanse *uoi*.

[33] Munro, ibid.

adulthood for both males and females.[34] After the second circumcision, Kamba women moved through three primary life stages. The second circumcision rendered girls marriageable women who helped older women with day-to-day tasks. After marriage, Kamba women became matrons, or *kiveti* in Kikamba, a status enhanced by successful childbearing, and were charged with achieving the social and physical reproduction of the household, including agricultural cultivation.[35] Elderly women, those past their reproductive years, did not occupy an "office" per se but had important voices in both family and community affairs.[36] For women of an *mbai* known for embodied *uoi*, however, the second circumcision did not constitute their initiation as the major reproducers of Kamba life. Rather, it coincided with the inauguration of their powers of social and physical destruction. The female "witch," the *mu'unde m'uoi*, initiated her daughters into *uoi* shortly after the girls underwent their second circumcision.[37]

The life stages of Kamba men, in contrast, were more numerous and diversified. Writing on the "natural grades through which the native can expect to pass during his life," Hobley explained that after the second circumcision, a Kamba male became a *mwanake* or "fully fledged warrior," next, an *nthele*, a young to middle-aged married man, and when a Kamba man had children old enough to be circumcised themselves he became eligible to participate in Kamba conciliar life.[38] "The male members of the family," British administration Charles Dundas noted in 1913, took "a very small share in the work of the village."[39] In old age, a Kamba male became a *mutumia*, or elder, and signaled his passage into this stage by hosting a feast during which he presented the principal invited elders with a goat and was thus received as an elder himself.[40] Once recognized as a

---

[34] Charles William Hobley, *Ethnology of A-kamba and Other African Tribes* (1910; reprint, London: Frank Cass & Co., 1971), 68–77; C. W. Hobley, "Further Researches into Kikuyu and Kamba Religious Beliefs and Customs," *Journal of the Royal Anthropological Institute of Great Britain and Ireland* 41 (July–December 1911): 416. Dundas suggests that the age of circumcision varied because circumcision ceremonies were not necessarily held on an annual basis. "History of Kitui," 522–523. More radically, Lindblom proposes the age at which the circumcisions occurred was fungible and contingent on the father's wishes. Lindblom, *The Akamba*, 43–46 .

[35] Dundas, "History of Kitui," 494–495.

[36] Lindblom, *The Akamba*, 446.

[37] Circumcision and *uoi* initiation are discussed in more detail in Chapter 3; David Kimilu, *Mukamba*, 113.

[38] Hobley, "Further Researches," 415.

[39] Dundas, "History of Kitui," 494.

[40] Tate, "Notes," 138.

mutumia, a Kamba man was able to serve on the *nzama*, a multi-village council, which met on demand to advise upon and mediate disputes. Both Dundas and Lindblom referred to the *nzama* as the "government" of Ukambani.[41] As he advanced in seniority, a Kamba man could serve on the *king'ole*, a council charged with investigating and adjudicating serious malfeasance such as thievery or *uoi*, offenses for which the *king'ole* could mete out capital punishment.[42] And a Kamba man could also become a *mutumia ma ithembo*, or "elder of the shrine."[43]

The office of *mutumia ma ithembo* is indicative of how Kamba people's sense of family extended from the tangible into the invisible world. The landscapes of Ukambani were populated by cadres of spirits, the most significant of whom were *aimu*, or spirits of the ancestors. Kamba households built shrines, called *ithembo* around groves of sacred fig trees where *aimu* were thought to reside, and shrine elders, called *atumia ma ithembo*, offered obligatory animal sacrifices, typically goats, to the *aimu* who in turn attended to the interests (or missteps) of their living kin.[44]

Aimu belonged to a broader Kamba cosmology in which supernatural actors of varying character and capacity figured. Coteries of foreign spirits, emanating from neighboring tribes like the Maasai, from the Swahili Coast, or even from as far away as *Ulaya*, or Europe, inhabited Ukambani. Categories of humans invested with supernatural powers included *athani* like Syokimau and Masuku, as well as the medium who could both channel and exorcise spirits, the diviner who diagnosed cases of *uoi*, the "witchdoctor" or *mu'unde m'uwe*, who straddled the bounds of *uoi* and *uwe* in order to treat people afflicted by *uoi*, the "witch," or *mu'unde m'uoi*, and cleansers, often imported from the Swahili Coast, who could strip the taint of evil from the *mu'unde m'uoi*.

Kamba people's exchange with the coast was not confined to the cosmological. With the famine of 1836, Kamba expanded their regional networks of trade to encompass the Swahili Coast. In the course of his travels in East Africa in the 1840s and 1850s, German missionary-explorer J. L. Krapf observed, "The Wakamba go in caravans, of from 200 to 300 persons, into the interior to fetch ivory, and form in a general way the commercial medium between the coast and the interior, into which they journey a distance of

---

[41] Dundas, "History of Kitui," 540. Also, Lindblom, *The Akamba*, 144. Lambert, "Land Tenure," 140–141.
[42] Munro, *Colonial Rule*, 56–57.
[43] Hobley, *Further Researches*, 416.
[44] Hobley, *Ethnology of A-kamba*, 89, 284.

from 200 to 250 leagues."⁴⁵ Kamba hunters, typically *anake*, supplied ivory, and *anake* and *nthele* served as porters and traders, exchanging the ivory for goods like fabric and beads.⁴⁶ In some instances, Kamba women served as support staff for the caravans or accompanied the caravans to do their own small-scale trading, and many of the *athani* who accompanied the caravans to offer prescience and protection were women.⁴⁷

In the 1860s, Swahili merchants became the dominant force in trade between Ukambani and the coast, while Kamba acted as middlemen, supplying ivory and foodstuffs to the passing coastal caravans, and served as porters.⁴⁸ Kamba oral histories indicate that as the nineteenth century wore on, Swahili caravans traversing Ukambani became less interested in ivory and increasingly engaged in "profiteering in persons," or slaving, and that Kamba middlemen and porters provided essential provision and labor to these caravans as well.⁴⁹

By the late 1880s, the Imperial British East Africa Company, the concessionary company "chartered to occupy Britain's sphere of influence," was, like the Swahili, sending caravans to Uganda for ivory, traversing Ukambani along the way.⁵⁰ In many cases, these caravans used Kamba porters. For example, in 1893 John Ainsworth wrote to his superior on the coast that Kamba men went "very willingly into the work of carrying loads, and hundreds of sturdy fellows are ready to go down to either Tzavo or Teita and bring up loads to this point, and if required take them on to Kikuyu."⁵¹ The IBEAC established a supply station at the "camp-market" of Machakos in 1889, a decision prompted by the Kamba's well-developed trading networks.⁵² The IBEAC was eager to buy foodstuffs from Kamba traders, who were equally keen to sell to the company as such transactions "boosted their commercial and political standing."⁵³ Overall, as Berman

---

⁴⁵ J. L. Krapf, *Travels, Researches, and Missionary Labors during an Eighteen Years Residence in East Africa* (Boston: Ticknor and Fields, 1860), 118.
⁴⁶ Robert J. Cummings, "Aspects of Human Porterage with Special Reference to the Akamba of Kenya: Towards an Economic History, 1820–1920" (PhD diss., University of California, Los Angeles, 1975), 168, 190; Robert J. Cummings, "The Early Development of Akamba Local Trade History, c. 1780–1820," *Kenya Historical Review* 4.1 (1976): 85–110.
⁴⁷ Cummings, "Aspects," 192.
⁴⁸ Ibid., 214, 225.
⁴⁹ Kimambo, "Economic History," 83.
⁵⁰ Berman and Lonsdale, *Unhappy Valley I*, 16.
⁵¹ PRO FO 2/59, Imperial British East Africa Company. Second bi-yearly Report from John Ainsworth, Commanding Officer at Machakos, to the Administrator, Mombasa. Machakos Station, 30 June 1893.
⁵² Munro, *Colonial Rule*, 32.
⁵³ Ibid., 35.

and Lonsdale note, in aim, structure, and staffing, the ivory caravans of the IBEAC "resembled" those of the Swahili with which the Kamba were well familiar.[54]

However, an important element distinguishing the company caravans from their Swahili counterparts was their "avowed hostility to slaving."[55] Both Machakos and Kitui were recognized as major sites of slaving activities that exceeded the mere provisioning of Swahili slaving caravans. As James McDonald, who worked as a surveyor for the company beginning in 1891, wrote, "Ulu had long been a favourite halting-place for Arab slave-caravans, as not only could food be cheaply obtained, but the Wakamba had captives for sale … once the Company's rule extended to Machakos's, the slave-dealer often found it convenient to leave a large number of slaves among the Wakamba, where they learned the language, and otherwise qualified themselves to pass as Swahilis at the coast the following season."[56] Ainsworth points to a similar scenario in Kitui, maintaining, "There is no doubt in my mind but that Kitwyi has for many years been a regular *rendezvous* for Swahili, etc. slave-traders."[57] The company actively engaged against the trade, interrupting it and freeing slaves whenever and wherever possible. For example, McDonald noted that a company official at Machakos "had succeeded in breaking up a large slave-caravan" and that his own caravan had offered sanctuary to runaway slaves.[58]

How the company's interference in the trade influenced relations between the British and the Kamba is a point of contention, some scholars regarding it as incidental and others treating it as an initiating factor in the violence of the piecemeal conquest period, which stretched from the 1890s into the early twentieth century.[59] What seems clear is that relations could shift rapidly, varied regionally, and were often a matter of how individual British officials operated vis-à-vis the Kamba. For instance, John Ainsworth, as a senior IBEAC official, initially armed Kamba militias to protect the food supply of the IBEAC station from

[54] Ibid., 22.
[55] Ibid., 22.
[56] James Ronald Leslie McDonald, *Soldiering and Surveying in British East Africa, 1891–1894* (London: Edward Arnold, 1897), 44; Kimambo, "Economic History," 84.
[57] John Ainsworth, "On a Journey from Machakos to Kitwyi," *Geographical Journal* 7.4 (April 1896): 409.
[58] McDonald, *Soldiering*, 45.
[59] Munro, *Colonial Rule*, 33–38. Kimambo, in contrast, suggests inept company administration at Machakos produced "constant fighting between the Kamba and the Company." "Economic History," 84–85.

Maasai attack, but ultimately mobilized them as tactical reserve against the more pastoral northern Kamba settlements, among whom the displaced Swahili found auxiliaries for ivory and slave-hunting farther afield.[60] Further, when the *atumia* of Mwala ignored his request to discuss the slave trade in their area, Ainsworth launched a series of raids. Prefiguring the Maji Maji Rebellion in Tanganyika and drawing upon the Kamba supernatural, Mwatu wa Ngoma, the leader of the Mwala *atumia*, planned to attack Machakos, his forces protected from British guns by a powerful *mu'unde m'uwe* whose potent medicine could render British bullets harmless.[61] Mwatu's plan was thwarted by a British raid on Mwala proper, and Mwatu ultimately acceded to an alliance with Ainsworth as a way to gain firearms and prestige with which to reinforce his own political position.[62]

Ainsworth was not the first British official to encounter the mixing of violent resistance and the Kamba supernatural. British-Kamba relations had first turned violent in the early 1890s when Ainsworth's predecessor had an *ithembo* tree near Iveti cut down with the object of turning it into a flagpole. Such sacrilege promoted the Iveti *anake* to attack the IBEAC station at Machakos. After firing on the *anake* with rifles, the superintendent "sent out a party which toured Iveti, burning down huts."[63] These early interactions helped to establish the Kamba supernatural as a space in which the Kamba and the British would consistently clash.

At the same time that the IBEAC was setting itself up militarily through a series of punitive missions against various pockets of recalcitrant Kamba, its economic position was withering. The Foreign Office took over direct control of Kenya, establishing the East Africa Protectorate in 1895 and taking charge of building a railway from the coast to Lake Victoria to replace the old caravan lines.[64] Though the railway bypassed Machakos, a span of the "Wakamba highway" between Kibwezi and Tsavo was nonetheless chosen as a link for the railway.[65] With the completion of the

---

[60] Berman and Lonsdale, *Unhappy Valley*, I, 26. Though the Maasai have a better-known image as warriors, prodigious hunters, especially of elephants, Maasai did not always come out on top in cattle raiding battles with the Kamba.
[61] Munro, *Colonial Rule*, 40; James Giblin and Jamie Monson, eds., *Lifting the Fog of War* (Boston: Brill, 2010).
[62] Munro, *Colonial Rule*, 41.
[63] Ibid., 36. See also, John Ndeti Somba, *Akamba Mirror: Some Notable Events in the Machakos District of Kenya, 1889–1929* (Nairobi: Kesho Publishing, 1979), 3.
[64] The Colonial Office took over from the Foreign Office in 1905.
[65] Cummings, "Aspects," 145.

railway in 1901–1902, Syokimau's prophecy that a "long narrow snake would move from the coast toward the setting sun" was realized.⁶⁶

The "patchwork of alliances and hostility" that had characterized earlier relationships between the Kamba and the British persisted, and Machakos, remaining under Ainsworth, served as a "forward base of conquest" in central Kenya.⁶⁷ As Munro notes, in contrast to the IBEAC, which had "limited goals" in Kenya's highlands, "the Foreign Office envisaged the establishment of a regular administrative system over the whole protectorate" organized on a provincial basis; a process that effectively transformed Kambaland into Ukamba Province.⁶⁸ Though conquest was achieved through battles, British rule was retrenched through bureaucratization.⁶⁹

As they built a bureaucracy increasingly hewing to the principles of Indirect Rule, British authorities aimed to refashion many of the institutions of Kamba sociopolitical life described earlier. For instance, the office of village headman, established through the Village Headman Ordinance of 1902, entailed representative responsibilities that were in many ways similar to those of the *atumia*.⁷⁰ British officials also created administrative offices where no Kamba model or precedent existed. For example, Ainsworth explained of the Kamba in 1893, "What they have been in want of is a general Head, which head should be in a position to wield authority over the whole, and which should be able to effect the general internal peace of the country."⁷¹ To rectify this state of affairs, the British appointed a cadre of Kamba "chiefs" although the position of "chief" was not part of the Kamba's largely egalitarian age-grade and council-based politics.⁷²

In other instances, the British sought to supplant Kamba authority. Significantly, they abolished *king'ole*, thereby claiming the state's

---

⁶⁶ Ambler, "What Is the World," 222.
⁶⁷ Berman and Lonsdale, *Unhappy Valley I*, 25–26. For a narrative of British expeditions and Kamba "primary resistance," see Munro, *Colonial Rule*, 41–47.
⁶⁸ Munro, *Colonial Rule*, 41; Berman, *Control and Crisis*, 211.
⁶⁹ Berman and Lonsdale, *Unhappy Valley I*, 32.
⁷⁰ Munro, *Colonial Rule*, 57.
⁷¹ PRO FO 2/59, Imperial British East Africa Company Second bi-yearly Report from John Ainsworth, Commanding Officer at Machakos, to the Administrator, Mombasa. Machakos Station, 30 June 1893.
⁷² Robert Tignor, "Colonial Chiefs in Chiefless Societies," *Journal of Modern African Studies* 9.3 (1971): 339–359. Explorers and travelers in Ukambani had referred to "chiefs" before the advent of colonial rule. For example, Krapf details his relationship with "Kivoi, chief of the Wakamba tribe of Kitui." However, such "chiefs" were typically powerful traders or *athani* or both as was the case with Kivoi. See Krapf, *Travels, Researches and Missionary Labours*, 207.

monopoly over juridical violence, but hobbling the Kamba system of justice, especially in regard to *uoi*. Indeed, as Munro notes, *king'ole* came to the attention of British authorities in large part via the execution of between thirty and forty "witches" in Kitui and through an alleged "witch" who sought sanctuary at the Machakos *boma* in 1901.[73] These early encounters with *king'ole* set the stage for colonial misunderstandings of the institution, especially its relationship to *uoi*, that emerged most spectacularly three decades later in the Wakamba Witch Trials.[74]

The corollary to Syokimau's prophecy concerning the railway was that Ukambani would be populated by men "with skins like raw meat" who spoke "like birds."[75] Her *mawathani*, or prophetic sayings, on this matter presaged not simply the advent of Company, and later Crown, rule, but also the arrival of Christian missionaries who by the mid-1890s had begun to set up stations in Ukambani. Though the East African Scottish Mission was first on the ground, the Africa Inland Mission (AIM), an American-based society with roots in revivalism, came to dominate Ukambani, establishing its first station in Machakos in the mid-1890s.[76] As Robert Tignor writes, the religion that AIM brought to Ukambani was "strongly evangelical, Bible centered, fundamentalist, socially conservative, and concerned above all to evangelize."[77] Additional AIM stations were established at Kangundo (1896), Machakos (1902), Mbooni (1908), Mukaa (1909), and Kilungu (1917), locations, which despite the mission presence, remained central sites of Kamba supernatural activities ranging from possession to prophecy to *uwe* and *uoi* throughout the century.[78]

White settlers would not begin to establish farms in Ukambani until the Kamba reserve was created in 1906. Though alienation of Kamba

---

[73] Munro, *Colonial Rule*, 56.
[74] Ibid., 56. Chapter 5 offers an in-depth analysis of the Wakamba Witch Trials.
[75] Ambler, "What Is the World," 222.
[76] It is possible to visit the fenced grave of Peter Cameron Scott, who established the AIM station at Nzawi in 1895 and died in 1898.
[77] Tignor, *Colonial Transformation of Kenya*, 116.
[78] James Muli Mbuva, "Witchcraft among the Akamba and the Africa Inland Church, Kenya" (M. A., Fuller Theological Seminary, 1992), 99. In his memoirs, James Juma Mbotela, a black Kenyan who evangelized on behalf of AIM in Kangundo in 1907, recollected the remoteness of Kangundo. Joseph B. Harris, *Recollections of James Joseph Mbotela* (Nairobi: East Africa Publishing House, 1977), 44–46. See also, Mahone, "Psychology," 241–258. Tignor writes, "The Kamba land losses were much less spectacular than those of the Kikuyu and Maasai, but annoying, nonetheless." Tignor, *Colonial Transformation of Kenya*, 39.

land occurred in steady increments over half a decade, the Kamba lost less land than did their Kikuyu and Maasai neighbors, and white settlement in Ukambani was much more limited than it was in Central Province and in the Rift Valley.[79] Nonetheless, as Munro notes, "the brusque manner" in which alienation had been carried out coupled with colonial disregard for Kamba land rights, produced "widespread distrust of colonial intentions."[80] The most notable account of settler-Kamba interactions found in colonial records was tied up in such distrust and in the Kamba supernatural. Colonial authorities regarded the brutality that a white farmer exhibited toward his Kamba laborers as a precipitating factor in the outbreak of a disruptive wave of spirit possession across Ukambani in the early twentieth century.[81]

In the last decades of the nineteenth century and the first decades of the twentieth, colonial actors developed attitudes about and models of engagement with the core elements of Kamba life that influenced British and Kamba interactions for the entirety of the colonial era. These early days gave rise to oft-times conflicting, but nonetheless consistent, tropes about Kamba people. Colonial accounts figured the Kamba variously as "industrious," and "lazy," as "hostile" and "friendly," as incorrigible drunks and natural soldiers. The most ready trope about the Kamba was that they were mired in the supernatural, particularly in *uoi* and *uwe*. The invocation of such images was largely dependent upon how Kamba people's behaviors meshed (or not) with colonial aims of the given moment. Overall, colonial records suggest that many administrators came to exhibit sentiments similar to that expressed by Ainsworth at the turn of the century: "I can assure you that it is at times uphill and tiring work breaking down the walls of barbaric ignorance and superstition and introducing in their places an acceptable form of civilisation."[82]

Kamba communities, in turn, had by the end of the first decade of the twentieth century experienced a variety of pronounced dislocations. Famine and disease had ravaged Kamba communities and their herds.

---

[79] Munro, *Colonial Rule*, 78–81. François Grignon writes, "Au sein du district, la réserve africaine de Machakos fut grossièrement délimitée en 1906, mais connut des modifications supplémentaires des colons sur les terres alors allouées aux africains." François Grignon, "*Le Politicien Entrepreneur en Son Terroir: Paul Ngei à Kangundo (Kenya), 1945–1900*" (PhD diss., Université de Montesquieu, 1997), annexe 7, 60.

[80] Munro, *Colonial Rule*, 79–80.

[81] PRO CO 533/92, "Case of Mr. Langridge," 18 November 1911; M. P. K. Sorrenson, *The Origins of European Settlement in Kenya* (London: Oxford University Press, 1968), 281.

[82] Ainsworth, "A Description," 187.

Some of these ecological dislocations were accompanied by the violence of conquest, perpetrated by newcomers who set about refashioning, co-opting, or eradicating key institutions of Kamba life. These renovations were keenly felt in terms of the space of the supernatural, as colonial rule disabled Kamba mechanisms for dealing with *uoi* and rendered *uwe* legally ambiguous at best.

But at the same moment, the advent of the British created fresh opportunities for some Kamba people. The establishment of the colonial administrative apparatus created new positions occupied by the *atumia* and *athani* of powerful clans. But the British did not limit these new positions to such elders and brokers, to "traditional authorities." In their quest for allies and intermediaries, colonial officials enabled a reshuffling of generation and genealogy in which the *anake* and *nthele*, along with members of less powerful lineages, who were typically excluded from authority, could exercise fresh power in positions as diverse as "native assessor" and "government witchdoctor." The next chapters engage these issues, focusing on the competing cosmologies of the Kamba and of the colonial state.

3

Understanding *Uoi, Uwe*, and *Kithitu* in Ukambani

> Whether witchcraft does or does not really work, it is sufficient to say that neither the practitioner, his victims, nor the general African public regard it as an imposture.[1]

In its broadest terms, "cosmology" denotes a critical contemplation of the universe and efforts to understand the place of human beings within the universe. Cosmology can also stand for a totalizing worldview, a consuming way of seeing and way of being in the world. Within the context of colonial Kenya, two competing cosmologies – dual ways-of-seeing and ways-of-being – existed. The next two chapters argue that from the opening moments of the colonial era, a Kamba cosmology centered on *uoi* (and *uwe*) beliefs and practices collided with a colonial cosmology focused around bureaucratic practices and beliefs. The collision of these two contrasting, totalizing worldviews produced various "critical events" through which the persistent sway of Kamba witchcraft challenged the ability of the state to secure law and order.

The colonial documentary record offers a clear picture of the ways in which British officials conceptualized and engaged with Kamba witchcraft and with other key supernatural practices like oathing, or *kithitu*. Colonial documents overwhelmingly figure such practices and beliefs as atavistic irrationalities, albeit ones that did work, challenging the "colonial order of things."[2] But how Kamba people have thought about and experienced *uoi, uwe*, and *kithitu* is more difficult to ascertain. As Steven Feierman

[1] KNA DC/MKS 1/1/25, Machakos District Annual Report 1933, 32.
[2] Ann Laura Stoler, *Race and the Education of Desire: Foucault's History of Sexuality and the Colonial Order of Things* (Durham, NC: Duke University Press, 1995), 13.

writes, "the particular domains of African life which the conquerors saw as irrational are precisely the ones most difficult for the historian to interpret. The European sources hang like a veil between the historian and the African actors of that period."[3]

The historian can begin by reading such written sources with an eye to the ethnographic rather than the merely extractive,[4] both attending to "fragments"[5] of non-state actors' voices in the archive and situating these voices within the broader makings of colonial "event" and "metaphor."[6] Stepping outside the archives into the field, the historian can also turn ethnographer, querying the living about the shape of the past *and* of the present. Through such investigatory labors, as Luise White notes, "historical facts emerge from social truths just as social truths develop from readings of historical facts."[7]

The body of ethnographic and historical literature about Ukambani is small, and available interview transcripts do not attend strongly to the contours and content of *uoi*, *uwe*, and *kithitu*.[8] In the colonial period, administrative documents were rife with mentions of witchcraft, and to a lesser extent of oathing, but unofficial ethnographic attention to Ukambani was somewhat sporadic, as early anthropological and administrative investigators produced relatively few articles and monographs on the Kamba before World War II. In the 1950s, a Machakos district commissioner authored a treatise on Kamba customary law, while Government Sociologist Godfrey Wilson and District Officer

[3] Steven Feierman, "Colonizers, Scholars, and the Creation of Invisible Histories," in *Beyond the Cultural Turn*, ed. Victoria E. Bonnell and Lynn Hunt (Berkeley: University of California Press, 1999), 186.
[4] Stoler, *Archival Grain*, 47.
[5] Gyanendra Pandey, "Voices from the Edge: The Struggle to Write Subaltern Histories," in *Mapping Subaltern Studies and the Postcolonial*, ed. Vinayak Chaturvedi (London: Verso, 2000), 282–283.
[6] Shahid Amin, *Event, Metaphor, Memory: Chauri Chaura, 1922–1992* (Berkeley: University of California Press, 1995), 3–5.
[7] Luise White, "True Stories: Narrative, Event, History, and Blood in the Lake Victoria Basin," in *African Words, African Voices: Critical Practices in Oral History*, ed. Luise White, Stephan Miescher, and David William Cohen (Bloomington: Indiana University Press, 2002), 287.
[8] Jeremy Newman, *Machakos Interviews*. Unpublished interview transcripts, 1974. Personal collection of François Grignon; William Mutemi Sungi and Raphael Nguli, eds., *Akamba Oral Historical Texts*. Unpublished interview transcripts, 1977. Nairobi: Kenya National Archives, Murembi Library Collection. In the 1970s, Japanese anthropologist Hitoshi Ueda studied Kamba cosmology in Kitui, producing a few seminar papers in English. For example, Hitoshi Ueda, "Witchcraft and Sorcery in Kitui of Kamba Tribe." Presented to Institute of African Studies, University of Nairobi, Research Seminar No 25. 22 June 1971. SOAS PP MS 42 Whiteley Collection File SL/14.

J. C. Nottingham conducted an extensive study of Kamba witchcraft in Machakos. The scope and limits of such documentary sources influence how finely the intricate tapestry of Kamba cosmology can be woven over a long period.[9]

After reading these sources, I spoke at length with elderly Kamba in Nairobi and Machakos. Most concretely, I hoped to ascertain if and how people recalled the "critical events" in the colonial compendium, if these events were indeed "*lieux de mémoire*."[10] More abstractly, I hoped to learn how contemporary understandings of *uoi*, *uwe*, and *kithitu* corresponded (or not) with colonial explanations. The first line of inquiry produced a notable absence of memory that is discussed in the following chapters. The second showed a remarkable continuity in understandings of *uoi*, *uwe*, and *kithitu*, both about the shape of these phenomena and their centrality to Kamba ways-of-being-in-the-world. As Harry West writes of "witchcraft," or *uwavi*, among Muedans of Mozambique, "*uwavi* both lived in the present *and* remembered the past."[11]

Across time and genre of evidence, *uoi*, *uwe*, and *kithitu* were understood, articulated, and experienced as nodes of invisible power imbued with varying degrees of malevolence or benevolence. Reading documentary and oral evidence together demonstrates a supernatural situation in Ukambani very similar to that described by West in the context of Mozambique's tumultuous twentieth century. He writes,

> Through it all, however, *uwavi* remained familiar to most Muedans. The complex discursive and material practices through which Muedans have engaged with the invisible realm of *uwavi* has sustained among them a distinct cultural schema concerning the workings of power – a schema drawing form from past Muedan experience while giving form to Muedan involvement in, and understanding of, ongoing historical events and processes.[12]

This chapter juxtaposes documentary records on Kamba witchcraft and oathing with the answers I received to the following core questions in 2004: How do people generally explain witchcraft? And oathing? How do you explain *uoi* and *uwe*? And *kithitu*? How do people generally describe the activities of men who practice *uoi* and/or *uwe*? Of women? How do

---

[9] D. J. Penwill, *Kamba Customary Law: Notes Taken in the Machakos District of the Kenya Colony* (London: Macillan, 1951).
[10] Nora, "Memory and History."
[11] West, *Kupilikula*, 19.
[12] Ibid., 84.

people generally explain how men and women come to be practitioners? What are generally held to be some of the motivations for practicing witchcraft? What sorts of events are associated with *uoi*? And *uwe*? How is *uoi* diagnosed? And dealt with? Following these lines of questioning, this chapter both depicts how *uoi*, *uwe*, and *kithitu* are articulated and experienced in contemporary Ukambani and illustrates what they stood for in the colonial era.[13]

KAMBA COSMOLOGY: *UOI*, *UWE*, AND *KITHITU*

Witchcraft is one of the true Mukamba acts.[14]
To the *kithitu* no one can lie, from the *kithitu* no one can hide.[15]

Kamba cosmology is complex and well developed, taking in beliefs and practices ranging from the simple wearing of protective amulets to the complicated processes of communication with Kamba spirits or *aimu*. This chapter addresses central, interrelated elements of Kamba cosmological beliefs and practices – *uoi*, *uwe*, and *kithitu* – that have been regarded by Kamba people themselves as fundamental to "Kamba-ness," what it means to be Kamba rather than Luo, Kikuyu, or even Giriama.[16] *Uoi*, *uwe*, and *kithitu* have also been central to external ideas of Kamba-ness, how members of other groups distinguish what it means to be Kamba as opposed to being a member of another tribe. The centrality of *uoi*, *uwe*, and *kithitu* to notions of Kamba-ness has been linked strongly to long-standing (and some might say well-proven) perceptions of Kamba *uoi* and *kithitu* as particularly permeating, efficacious, and lethal.

Further, *uoi*, *uwe*, and *kithitu* have been historically intermeshed with issues and institutions of law and order. In precolonial and colonial-era Kamba societies, *uoi*, *uwe*, and *kithitu* were central concerns of the bodies of elders responsible for maintaining law and order. Throughout the colonial period, Kamba witchcraft and oathing attracted the interest of British authorities as well, emerging as consistent foci of British anthro-

---

[13] Luise White asks, "How do historians access what shaped the past, and how can they use oral sources to discern these causes?" "Such a question" she notes is "categorically different from that of what really happened." See White, "True Stories," 282–283.
[14] Kimilu, *Mukamba*, 113.
[15] François Grignon, "The *Kithitu* Oath in Ukambani Politics: A Moral Contract in Kenyan Politics," paper presented at the ASA-UK Bi-annual Meeting, London, Great Britain, 1998, 5.
[16] While "witchcraft" is practiced among all these groups, Kamba people retain an internal and external reputation as Kenya's foremost "witches."

administrative inquiries into local mechanisms and understandings of justice. At the same time, the intersection of witchcraft and oathing with British institutions and ideals concerning justice created many of the "critical moments" at which local practices and beliefs challenged the authority of the colonial state to establish law and order. Finally, *uoi*, *uwe*, and *kithitu* continue to hold enormous cachet across the postcolonial Kenyan political arena, and many politicians have mobilized them in their bids for political success.[17]

UOI VERSUS *UWE*

Kikamba *uoi* is the equivalent of the Kiswahili term *uchawi*, and the fundamental meanings of *uoi* and *uchawi* are not far removed from that of "witchcraft" in the Euro-American sense of the word – "magical harm."[18] Writing on witchcraft in contemporary South Africa, Nelson Tebbe posits, "Witchcraft, then, is the practice of secretly using supernatural power for evil – in order to harm others or to help oneself at the expense of others," noting that "this definition is one that many Africans would accept."[19] Historical and contemporary sources suggest that Kamba people would be open to defining *uoi* along such lines. In Kikamba, the witch herself (or more rarely, himself), the person perpetrating *uoi*, is called *mu'unde m'uoi*, the literal translation of which is "witch person."

In his foundational text on the supernatural in Sudan, Evans-Pritchard recounted how Azande people distinguished between "witchcraft," the use of inherited, embodied, supernatural power to do malevolence, and "sorcery," the use of external means in pursuit of the same aims. "Magic," in turn, stood for the "supernatural" power to countermand "witchcraft" and "sorcery."[20] Although Kamba people have distinguished similarly between "embodied" and "bought" *uoi*, no linguistic distinction exists in Kikamba. Malevolent supernatural harm is *uoi* and its practitioner is

---

[17] See Katherine Luongo, "Polling Places and Slow-Punctured Provocation: Occult-Driven Cases in Postcolonial Kenya's High Courts," *Journal of Eastern African Studies* 4.3 (2010): 577–591. Hervé Maupeu, "Les Élections Comme Moment Prophétique. Narrations Kikuyu Des Élections Générales de 2002 (Kenya)," *Politique Africaine* 90 (Juin 2003): 56–77.

[18] Diane Ciekawy, "Witchcraft and Statecraft." Employing the present tense does not mean that the researcher or her informants subscribe to a stable notion of an immutable "ethnographic present." Rather, discussions about what "witchcraft" and "oathing" *are* rather than what they *were* foreground the challenge of doing historicized ethnographies of Kamba witchcraft and oathing.

[19] Nelson Tebbe, "Witchcraft and Statecraft: Liberal Democracy in Africa," *Georgetown Law Journal* 96 (2007): 190.

[20] Evans-Pritchard, *Witchcraft*, 177.

a *mu'unde m'uoi*. "Magic," in Evans-Pritchard's sense of the term, is the Kikamba "*uwe*." Very similar to the Kiswahili word *uganga*, *uwe* can be broadly conceived of as "healing," very often with the purpose of undoing *uoi*. In Kikamba, a person engaged in *uwe* is known as a *mu'unde m'uwe*, the literal translation of which is "healing person," but which is also often translated as "witchdoctor."[21]

The primary distinction between *uoi* and *uwe* then is that of black magic versus white magic. As Evans-Pritchard wrote,

> The use of magic for socially approved ends, such as combating witchcraft, is sharply distinguished by Azande from its evil and anti-social use in sorcery. To them, the difference between a sorcerer and a witch is that the former uses the technique of magic and derives his power from medicines, while the latter acts with rites and spells and uses hereditary psycho-physical powers to attain his ends. Both alike are enemies of men, and Azande class them together. Witchcraft and sorcery are opposed to, and opposed by, good magic.[22]

More recently, Geschiere has neatly expressed such distinctions as "sorcery of construction" versus "sorcery of destruction," notions that West also cites as underpinning the Muedan formulation, *kupilikula*.[23] In understanding *uoi* and *uwe* it is important to note that *uoi* is always used for harm and for the creation of *lack* – lack of life, lack of mental and physical health, lack of property, and so on. *Uwe* is always used as a remedy and for rectifying lack – for restoring health, love, property, and so on.

While acknowledging *uwe* and its practitioners, this study focuses primarily on *uoi*. *Uoi* is much more widely practiced than *uwe*, and proficiency at *uoi*, rather than at *uwe*, is the primary source of the Kamba reputation for widespread and powerful "witchcraft." As Machakos District Commissioner D. J. Penwill noted in the 1950s, "Witchcraft – 'uchawi,' in Kamba 'woi' – is a field in which Kamba are reputed by

---

[21] This book typically employs "witchcraft," "witch," and "oathing" and so on when addressing British colonial perspectives or in reference to literature not having to do with Ukambani and typically uses *uoi*, *mu'unde m'uoi*, and so on when writing on the Kamba perspective. Kamba people also alternate between *mu'unde m'uoi* and *mu'unde m'uwe* to refer to the category of supernatural specialist glossed as "witchdoctor" in English. They do so in a contextually contingent manner, depending on whether this variety of practitioner uses his or her knowledge of *uoi* and *uwe* for harm or for help. This book uses "witchdoctor" for both types of practitioner in order to provide clarity for English-speaking readers and to highlight the ambiguous nature of the practitioner's knowledge and activities.

[22] Evans-Pritchard, *Witchcraft*, 177.

[23] Geschiere, *The Modernity of Witchcraft*, 50. Also West, *Kupilikula*, 74–75.

the other tribes to have high accomplishments."[24] Further, Kamba beliefs and practices related to *uoi* produced the majority of "critical events" through which witchcraft challenged colonial administration.

Writing in the 1970s on the pervasiveness of *uoi*, anthropologist Hitoshi Ueda offered observations borne out by both historical and contemporary sources. He observed,

> Villagers use the word *uoi* very often in their daily life. You often hear them saying "That person was killed by *uoi*. My friend bought a very strong *uoi* in Mombasa. That woman is very famous for giving *uoi* to villagers. *Uoi* of woman is not so strong. Witchdoctors in Tharaka are experts to remove *uoi*, etc." *Uoi* is defined as a magical power by which evil intentions, such as killing enemy or human ill-feelings such as envy, anger, hostility etc., can be attained.[25]

Uoi therefore can be most easily understood as the harnessing of malevolent supernatural power to harm a person or property. But within Kamba cosmology, *uoi* is at the same time more complex. It is not simply the act itself of doing harm through supernatural methods and means but can also be a substance, a power, and even a way-of-being-in-the-world. *Uoi* has existed simultaneously as substances and articles that are used to do malevolent harm and also as the power that renders them harmful. Indeed, writing on the various aspects of Kamba witchcraft in the early 1900s, Lindblom emphasized, "The concrete means is also called *uoi*."[26] Overall, *uoi* is both material and experiential.

Foremost, the female Kamba *mu'unde m'uoi* herself is imbued with *uoi* as is the witchcraft lineage from which she typically springs.[27] For the female *mu'unde m'uoi*, *uoi* is both embodied and affective. The female *mu'unde m'uoi* is an embodiment of *uoi*; she carries the power of *uoi* in her body and activates it through her body.[28] At the same time, *uoi* has affective resonances for both the male and the female *mu'unde m'uoi*. The use of *uoi* often has its roots in the excitement of emotions, and the *mu'unde m'uoi* often exercises *uoi* for the simple pleasure of doing harm.

---

[24] Penwill, *Kamba Customary*, 93. *Uoi* and related Kikamba cosmological terms have various spellings in anthro-historical literature. I have preserved the original spellings except in cases in which the author used a period-specific phonetic alphabet. In such cases I have substituted the present-day spelling of the term in question.

[25] Ueda, "Witchcraft," n.p.

[26] Lindblom, *The Akamba*, 278.

[27] See Chapter 2.

[28] While male witches do not come from "witchcraft lineages" or necessarily embody *uoi*, they nonetheless activate *uoi* by harnessing malevolent supernatural power through their speech. The gendered nature of *uoi* as well as the ambiguous relationship between witchdoctors and *uoi* is discussed further later in the chapter.

For its victims too, *uoi* is a way-of-being-in-the-world. When a person is bewitched, he or she often becomes bodily and/or emotionally and psychologically saturated with *uoi*. The most regularly practiced forms of *uoi* are those aimed at harming or even destroying bodies. Yet whether the *uoi* is directed toward killing a person, harming a person's body, or destroying a person's property or kin, the victim's experience of having had *uoi* turned against him or her has adverse effects on his or her spirit and psychology as well.[29] When a person is bewitched, particularly if the bewitchment takes place over a long period of time, the experience of being bewitched often becomes the determining factor in how the person regards himself or herself, and also the primary experience through which others in the community come to identify the bewitched person.

Uoi is a way-of-being-in-the-world across communities as well. As Penwill noted in the 1950s, "The Kamba did, and still do, fear witchcraft greatly; and their chief concern with it is to protect themselves against it."[30] The agreed-upon permeating presence and potentials of *uoi* imbue community members with a consistent, cyclical unease while at the same moment resolving seemingly irresolvable questions. For example, *uoi* might provide a simple, assimilable answer to the question of why a healthy young man has died suddenly while at the same time drawing attention to the omnipresence of *uoi* and its results.

Uoi also produces quotidian social interactions predicated on fear, distrust, and avoidance as opposed to those based on cohesion and harmony. The affective environment of Ukambani is similar to that described by West who writes, "Fear has long been woven into the tapestry of Muedan life."[31] For example, a piece of essential local knowledge in a given community might be to forgo the hospitality offered at a particular homestead because the women there are reputed to practice *uoi* and it is thus unsafe to accept their food.[32] Indeed, Lindblom focused on such an intersection of witchcraft and poisoning. He wrote,

> In times past murder by means of witch-craft and also by poison was very common and now-a-days it is said to occur. The murder was

---

[29] Adam Ashforth, *Madumo: A Man Bewitched* (Chicago: University of Chicago Press, 2000).
[30] Penwill, *Kamba Customary*, 94.
[31] West, *Kupilikula*, 78.
[32] When staying with a family in Kilungu, I was warned by various family members that surrounding homesteads housed "witches" and thus that neither my research assistant nor I should not accept food at these homesteads.

generally done by putting poison in beer or a woman would sometimes kill a guest by poisoning his food.[33]

Uoi can thus create a collective affective state of always already being afraid and distrustful; a way-of-being-in-the-world in which to live among others (and especially to prosper) is to court myriad risks.

Yet, despite the negative emotions and relations that *uoi* produces, it is rarely a source of shame or even reticence. While practicing *uoi* may be a hidden activity and evidencing too much knowledge of its particulars viewed as impolitic, talking about the people, power, and pervasiveness associated with *uoi* is not. Indeed, most Kamba people regard *uoi* as a central part of "Kamba-ness" and do not dispute outsiders' identifications of Kamba people with witchcraft. Such matter-of-fact attitudes about *uoi* result from a range of reasons, the most central of which is that for many people, *uoi* is not refutable or contestable – it just *is*. So it follows that if *uoi* exists (and exists everywhere) it is better to belong to a tribe with a reputation for powerful witchcraft than to one without.

Uoi is divided into numerous subtypes, and again the most basic distinction is between bought *uoi* and inherited *uoi*. These two types of *uoi* in turn break down along gendered lines. They also correspond to different levels of professionalization. The two genres of *uoi* also emerged in different periods. Of the two types of Kamba witchcraft, bought *uoi* – described as a substance rather than a power – is the newer and less elaborate. As one Kamba witchdoctor explained,

> I don't know [what it is] because I don't practice, but I guess you could say it's a substance or knowledge; a substance like *muthea* – the same as *muti* – a mixture of herbs available in containers. It can be bought. *Uoi* can be in different forms depending on where you buy it from. It can be a powder, an object, and then you are told how to apply [it].[34]

Bought *uoi* is often figured as a poison administered through food. An elderly Kamba man's explanation that bought *uoi* is "substances mixed into food to kill" is typical. While some Kamba people explain that bought *uoi* is already imbued with magic when it is purchased, others explain that extra steps are needed to activate it. For example, one elderly Kamba man noted, "You boil it [*uoi*] in a pot and put it in food to kill. When treated further with words, it can be called 'uoi'." Using the same terminology as the witchdoctor cited above, this man elaborated

---

[33] Lindblom, *The Akamba*, 95.
[34] R. K., Kilungu, September 2004.

that bought *uoi* "can be packed in a container and sold in strips. The container is *mulungu*. The substance is *muti*."[35]

Bought *uoi* is available from witchdoctors, a category of supernatural "middle figures" whose activities we will turn to in more detail later in the chapter. Bought *uoi* has historically been available locally from Kamba purveyors but can also be obtained from witchdoctors from other tribes traveling through Nairobi or Ukambani or through visits to these witchdoctors in their home locations. Many people concur that *uoi* has been typically purchased by men because of materially driven conflicts – for example, disputes over land or other types of property. One elderly Kamba man explained, "With men, men will only use that [*uoi*] when they are competing over something, if there is some struggle somewhere or if you are progressive."[36] Despite various differences in the explanations of bought *uoi*, its origins and how it works, it has been generally agreed that men are the primary buyers and sellers of bought *uoi*. Bought *uoi* then is synonymous with the "witchcraft of men."

Inherited *uoi*, in contrast, is much more complex. Varying types of inherited *uoi* are known by different names. For example, the *uoi* called *ndia* refers to *uoi* causing deafness while *konzesya* is the name of the *uoi* that causes a prolonged, wasting illness. Inherited *uoi* does not necessarily entail substances but always requires the mobilization of the practitioner's embodied powers of malfeasance. Unlike bought *uoi*, which has a finite use-value, inherited *uoi* is witchcraft of a "permanent kind."[37] Inherited *uoi* is only passed from mother to daughter and is thus synonymous with "women's witchcraft." Indeed, colonial official Charles Dundas explained in the early 1900s that "If a woman is a witch her daughter will be one too."[38] As one elderly Kamba succinctly explained, "Witchcraft is an inherited practice that is used for destruction. It is very old and it is there even today."[39]

Many Kamba explain that "lineage is a determinant" of who inherits *uoi* and are able to cite particular *uoi* clans.[40] Though *uoi* is inborn, a

---

[35] J. K., Kilungu, August 2004; P. M., Kangundo, August 2004. Colonial officials were well aware of the frequency of poisonings. For example, in response to reports about outbreaks of poisoning allegations in Kenya's Native Reserves, J. E. W. Flood of the Colonial Office Legal Department wrote simply, "The usual sort of story!" PRO CO 533/431, Poisoning Allegations in Native Reserves 1933.
[36] K. M., Kangundo, August 2004.
[37] P. M., Kilungu, August 2004.
[38] Dundas, "History of Kitui," 531.
[39] M. M., Tawa, August 2004.
[40] K. N., Nzawi, September 2004. See Chapter 2.

girl's status as a *mu'unde m'uoi* must be acknowledged and activated secretly through a two-step process. First, when a girl reaches puberty, her mother initiates her as a *mu'unde m'uoi*. This initiation takes place at night in a secluded location. Some accounts stipulate that the novice *mu'unde m'uoi* is inoculated with *uoi* by her mother who cuts her daughter, or helps the girl to cut herself, at various pulse points on her body and who then rubs *uoi* substances into the cuts. As one elderly Kamba explained, "They [witches] cut themselves four times near the spine and apply a substance so *uoi* gets into the blood."[41] Other explanations point to a ceremony in which mother and daughter "stand back-to-back, naked, and exchange paraphernalia."[42] Two elderly Kamba women were able to flesh out the details of this type of initiation. They explained,

> Mothers and daughters go to a shrine, preferably with a friend who is also a *mu'unde m'uoi*. Her presence enhances the power. The mother and daughter stand back-to-back, naked. They bring their buttocks together and say some words. Then there is dancing. Sometimes they sacrifice at shrines, but that is not a "must." The recipient would say after receiving the *uoi*, "I do not know what you have given me" meaning that she will not reveal her *uoi* in her lifetime.[43]

Although a girl is initiated and instructed in *uoi* at puberty, she does not inaugurate her practice until she has married and had children. While some informants explain, "A girl must wait until she is married and has a boy and girl," other elderly Kamba suggest that a novice witch must have three children (whose sex is insignificant) before she can commence practicing.[44] Despite these differences, both accounts show that motherhood is a prerequisite for activating *uoi*, perhaps because a novice *mu'unde m'uoi* makes the initial test of her *uoi* by killing children. One elderly Kamba man explained that killing children to inaugurate *uoi* is "a trial called *kusyimithya* to see if your *uoi* will work."[45] While some accounts suggest that a Kamba *mu'unde m'uoi* inaugurates her practice of *uoi* by using it against her own firstborn, others explain that she turns her *uoi* on other close associates. As one elderly Kamba man noted, "She

---

[41] Ibid. Some colonial accounts explain somewhat ambiguously that young women are inoculated with witchcraft at the time of their circumcisions. Oral evidence suggests that young women are inoculated with witchcraft at the *age* for circumcision rather than through the circumcision ceremony itself.
[42] J. K., Kilungu, August 2004.
[43] M. N., Kilungu, September 2004; B. M., Kilungu, September 2004.
[44] K. N., Nzawi, September 2004; M. W., Imani, September 2004.
[45] P. M., Kangundo, August 2004.

[the novice *mu'unde m'uoi*] starts with children at home. Not her own children, other people's."[46] In either case, the novice *mu'unde m'uoi* inaugurates her *uoi* by proving her reproductive and destructive capacities.

The actual ways in which a woman practices *uoi* are somewhat obscure for a number of reasons. First, as noted, initiation into *uoi* entails vows of secrecy. While most Kamba people are willing to speak freely about *uoi* on a generalized basis, they are often reluctant to evidence too much specific knowledge about how inherited *uoi* is actually practiced because such knowledge can invite accusations that the speaker is a *mu'unde m'uoi* or at least maintains close ties with others who are. And many members of conservative evangelical churches such as the Africa Inland Mission/ Africa Inland Church to which many Kamba belong regard speaking of *uoi* or even acknowledging its existence as taboo.[47] Nonetheless, a general consensus exists that the female *mu'unde m'uoi* uses *uoi* primarily by mobilizing malevolent powers within herself and directing these powers to harm others. Despite most Kamba people's reticence regarding practices associated with women's *uoi*, an elderly Kamba man was willing to shed light on how a female witch might deploy her *uoi*. He explained,

> Usually a person who practices that [*uoi*] has a small bag, very small, filled with paraphernalia. That bag is somewhere, maybe in the pocket. And when she wants to perform that act of bewitching somebody, she does some funny things. She can do like this (touches the wrists and scratches the heels). She claps the hands. While doing that, she can say what she wants now. She can send those words to a certain person. And that will happen.[48]

Kamba women's *uoi* is *ineluctably* embodied. As it is inherited, women's *uoi* acts from within the body of the novice *mu'unde m'uoi* whether initiation occurs through contact with the body of a senior *mu'unde m'uoi* or through the introduction of *uoi* substances into the novice's body. Further, the *uoi* of the novice – her destructive power – is inaugurated when she demonstrates the reproductive capacities of her body. Even

---

[46] M. W., Imani, September 2004.
[47] For a brief history of Christianity in Ukambani, see David Sandgren, "Kamba Christianity: From Africa Inland Church to African Brotherhood Church," in *East African Expressions of Christianity*, ed. Thomas Spear and Isaria Kimambo (Oxford: James Currey, 1999), 169–195. The Africa Inland Mission and its relationship to *uoi* are discussed further in Chapter 8.
[48] K. N., Nzawi, September 2004. This account accords with testimony offered by witches at the Machakos witch-cleansings and recorded by J. C. Nottingham and Godfrey Wilson in the 1950s. See Chapters 7 and 8.

uoi entailing the use of paraphernalia is embodied when mobilized by a hereditary *mu'unde m'uoi* because the power that renders the paraphernalia efficacious originates in the body of the *mu'unde m'uoi*. And, most significantly, if the novice witch refuses the *uoi* embodied in her, her body will turn against her and she may even die. As one elderly Kamba woman explained, "The mother promises to pass *uoi* on to her daughter. If the daughter refuses it, she can be bewitched."[49]

The initial exercise of inherited *uoi* is driven by an embodied imperative, but subsequent acts are motivated by emotions, often "hatred" with an unattributable source. *Uoi* is also described as being driven by jealousy of things related to women's reproduction – successful *mashamba*, thriving children, and so on. Thus, while men's *uoi* draws on the provider's professional expertise and is motivated by men's material concerns, a woman's *uoi* and her reasons for using it come from within herself. Many Kamba people regard men's *uoi* as logical and women's *uoi* as ephemeral. Simply put, "Men usually have a reason. Sometimes women just use it [*uoi*]." Another elderly Kamba man fleshed out this succinct explanation. He explained,

> Women – first they practice that because it is a tradition. They don't need even to quarrel with somebody. They can just practice out of jealousy, from nothing. They can also use it when there is some dispute over something, when you are struggling.[50]

This constellation of female-centered factors was also described by Ueda,

> This magical power is originated by such women themselves, not by the witchdoctor, even the female witchdoctor. People explain that this magical power comes from the inside of such women's bodies, or from their blood. If such women feel jealous, angry, or have bad-will, *uoi* of such women can be sent to harm others directly, without getting the help of witchdoctor. *Uoi* of woman is suitable for witchcraft. It is said that *uoi* of woman is inherited through the female line. IF a mother is a witch, every real daughter is regarded (potentially) as a witch.[51]

Asked what some of the typical results of women's *uoi* are, one elderly Kamba man simply enumerated: "Kids stop going to school. Girls don't marry. People die."[52] In sum, as Smith notes of "witchcraft" in Taita, *uoi*

---

[49] M. N., Kilungu, August 2004.
[50] J. K., Kilungu, August 2004; M. M., Tawa, September 2004.
[51] Ueda, "Witchcraft," n.p.
[52] P. M., Kangundo, August 2004.

in Ukambani has also been conceived of as "the destructive power of selfish desire, which sometimes causes fantastic things to happen."[53]

The middling figure of the witchdoctor is present in both men's and women's *uoi*. As noted above, the status of the witchdoctor as a practitioner of *uwe* and/or *uoi* is somewhat muddled. Like the female *mu'unde m'uoi*, the witchdoctor inherits his or her abilities to do *uwe* and/or *uoi*, and the witchdoctor's capacities are embodied. One elderly Kamba man explained,

> They [witchdoctors] are born. When they are born they are holding *mbuu*, "beads" in their hand. Their *mbuu* are kept in a special gourd, *kititi*, until they come of age. They may be initiated by an older male or female, but this is not a "must."[54]

In writing on Kamba witchdoctors (often referred to as "medicine men" in colonial anthropological parlance), Lindblom cited similar elements. He explained,

> It is not everyone who can be a medicine man, as a rule only those who have shown themselves predestined to this position from birth are eligible. The proof of this is that the child should be born with what one might call appendages, which constitute an indication from the ancestral spirits that he is to be a medicine-man. Thus some have been born with a little peg in their hands and in the case of another new-born child there were found in the afterbirth five small stones, such as the medicine man uses in his calabashes for divination.[55]

Explaining her own experience, an elderly Kamba witchdoctor in Nairobi's Pipeline location stated, "My mother was a *mu'unde m'uwe*. I was initiated after the birth of my first child. I was born holding beads."[56] However, despite the embodied nature of his or her power, the *mu'unde m'uwe* practices *uwe* (and sometimes *uoi*) as a matter of choice rather than as the result of a physical imperative.

The avowed aim of the *mu'unde m'uwe* is to offer remedies for the suffering and lack caused by *uoi* and to provide protective magic to ward off or counteract the effects of *uoi*. This role is consistently cited by elderly people from across Machakos and Nairobi. One Kamba man summed up the difference between a witch and a witchdoctor: "A *mu'unde m'uoi* always does harm. A *mu'unde m'uwe* often tries to help." A contemporary

---

[53] Smith, *Bewitching*, 16.
[54] M. W., Imani, September 2004; R. K., Kilungu, September 2004.
[55] Lindblom, *The Akamba*, 255.
[56] B. W., Pipeline, August 2004; M. W., Imani, September 2004; J. K. S., Kilungu, September 2004; R. K., Kilungu September 2004.

pointed out, "The *mu'unde m'uwe* tries to stop *uoi*. The *mu'unde m'uoi* does his or her work separately from the *mu'unde m'uwe*." A Kamba *mu'unde m'uwe* explained in more detail, "A *mu'unde m'uoi* uses his or her paraphernalia to destroy while a *mu'unde m'uwe* is there to undo what a *mu'unde m'uoi* has done."[57]

But in order to counteract *uoi*, the *mu'unde m'uwe* must have a working knowledge of the full complement of *uoi*. Such knowledge can be slippery, treacherous, and tempting. Ultimately, what the *mu'unde m'uwe* chooses to do with his or her knowledge of *uoi* is entirely up to him or her, and often a *mu'unde m'uwe* moves between practicing and dispensing *uwe* and *uoi*. In response to a question about whether witchdoctors have harmful paraphernalia, a Kamba *mu'unde m'uwe* stated without hesitation, "Yes, they sell it [harmful paraphernalia] to other people who want to use it or the *mu'unde m'uwe* can use it himself or herself when angry." Her views were borne out in the replies of most elderly Kamba to the question of the witchdoctor's malevolent powers. The reply of one Kamba man from Kangundo, that "Yes, they [witchdoctors] have it [*uoi*]. And they sell it to people who want to use it," is typical.[58] Thus, while the primary purpose of the *mu'unde m'uwe* is to counter *uoi* by doing and dispensing benevolent, palliative magic, the necessary knowledge of harmful magic makes it easy and oftentimes inviting for the witchdoctor to move between *uwe* and *uoi*.[59]

A final category of supernatural practitioner involved in *uwe* and *uoi* is the diviner. Diviners are most often women and, like the *mu'unde m'uoi* and *mu'unde m'uwe*, a diviner is imbued with inherited supernatural powers.[60] However, the diviner's powers do not enable her to do or dispense magic per se. Rather, they enable her to function as a supernatural diagnostician, deducing and identifying the origin of *uoi*. Less frequently, the diviner's powers enable her to do work more in keeping with the Euro-American sense of divination – the ferreting out of another's secret self and the prediction of the future.[61] However, people most often

[57] R. K., Kilungu September 2004; J. K. S., Kilungu, September 2004; B. W., Pipeline, August 2004.
[58] B. W., Pipeline, August 2004.
[59] Eric de Rosny, "Justice and Sorcellerie." Unpublished Paper. November, 2005.
[60] The diviner is also called "*mu'unde m'uoi*" in Kikamba. For the purposes of clarity, this book uses the English gloss, "diviner," when discussing practitioners who use "supernatural" power benevolently to diagnose cases of *uoi*.
[61] I visited a diviner based in Nairobi's Kibera shantytown. I did not have a specific complaint to address to the diviner, and the diviner concluded that I had been "lucky" in life and offered to review past events in my life in order to establish her credibility as a diviner and then to predict future events in my life. The diviner proceeded to do so with varying degrees of success.

PHOTOGRAPH 2. A Kamba diviner in her Kibera home and place of business. She is holding a Koran. Photograph by the author.

approach diviners when they suspect that they or someone close to them has been bewitched.

The diviner does her work through consultations with spirits of diverse origins who advise her on the origin of a client's misfortune. The spirits may request a consultation with the diviner or she may summon them for advice. Consultations at the request of the spirits or of the diviner are opened by the diviner donning a particular *kikoi*, a solid white or solid black sarong with a narrow, windowpane pattern in red, and by the diviner drawing patterns out of a chalky substance on the ground.[62]

---

[62] A *kikoi* (pl. *vikoi*) is a finished piece of lightweight cotton fabric, approximately 1 yard in width and 2 yards in length. Initially worn as a wrap-skirt by Muslim men on the

Both the *kikoi* and the patterns are said to be attractive to the spirits, and diviners put on the special *kikoi* and draw with chalk either in response to direct requests from the spirits or in unsolicited efforts to attract them. Once a diviner is in consultation with the spirits, she often flips through a holy book like the Koran or the Bible at the direction of the spirits. The diviner gains insight from heeding the spirits' directions rather than from the text itself as in many cases diviners are themselves illiterate.[63] The diviner's primary work is not doing or dispensing *uoi* or *uwe*, but rather identifying those who have practiced *uoi* and matching a *mu'unde m'uoi* with his or her misdeeds. In doing her work, the diviner is not so much exercising her will over her supernatural powers as she is allowing herself to act as a channel for the knowledge of the spirits. A diviner's diagnosis generally leads to the cleansing or killing of a *mu'unde m'uoi*.

Kamba institutions and authorities existed to deal with *uoi* well into the colonial era and many of them linger today in modified forms. As the practice of *uoi* disrupts and destroys not only individual lives but community life as well, conciliar mechanisms have existed to deal with *uoi*. In the precolonial and early colonial periods, upon diagnosis by a diviner, the *mu'unde m'uoi* was referred to the *king'ole* for discipline. The term *king'ole* carries multiple meanings: law, act, institution. A *king'ole* council was composed of select *atumia* or respected community elders. As one interviewee explained, "Old men and women who could keep a secret" made up *king'ole* councils.[64] The role of the *king'ole* was to restore and ensure order in the community; as one Kamba man put it, "They

---

East Coast of Africa, *vikoi* are now used by East Africans for a variety of sartorial and decorative functions. Their popularity has carried over into the tourist industry, and shops and stalls devoted to selling *vikoi* and clothing and accessories made from them have blossomed in Nairobi and Dar es Salaam and on the East African Coast. *Vikoi* can even be found in stylish boutiques in Paris's *bobo chic* shopping district. It is, however, rare to see the white and black *vikoi* used by diviners in ordinary shops. I was able to purchase one of each at a shop with a reputation for selling these *vikoi* outside Nairobi's Gikomba market.

[63] Kamba people have had long-standing interactions with communities on Kenya's Coast, and many Kamba people have historically believed supernatural practitioners and "spirits" from the coastal region to be more powerful than local ones. When I inquired of the pictured diviner, M. K., if she was a Muslim and why she utilized a Koran, the diviner explained that she was not a Muslim, but that the spirits with whom she was in contact asked that she use a Koran. She added that she was illiterate and not reading the Koran, but simply flipping through the pages for the pleasure of the spirits.

[64] J. M., Kilungu, August 2004. Colonial-era anthropology and many contemporary sources explain the *king'ole* as an exclusively male council. However, claims that both men and women served on the *king'ole* appear regularly enough in informant testimony to suggest that women may have participated in some locations and not in others.

were like the *serikali* of the Kamba."⁶⁵ And an elderly Kamba woman reiterated, "This [*king'ole*] is a group that organized themselves to control society."⁶⁶

A central part of this role was disciplining severe social malefactors like the *mu'unde m'uoi* and the thief. In dealing with such "categories of dangerous persons," the *king'ole* council exercised *king'ole* law, a juridical process in which the council warned social malefactors to cease their activities and then saw to the cleansing or removal of a *mu'unde m'uoi* or thief who agreed to desist.⁶⁷ Under *king'ole* law, the council was also empowered to kill dangerous persons who refused to comply with the council's order to stop their activities. Simply put in the words of one elderly Kamba man, "*King'ole* does the killing of the bad ones."⁶⁸ A contemporary noted, "They [the *king'ole*] punished the *mu'unde m'uoi*, the thieves, and other criminal activities."⁶⁹ The act of killing a recidivist *mu'unde m'uoi* or thief was also called *king'ole*. The elderly Kamba woman cited above elaborated, "A long time ago the community could kill the *mu'unde m'uoi*. This was called *king'ole*."⁷⁰

Oral and anthro-historical sources propose that particularly virulent, brazen, and widespread *uoi* activities brought a *mu'unde m'uoi* to the attention of the *king'ole*. One elderly Kamba woman explained that a recidivist *mu'unde m'uoi* is one who "kills with fear. Continuously. She can't be contained."⁷¹ Dundas emphasized the recidivist nature of those subject to *king'ole* discipline. He wrote,

> When a man had repeatedly committed serious crimes, or was a notorious wizard, so that he came to be regarded as a public danger, the assembled elders might decide that he must be put to death. In such case elders from remote parts were summoned, and the accusations made were deposed to in a form of oath, which is believed to be fatal to the perjurer.⁷²

---

⁶⁵ L. N. N., Kangundo, August 2004. *Serikali* is the Kiswahili word for "government." For example, the British colonial government is called *serikali ya ukoloni* and the contemporary government *serikali ya leo*.

⁶⁶ R. K., Kilungu, September 2004.

⁶⁷ Suzette Heald, *Controlling Anger: The Anthropology of Gisu Violence* (Oxford: James Currey, 1998), 12.

⁶⁸ L. N. N., Kangundo, August 2004.

⁶⁹ R. K., Kilungu, September 2004.

⁷⁰ Ibid.

⁷¹ M. N., Kilungu, August 2004.

⁷² Charles Dundas, "Native Laws of Some Bantu Tribes of East Africa," *Journal of the Royal Anthropological Society of Great Britain and Ireland*, 51 (January–June 1921): 234.

And Lindblom also noted how "categories of dangerous persons" were dealt with by *king'ole* justice.[73] He explained,

> Persons who are suspected of causing the death of other people by means of *uoi* (that is, witchcraft) and are thus dangerous to the public safety, can be killed with impunity by the united intervention of all the adult male inhabitants in the district. This is also true of incorrigible thieves.[74]

Sometimes, albeit rarely, a *mu'unde m'uoi* would invite the interest of the *king'ole* through her public practice or threats of *uoi*. More commonly, victims of *uoi* reported the activities of the *mu'unde m'uoi* to the *king'ole* after consultation with a diviner. Subtle differences exist in ethnographic and documentary information on how the *king'ole* would proceed after hearing accusations of recidivist *uoi*, but the majority of accounts point to a process of warning, corporal punishment, cleansing and/or exile, and ultimately killing if the *mu'unde m'uoi* refused to subject herself (or more rarely, himself) to cleansing or removal from the community. As one elderly Kamba man neatly explained,

> The *mu'unde m'uoi* was killed if she ignored the warning of the *atumia* to stop. She was beaten, then moved, then killed. The *atumia* called *king'ole* to discuss the issue and resolve it. The goal was to move the *mu'unde m'uoi* away. If she refused, she was beaten, and then killed.[75]

In rarer instances, the *king'ole* took action to prompt a reluctant *mu'unde mu'uoi* to confess. An elderly Kamba woman cited the *king'ole*'s employ of a sort of "truth serum." She explained,

> The *mu'unde m'uoi* needed to be beaten hard. The *king'ole* used to give the suspect *kivala* – a stimulant to get the *mu'unde m'uoi* to confess all the people she has bewitched. After that, the *king'ole* decided what to do with the *mu'unde m'uoi*.[76]

Accounts vary regarding the degree to which the family of the *mu'unde m'uoi* was involved in the deliberations and administration of *king'ole*. Some sources

---

[73] Heald, *Controlling Anger*, 12.
[74] Lindblom, *The Akamba*, 176.
[75] M. K., Tawa, September 2004.
[76] M. N., Kilungu, August 2004. This informant's mention of the use of *kivala* as part of *king'ole* justice is unusual. Discussions of *kivala* emerge more regularly in accounts of witch-cleansings in the 1940s and 1950s, particularly those addressing cleansings conducted in Machakos by coastal witchdoctors. See Chapters 7 and 8.

assert that the family had no knowledge of *king'ole* justice until after the fact. One interviewee explained, "They [the family] weren't supposed to know. After they would sacrifice a bull."[77] Other accounts stipulate that the families were aware of or even present at *king'ole* proceedings and executions, but were powerless to intervene in the deliberations and decisions of the *king'ole*. For example, an elderly Kamba woman explained, "The family members could be around but they were helpless since *king'ole* was final. They were not consulted."[78] Some informants stipulate that the family was made aware of the *king'ole*'s interest in their relative when the *king'ole* offered its warning to the *mu'unde m'uoi* to cease and desist. One elderly Kamba man noted, "The family and clan of the *mu'unde m'uoi* were informed. If she continued to practice, she was hanged."[79]

Other discussions propose that the *king'ole* notified the family of impending proceedings as a type of "insurance" against later claims by the family for compensation for the life of their relative. Another elderly Kamba informant noted, "Permission was granted by the family so later the person couldn't be claimed from *king'ole*. 'Claimed' means that if the family participated, then they couldn't say later that the *king'ole* had killed an innocent person."[80] And, in describing *king'ole* procedures, Hobley focused strongly on the element of compensation. He noted in the early 1900s,

> They [*king'ole* council] then call the brothers of the suspect to the assembly and ask them why their brother or sister has killed so and so, and so and so, naming each victim; the brothers of course deny any knowledge of the matter and then each elder who has lost a man from his village demands compensation from the brothers of the accused for the life of his man. In nearly every case these brothers refuse saying: How can we pay compensation for the lives of all these people? The principal elder then calls out with a loud voice and says, "If one man kills the accused it means compensation so we will do it all together and then no one will be able to say that any one man killed him," and then all rush to the place where the accused is to be found and the people follow in a great crowd and they kill the accused: a man is killed by arrows and a woman is stoned to death ... the custom is called *king'ole*.[81]

---

[77] M. W., Imani, September 2004. Files pertaining to the Machakos Panels on Customary Law indicate that compensation was the "customary" form of punishment death and that animal sacrifice was often part of the Kamba legal process. KNA BB/22/2, Law Panels, Machakos, June 1955–October 1956.
[78] R. K., Kilungu, September 2004.
[79] J. N. K., Kilungu, September 2004.
[80] L. N. N., Kangundo, August 2004.
[81] Hobley, *Ethnology of A-kamba*, 96.

Many discussions of *king'ole* also foreground the presence and participation of the family throughout various stages of *king'ole* activity. For example, an elderly Kamba woman noted, "The family was part of the *king'ole* and would have thus been present when the decision was made. The family members were also fed up."[82] These varying accounts thus produce a continuum of family involvement in *king'ole* proceedings against a *mu'unde m'uoi*. Whether family members participated actively in *king'ole* or were simply informed of the events, in no case were family members able to appeal a judgment. In *uoi* cases, the authority of the *king'ole* was final.

In cases of *non-magical* murder, Kamba codes prescribed a compensatory system in which the killer compensated the victim's family with animal offerings. Lethal *king'ole* justice typically settled magical murder cases in which the murderer refused to confess and repent. The recidivist and unrepentant *mu'unde m'uoi* was killed because she (or he) was regarded as a serial killer who had killed often and would continue to do so.

Ethnographic and documentary accounts also differ as to the means by which the recalcitrant *mu'unde m'uoi* was killed by *king'ole*. In some instances, the disciplinary beatings that seem to have constituted a regular step in the administration of *king'ole* justice segued into lethal beatings. One elderly Kamba man noted simply, "They beat them with sticks."[83] Indeed, Hobley described *king'ole* killing in this way.[84] And Mwaiki, the most famous (alleged) Kamba *mu'unde m'uoi* to be subjected to *king'ole* justice died from a mass beating.[85] Other accounts suggest that a variety of methods were used to kill the *mu'unde m'uoi* according to the *king'ole* members' preferences. One elderly Kamba woman elaborated, "They [the *king'ole*] used to hang them [witches], throw them in a ditch and kill them using arrows or beat them to death or use *panga*."[86] Another interviewee cited burning as a preferred method, explaining, "The *atumia* gathered and asked the *mu'unde m'uoi* for her paraphernalia to be burned. If the *mu'unde m'uoi* refused, she could be burned."[87] Regardless of the

---

[82] B. M., Kilungu, August 2004.
[83] L. N. N., Kangundo, August 2004.
[84] Hobley, *Ethnology of A-kamba*, 95. For more of Hobley's general musings on witchcraft, see C. W. Hobley, "Some Reflections on Native Magic in Relation to Witchcraft," *Journal of the African Society* 33.132 (July 1934): 243–249.
[85] See Chapter 5 for a full discussion of Mwaiki's death.
[86] R. K., Kilungu, August 2004. A *panga* is a large, scythe-like knife generally used in agriculture work like cutting sugarcane or clearing brush.
[87] M. K., Kilungu, August 2004. This informant's statement about burning paraphernalia is not typical. Discussions of burning paraphernalia are regularly present in accounts of "witch-cleansings" in the 1940s and 1950s. See Chapters 7 and 8.

method, the goal of the *king'ole* was to discipline the practice of *uoi* through destroying the body of recalcitrant, recidivist *mu'unde m'uoi*.

King'ole is figured in oral and documentary sources as a precolonial and early colonial institution that was eventually supplanted through the colonial co-option of the Kamba *nzama* councils and through people's reliance on colonial courts. As one elderly Kamba man noted, with the advent of British colonial administration in Ukambani, the *king'ole*'s "operations were gradually curtailed."[88] Some informants and texts cite ways of dealing with *uoi* without seeking recourse in colonial or contemporary courts. An elderly Kamba woman explained the options: "Sometimes individuals seek revenge, but the community has had ways of dealing with the *mu'unde m'uoi*. They could use protective or counter paraphernalia."[89] As this comment hints, *king'ole*-style justice did not necessarily disappear with the coming of colonialism even if *king'ole* as an institution was marginalized or eradicated by colonial authority.[90] Rather Kamba people have continued to act against *uoi* as ad hoc *king'ole* councils, even when the composition of their groups or the content and the form of their *king'ole* proceedings contravenes earlier Kamba norms concerning *king'ole*.[91] Sometimes individuals have taken *king'ole*-style justice into their own hands without any broader sanction. In these ways, *king'ole* justice can be said to have existed alongside that of the colonial and postcolonial governments into the present day.

KAMBA OATHING – *NDUNDU* TO *KITHITU*

Like *uoi*, *uwe*, and *king'ole*, the term *kithitu* has multiple resonances. First, *kithitu* is the oath itself; the actual words spoken, the real promises made. *Kithitu* also refers to the substances and articles employed in the ceremony in which the oath is spoken. And *kithitu* is the (lethal) power that renders the oath efficacious. Neither documentary nor oral sources

---

[88] R. K., Kilungu, August 2004.
[89] J. M., Kilungu, August 2004.
[90] The timing at which *king'ole* was marginalized and Kamba people turned to colonial councils and courts is not clear from archival or ethnographic sources. Lindblom wrote, "Nowadays, when the whole of Ukamba is under British rule, *king'ole* is forbidden. However, some of the officials think that it is still practiced in the more remote regions." Lindblom, *The Akamba*, 180. Lindblom's work was originally published as a dissertation in 1916. He conducted fieldwork in Kenya before World War I. His comment suggests that colonial efforts to supplant *king'ole* began early in the colonial era.
[91] For specific discussions of this behavior, see Chapter 5.

are clear about the source of *kithitu*'s power, asserting simply that its power is in its killing capacity and "special ingredients."[92] *Kithitu* is processual, and it is accurate to say, "*Kithitu* is at the same time the generic name for oathing and the active factor of the oath."[93] The act of engaging in *kithitu* is called *kuusya kithitu*, literally "to eat *kithitu*," referring to the ingestion of the *kithitu* substances contained in a *kithitu* object such as a pot or calabash, a central element of the oathing process. A *kithitu* ceremony is managed by a specialist called *mu'unde wa kuuysa kithitu*, a term broadly translatable as "man of eating *kithitu*." In contrast to certain documentary sources that conflate the *mu'unde wa kuuysa kithitu* with the witchdoctor or the even less precise colonial category of the "medicine man," Kamba people are often quick to emphasize that the *mu'unde wa kuuysa kithitu* is *not* a witchdoctor, but a category of oath administrator unto himself.[94]

Oathing – like *uoi* and *uwe* – is figured by Kamba and non-Kamba people alike as a central Kamba way-of-being-in-the-world. Respect for the omnipresent power that *kithitu* has in decision making and in competitive interactions is a key element of "Kamba-ness." Indeed, the strength of *kithitu* is recognized even outside Kamba communities.

Accordingly, *kithitu* has a number of functions and is invoked in a range of politico-juridical settings. *Kithitu* is used to cleanse people of social transgressions. It is used for the settlement of disputes between individuals. And as *uoi* has been the subject of social regulation by *non*-magical authorities, so has *kithitu* been intertwined with institutions of Kamba and Kenyan governance. In the precolonial and colonial periods, *kithitu* was used by *nzama* – councils of *atumia* similar to the *king'ole* but having broader functions – in deciding conflicts between individuals and/or parties.[95] Since independence, *kithitu* has been increasingly linked to political loyalty in Ukambani. Therefore, "swearing over the *kithitu* is connected with law, morals, values, legal procedure, clan conferences (*mbai*), political power and so on."[96] In all of these instances, the role of *kithitu* is to guarantee

---

[92] Anthony E. Thomas, "Oaths, Ordeals, and the Kenyan Courts: A Policy Analysis," *Human Organization* 33.1 (1974): 60.
[93] Grignon, "The *Kithitu*," 5.
[94] E. M. M., Tawa, September 2004; N. D. M., Tawa, September 2004; M. K., Tawa, September 2004; M. N., Kangundo, August 2004.
[95] *Nzama* were ultimately co-opted into the colonial administration. *Nzama* are discussed in more detail later in the chapter.
[96] Hitoshi Ueda, "Kithitu among the Kamba of Kenya – the Case Study of Kilonzo's Kithitu." Kenya National Archives Mss. 83–821 390 EUD; n.d.

the oath-taker's incontrovertible fidelity to the promises that the particular situation and setting have that demanded he or she make.[97]

Kithitu works as guarantor because of its killing capacity. Depending on the particular type of *kithitu* taken, to contravene *kithitu* is certainly to invite one's own death and in some instances, the deaths of one's kin and close associates as well. Further, through the act of "eating the oath," *kithitu*, like *uoi*, becomes embodied. The embodied nature of *kithitu* thus renders it impossible for the oath-taker to escape from the promise made over *kithitu* and from the killing capacity of *kithitu* that has become part of his or her body through ingestion. And like *uoi*, *kithitu* has affective resonances that contribute to its power. *Kithitu* is efficacious because people fear its consequences. As Ueda neatly explains, "There are many oral traditions and much gossip about the *kithitu* in which its potency and the people's fear of it are always expressed."[98]

However, while *kithitu*, like *uoi* is embodied, affective, and deadly, *kithitu* is not *uoi* or *uwe*. Kamba people rarely conflate the two.[99] Nonetheless, Onesmus Mutungi, a noted scholar of Kamba law and cosmology, has proposed that *kithitu* is a sort of *uoi*. He writes, "In a nutshell, in the absence of a belief in a supernatural power, capable of inflicting death and similar misfortunes, the *kithitu* oath has no functional basis. And this is the same power one encounters in examining witchcraft and beliefs incidental thereto."[100] While Mutungi is correct to suggest that *kithitu*'s power is rooted in its "supernatural" killing capacity, he is mistaken in his assertion that *kithitu* is imbued with the same brand of supernatural power that drives *uoi*. *Uoi* always already entails a malevolent supernatural power. The supernatural power of *kithitu*, in contrast, removes the stain of or prevents the use of malevolent power. Unlike *uoi*, the supernatural power of *kithitu* is directed toward the preservation or restoration of community relations. As François Grignon succinctly explains, "The oath, in short, is a remedy against any threat of disunity or conflict that can hit the community."[101]

---

[97] Some documentary sources claim that *kithitu* is a solely male affair. However, women are known to engage in *ndundu*, itself a type of *kithitu*.

[98] Ueda, "Kilonzo's *Kithitu*," n.p.

[99] In targeted interviews and casual conversations conducted over a year, only once did the author hear *kithitu* described by a Kamba person as a type of *uoi*. M. N., Kangundo, September 2004.

[100] Onesmus K. Mutungi, *The Legal Aspects of Witchcraft in East Africa* (Nairobi: East Africa Literature Bureau, 1977), 78. Mutungi uses the term "witchcraft" to designate black magic or *uoi* rather than white magic or *uwe*.

[101] Grignon, "The *Kithitu*," 5.

Understanding Uoi, Uwe, and Kithitu

In sum, then, *kithitu* is "a most deadly Kamba oath" that can be classified into four basic types: (1) the *ndundu*, (2) *kithitu kya ndata mwanza* or "oath of the seven sticks," (3) *kithitu kya matuka* or "oath of the seven days," and (4) *kithitu kya mbisu* or "oath of the cooking pot."[102] It has been largely through *ndundu* – the *uoi*-cleansing oath – that the institutions and actors of *uoi*, *king'ole*, *kithitu*, *nzama*, and the state have intersected.

Though many a *mu'unde m'uoi* resisted *king'ole* warnings, others did indeed assent to *king'ole* demands that they cease their practice of *uoi*. While some were simply "chased away," others underwent cleansing ceremonies involving the taking of *ndundu* oaths administered by specialized cleansers. An informant explained the procedure, noting, "Old men accuse the *mu'unde m'uoi* and then call in a cleansing specialist. The cleansing is called *kithitu*."[103]

Other documentary and oral sources point more specifically to the existence and widespread use of the *ndundu* oath, the type of *kithitu* whose exclusive function was to cleanse *uoi*.[104] While some sources suggest that *ndundu* is administered exclusively to the repentant *mu'unde m'uoi*, others propose that *ndundu* is sometimes administered to the entire female village populations to simultaneously weed out and cleanse *uoi*. Like many types of *kithitu*, the *ndundu* oath involved acts, speech, and substances. As one elderly Kamba man explained, "The *mu'unde m'uoi* got cleansed with the *ndundu* oath. There was a pot with blood and herbs. The *mu'unde m'uoi* stirred the pot and ingested another mixture. She jumped over the pot. Then she would never practice again."[105] Such was the type of oathing conducted under the auspices of the *nzama* and the colonial state during the Mau Mau period, and similar "cleansings" persist into the present.[106]

Whatever the circumstances under which *uoi* "cleansing" oaths are administered, they retain a killing capacity directed against oath-takers who renege on their oaths. The role of the anti-*uoi* oath is not simply to

---

[102] M. N., Kangundo, August 2004. The author and her research assistant inquired on numerous occasions about the significance of the number seven vis-à-vis Kamba oathing but were unable to elicit satisfactory responses. Numerology is not discussed in texts on Kamba cosmology.

[103] M. W., Imani, September 2004. *Kithitu* is the basic term given to Kamba oaths with the capacity to kill oath-takers who renege on their oaths. See the next section of this chapter.

[104] M. W., Imani, September 2004; J. K. S., Kilungu, September 2004; M. K., Tawa, September 2004; M. N., Kangundo, August 2004.

[105] M. K., Tawa, September 2004.

[106] See Chapters 6 and 7.

cleanse a *mu'unde m'uoi* of prior bad acts, but also to ensure the end of a witch's *uoi* practices. Once cleansed of *uoi* and prevented from further practice by the taking of an anti-*uoi kithitu*, a *mu'unde m'uoi* no longer belonged to a category of dangerous persons and could thus be reintegrated into her community as a "good" person.

Overall, *uoi, uwe,* and *kithitu* have long constituted central elements both of what it means to be Kamba and how Kamba people have themselves made sense of being in the world. But *uoi, uwe,* and *kithitu* have been also been significant because their entanglement with spectacular violence has caused them to be subject to the sort of consistent scrutiny and discipline by the state which has produced many of the "critical moments" at which witchcraft beliefs and practices have challenged state authority from the colonial era to the present. Accordingly, the next chapter traces how witchcraft and oathing have become engrained in the state's anthro-administrative lexicon, working to explain away persistent disorder and underdevelopment and to reproduce narratives of governmental best practice in response to witchcraft-centered challenges to state authority.

4

The "Cosmology" of the Colonial State

AN ANTHROPOLOGIZING AND ARCHIVING BUREAUCRACY

At the beginning of the colonial era, British authorities stepped into the dynamic sociopolitical, supernatural situations of the Kamba people. And, like the Kamba, British officials had their own way-of-being-in-the-world, a brand of "cosmology" centered on the core beliefs, practices, institutions, and authorities encompassed by colonial governmentality. In colonial imaginations, this "modern" colonial cosmology operated in stark, deliberate opposition to the "traditional" Kamba one. Yet, at the same time, the claims of colonial cosmology also worked to obscure the moments at which colonial authorities had to adapt to Kamba ways and means.

The cosmology of British officials quickly brought the institutions and actors of the state into conflict and competition with those of the Kamba. In the context of witchcraft and oathing, clashes resulted because British officials sought simultaneously to discipline and deny the efficacy of Kamba practices and beliefs while Kamba people refused to surrender authoritative sway over *uoi* to the state. And, more broadly, conflicts took place because both the colonial state and Kamba authorities claimed the right to exercise judicial violence through their own institutions – the colonial courts or the Kamba *king'ole*.

The colonial state's legal and administrative efforts to deal with "witchcraft" in Ukambani during the twentieth century entailed the development of the Witchcraft Ordinances and the burgeoning of Kamba witchcraft as an area of anthro-administrative investigative concern. Colonial discourse reflects British authorities' recognition of the affective and embodied elements of Kamba witchcraft. Such knowledge, in turn, strongly influenced the development of administrative and judicial strategies and institutions that comprised the cosmology of the colonial state.

This chapter argues that colonial-era conflicts and clashes point to how challenges to state authority transpired beyond moments of unambiguous civil or martial rebellion. Rather, challenges also occurred on a more quotidian basis through Kamba people's continued adherence to beliefs, practices, and institutions like those concerned with *uoi*, *kithitu*, and *king'ole*. The consistency of such challenges produced a type of colonial governance conducted within an "idiom of crisis"; a heightening of stakes and hardening of approaches which in turn led to many of the "critical events" that buffeted the state in the first half of the twentieth century.

CONTOURS OF COLONIAL ADMINISTRATION

After the conquest period, the emphasis of colonial authorities shifted from coercion and rule via violence to coercion and rule via bureaucratization. Yet, the somewhat improvisational and often individualistic style of colonial administration that developed in Kenya created resentments and mismanagements that contributed strongly to conflicts throughout the first half of the twentieth century. "Colonial domination," Berman notes, "turns out, in fact to have been an extraordinarily complex social process involving far more than the use of force."[1]

The structure of government in Kenya was at once hierarchical and ad hoc, and the development of the protectorate, and shortly after the colonial state, involved both institutions and individuals. The basic governmental structure was as follows: Governor, Chief Justice, Legislative Council, Department Heads, and Administrators at the Provincial and District levels.[2] Despite the existence of a clear governmental structure, factors like distance, poor communications, and spotty knowledge of the people being governed limited the reach of the Executive. Aware of such limits, imperial authorities organized administration along a prefectural model in order to create a corps of administrators who would share the mind-sets and goals of the Executive even if they were not under direct

---

[1] Berman and Lonsdale, *Unhappy Valley I*, 152.
[2] Y. P. Ghai and J. P. W. B. McAuslan note that a "striking feature" of the East Africa Order in Council 1897 was its "emphasis on judicial power and institutions." Y. P. Ghai and J. P. W. B. McAuslan, *Public Law and Political Change in Kenya* (London: Oxford University Press), 37. See also, the 1942 diagram, "Typical Colonial Establishment," helpfully reprinted in Lewis, *Empire and State-building*, xv.

Executive control and supervision at all times.³ The administrators were to be taken from an elite pool with the education and background to carry out an administration based on paternalistic authoritarianism.⁴ As a result of this system, a great deal of power resided in the "men-on-the-spot," district and provincial administrators. As Berman underscores, "The looseness of central control, a common feature of British colonies in Africa, was what made the local prefectural agent the most important figure in establishing and sustaining effective control and the legitimacy of the colonial state."⁵

The development of the state apparatus in Kenya was also predicated on British fantasies about what colonial authorities might find as the material for governance and how colonial governance might proceed. First, British officials imagined their "imperial tutelage" would result in gradual evolution of a uniform African consciousness from a state of "primitivism" to one of "civilization." Also, British authorities had a "mental map" of Africa in which Africans were divided neatly into tribal groups that colonial authorities expected to act in particular ways. "Tribes," as Shadle notes, were in the colonial imagination, "discrete collections of people attached to unique cultural, political, and societal norms, ruled by strong chiefs."⁶ Colonial administrators conceived of Kamba people as prosperous and pliable and as a potential, though resistant, source of labor for colonial markets. At the same time, "men-on-the-spot" in Ukambani also figured Kamba people as awash in the supernatural, and as a result administratively intractable, an initial characterization that persists into the present day.

Such observations about the Kamba were part of a central element of colonial administration – the production of knowledge about colonized peoples. A key component of an administrator's role was to make "knowable" the formerly "unknown" people under his control; to collect, organize, and report anthro-administrative data on a colony's neatly demarcated tribes and then present this information in equally neat record books.⁷ Indeed, as early as 1905, the government of Kenya required

---

³ Berman, *Control and Crisis*, 73–75; Charles Chevenix Trench, *The Men Who Ruled Kenya* (London: Radcliffe Press, 1993).
⁴ Berman and Lonsdale, *Unhappy Valley I*, 33.
⁵ Berman, *Crisis and Control*, 81.
⁶ Shadle, "*Girl Cases*," 64.
⁷ John Lonsdale, "When Did the Gusii (or Any Other Group) Become a Tribe?" *Kenya Historical Review* 5.1 (1997): 122–133. "Native Research Work," *Habari: A Newspaper for the Nations of the Kenya Colony* 6.2 (May 1927): 3–5.

that colonial officers submit specifically formatted Annual and Quarterly Reports on their individual districts.

By 1910, a memorandum from the governor's office demanded that colonial officials submit Political Record Books, extensive reports designed to "constitute a complete history of the native administration of the country,"[8] taking in "current information of a statistical nature" as well as "records of local tribal history and custom, the family history and connexions of native authorities, and observations heard on appeal or revision from native courts."[9] The overarching purpose of such systematized record books, William Hailey explained in his 1938 monograph assessing Indirect Rule, was not "a systematic statement of custom, but the recording of information which may prove useful to the administration."[10] Overall, a primary goal of the archived and archiving colonial state was to render subject peoples more easily governable by making their unfamiliar cultures, customs, and institutions known quantities.

The anthro-administrative knowledge generated by the "men-on-the-spot" was not confined to official reports. Rather, numerous colonial officials, particularly those stationed in the central portion of the country, produced their own articles and monographs based on information they had gleaned in the course of their administrative duties.[11] As their writings reflect, the "men-on-the-spot" in Ukambani, took a deep interest in Kamba cosmology, in many instances working as administrators-cum-anthropologists. C. W. Hobley, the most prolific and one of the best known of the early Ukambani administrators, had already by 1910 published an anthropological monograph on the Kamba which focused strongly on cosmology and which was derived in part from his administrative writings.[12] The anthro-administrative knowledge produced by officials like Hobley was circulated through topical, imperial networks

---

[8] Robert G. Gregory, Robert M. Maxon, and Leon P. Spencer, eds., *A Guide to the Kenya National Archives* (Syracuse: Program of Eastern African Studies, 1968), 5.

[9] William Malcolm Hailey, *An African Survey* (London: Oxford University Press, 1938), 49. By the 1930s, a range of foundations in Europe and America were sponsoring research on Africa. Hailey's work was in part sponsored by the Carnegie Corporation. And the Africa Institute at the London School of Economics was closely tied to the Rockefeller Foundation. Papers related to the Africa Institute are split between the London School of Economics Archives and the Rockefeller Archives Center in Sleepy Hollow, New York.

[10] Ibid.

[11] G. St. J. Orde Browne, "Mount Kenya and Its People: Some Notes on the Chuka Tribe," *Journal of the Royal African Society* 15.59 (April 1916): 225–233.

[12] Hobley, *Ethnology of A-kamba*. For succinct biographical information about of Hobley, see A. T. Matson and Thomas P. Ofcansky, "A Bio-Bibliography of C. W. Hobley," *History in Africa* 8 (1981): 253–260; Mutongi, *Worries*, 17–22.

of varying scale throughout the colonial era. Indeed, the 1909–1910 Machakos District Annual Report shows that Hobley's text was immediately put into use as a reference for other administrators.[13]

Yet, while district and provincial officers worked individually to develop a corpus of information about the people under their authority, the distances that administrators had to cover combined with the scope of their duties provided incentives for a co-optive form of government throughout the colonial period. Throughout their African Empire, the British instituted, in an assortment of forms and to varying degrees, the system of Indirect Rule, a mode of governmentality initially developed by Lord Frederick Lugard during the latter part of the nineteenth century in Nigeria. Broadly, Indirect Rule was premised on maintaining local authority and "customs" under the direction of British administrators.[14] Pragmatically speaking, it was intended to provide a cheap system of administration that would require a minimum of British staff, maintain law and order, and facilitate economic exploitation. On a more abstract level, Indirect Rule was envisioned as part of a system of "imperial tutelage" aimed at promoting the moral and intellectual progress of Africans along European lines.

This context necessitated that British officials work through an assortment of African institutions and actors, both in the administrative and legal arenas. In the latter, as Stacey Hynd succinctly summarizes, the "treatment of crime and punishment" entailed a "bifurcation of legal and penal systems, with lesser offences and punishments being dealt with by Native Authorities in Native Courts, and serious crimes being sentenced by British magistrates in Subordinate Courts, or in the High Court by British judges."[15]

Customary law emerged as one of the most significant foci of the legal system. The meaning and content of customary law has been historically contentious. Generally speaking, customary law comprised a variety of legally recognized rules, norms, and processes derived from an administratively driven effort to develop a system of laws supposedly originating from the "laws" of precolonial African societies. Many anthro-administrators concerned themselves with cataloguing

---

[13] KNA DC/MKS 1/1/2, Machakos District Annual Report 1909–1910. See the insert of Hobley's text.
[14] Lugard, *The Dual Mandate*.
[15] Stacey Hynd, "Imperial Gallows: Capital Punishment, Violence and Colonial Rule in Britain's African Territories, c.1908–68" (PhD diss., Oxford University, 2007), 15; Ghai and McAuslan, *Public Law*, 138–144, 166–172.

customary law, imagining it as bounded and unchanging. In reality, it was a supple corpus of rules and norms often predating colonialism and modifiable by colonial and local authorities alike as circumstance demanded. In the colonial period, a primary focus of the constitutive debates over customary law was the degree to which local cosmological practices and beliefs such as *kithitu* should be integrated into colonial legal proceedings.

In general then, while administrative officers often advocated an expansion of the body of law rooted in local customs and judicial authorities typically promoted the expansion of law that was based on the Indian Penal Code and referred to precedents of British Common Law, both groups were willing to consider that local sources of order and justice existed before the advent of British rule. It is important to note, however, that customary law overwhelmingly governed the *civil* arena. In working with customary law, the colonial state showed that it was prepared to negotiate about local customs and beliefs pertaining to civil matters like marriage.[16] Members of the colonial administration were *not* prepared to step away from British mores and means concerning capital crimes. Overall, the colonial state was unwilling to compromise its monopoly on juridical violence by integrating or sanctioning *local* forms of juridical violence, like *king'ole*.

Competing notions of law and justice collided in an uncomfortable nexus around witchcraft generally and *uoi* in particular. British law criminalized witchcraft practices and beliefs like *uoi*, but provided no viable means for prosecution and punishment. At the same time, in maintaining an exclusive hold over the exercise of juridical violence, state codes both outlawed local, institutional approaches (like *king'ole*) for dealing with lethal, recidivist witches and prescribed capital punishment of people who stepped into the authoritative vacuum created by the state and who practiced informal, ad hoc violence against murderous witches. Both the Indian Penal Code, the body of law transferred to Kenya with few amendments at the beginning of the colonial period, and the Kenya Penal Code, which replaced the Indian Penal Code in 1930, reflect the state's monopoly on juridical violence.

---

[16] Shadle, *"Girl Cases."* Also, H. F. Morris and James S. Read, *Indirect Rule and the Search for Justice* (Oxford: Clarendon Press, 1972); Falk Moore, "Treating Law." Falk Moore focuses on the administration of justice in the *civil arena* as a function of the colonial imaginary. However, discourses about crime and justice expressed by colonial authorities in documents pertaining to the administration of justice in criminal matters can be profitably theorized as products of the colonial imaginary as well.

Yet, despite the powers they were ascribed and the knowledge they succeeded in acquiring, colonial administrators' limited numbers and broad duties necessitated Africans' assistance in everyday rule and mediation. Under the colonial regime in Kenya and elsewhere in Africa, various categories of African "middle figures" had their origin in a variety of actual preexisting (and imagined) positions of local authority.[17] These "linchpins of colonial rule," as Benjamin Lawrance, Emily Osborne, and Richard Roberts note, were important, influential actors who "shaped the interactions of subject populations with European officials."[18] Generally, Africans in the employ of the colonial state can be loosely grouped into two, sometimes overlapping, categories – functionaries and "experts-of-the-local." Functionaries occupied hierarchically organized administrative positions like those of chief, sub-chief, headmen, assistant-headman, and so on.[19] In both ad hoc and official capacities, experts-of-the-local facilitated colonial authorities' comprehension of the workings of African societies by providing context for and interpretation of various elements of local cultures.

The origins of such intermediary posts were diverse, some having loose origins in preexisting structures of authority, others imagined into existence by the colonial state. In many cases, Africans occupying intermediary roles had already been recognized as elders within their own communities, for example, the *atumia* of Ukambani. But, as Berman and Lonsdale explain, "Where willing collaborators could not be found within indigenous precolonial structures they were created, and the actual practice in the field was formulated by the administrative officers on the spot in response to local exigencies."[20] Such was the situation in Ukambani. A 1909 report aptly explained, "The prestige of the Chiefs is in the process of being created in most cases."[21]

In other instances, the constitution of intermediary groups was in fact a co-option of actual precolonial bodies, in the Kamba case, the *nzama*. Indeed, in discussions about the obsolescence of *king'ole* and the evolution

---

[17] Hunt, *Colonial Lexicon*.
[18] Benjamin N. Lawrance, Emily Osborne, and Richard L. Roberts, "Introduction: African Intermediaries and the 'Bargain' of Collaboration," in *Intermediaries, Interpreters, and Clerks: African Employees in the Making of Colonial Africa*, ed. Benjamin N. Lawrance, Emily Osborne, and Richard L. Roberts (Madison: University of Wisconsin Press, 2006), 4.
[19] For example, as John Middleton notes, "The Native Authority Ordinance of 1912 enlarged the formerly relatively minor powers of headmen and laid down that they were appointed over specific areas, later to be known as locations, and whose boundaries were in most cases drawn on tribal or ethnical basis." Middleton, "Kenya," 352.
[20] Berman and Lonsdale, *Unhappy Valley I*, 161.
[21] KNA DC/MKS 1/1/3, Machakos District Quarterly Report 1909, 42.

of *nzama*, elderly Kamba people point to the merging of the *nzama* with colonial administrative institutions and actors. As one couple explained,

> They [*nzama* members] worked under the chief's authority. They followed colonial rules. They met with and without the chief. They were appointed by the chief. They then slaughtered a goat for eating.[22]

Describing the colonial-era role of the *nzama*, a contemporary noted that "The *nzama* was used by the colonial government in deciding local issues" while another elderly Kamba man explained that the colonial government granted the *nzama* permits to deal with "witchcraft, general conflicts ... all cases needing resolution."[23]

The *nzama*'s role in conflict resolution hinted at by the Kamba man cited here is generally in keeping with how scholars have described *nzama*. Munro describes *nzama*, as a "small *ad hoc* body" responsible for mediating quotidian conflicts "between individuals and families." A group of "four to six elders, selected by the litigants and *motui*, comprised an *nzama*." Sometimes, Munro notes, the *nzama* also included an *nzili* whose purpose was to lend greater "impartiality" to the proceedings and to provide a "special knowledge of customary laws."[24]

Functionaries like chiefs, headmen, and *nzama* members were integrated into the colonial judicial system through the passage of a variety of statutes, although the exercise of juridical violence remained off limits to them.[25] Colonial documents initially tended to use the terms *nzama* and "Native Courts" interchangeably and later situated them under the heading of "Native Tribunals."[26]

As suggested, issues of law and justice presented problems to the colonial administration, coalescing around the questions of how much and what kind of judicial powers functionaries like chiefs or *nzama* members

---

[22] L. N. N., Kangundo, August 2004; M. N. N., Kangundo, August 2004.
[23] J. K. S., Kilungu, September 2004; M. W., Imani, September 2004.
[24] Munro, *Colonial Rule*, 55. My research assistant and I consistently questioned interviewees about the existence in the precolonial and colonial eras or in the present of local "experts" with special knowledge of customary law. In almost every instance, interviewees claimed no knowledge of such persons or conflated them with translators. Perhaps the more than thirty years between the author's fieldwork and Munro's explains why Kamba people in 2004 were unable to cite or explain the category *nzili* identified in Munro's text. Munro's notes and tapes are not available at the Kenya National Archives.
[25] In 1911, a Kikuyu *kiama*, the Kikuyu equivalent of a Kamba *nzama*, asserted its right to have burned two men found to be witches. The case against the *kiama* was tried in the High Court of Kenya. KNA DC/KBU/3/25, Kiama Case. See also, Chapter 5.
[26] KNA DC/KTI 1/1/1, Kitui District Annual Report 1911, 19; KNA DC/MKS 1/3/12, Kitui District Annual Report 1925, 11.

should have since at the outset of the colonial period "there were no indigenous judicial authorities other than informal councils of elders" and "traditional sanctions had usually been destroyed by the prohibition of the use of force by any but agents of the central government."[27] The 1909 Machakos District Quarterly Report reflects this situation, complaining that "[chiefs] have no legal powers of enforcing obedience beyond native law" and explaining, "British law is applied where Native law is contrary to humanity or morality.... Serious Criminal Cases such as murder have been forbidden to Native Courts as also the System of Blood Money – Such Cases must be brought before the British Court."[28]

Accordingly, the Native Tribunals Act of 1911 officially made the *nzama* the "recognized judicial bodies with authority to try all cases cognizable to Kamba law and arising within their areas of jurisdiction with the exception of such cases as homicide and serious assault."[29] Functionaries were thus integrated into the colonial judicial administration in varying degrees through positions that were rooted in precolonial judicial structures and status or in posts that were colonial-era inventions.

Although a central element of a colonial officer's role was the production of useable anthro-administrative knowledge, in many instances this knowledge was insufficient for thorough governance. As Berman notes, although "several administrators were talented amateur anthropologists," generally speaking "the information collected by administrators in the reserves reflected a very limited knowledge of indigenous culture and institutions."[30] To fill in such gaps, the colonial administration enlisted Africans in a range of support positions as experts-of-the-local. They often facilitated British officers' work within the colonial courts, serving as translators or "native assessors."

The task of translators was fairly straightforward, translating various local languages into the Kiswahili that was spoken by British officers. Unlike most functionaries selected from pools of elders, translators were generally younger men who had either been employed in a Kiswahili-speaking environment or who had been educated in Kiswahili.[31] Translators were

---

[27] Middleton, "Kenya," 351.
[28] KNA DC/MKS 1/1/3, Machakos District Quarterly Report 1909, 37.
[29] Munro, *Colonial Rule*, 66. The Native Courts Ordinance of 1907 had recognized tribunals under the direct authority of chiefs and headmen and the Native Tribunal Rules of 1911 "recognized the constitution of councils of elders in accordance with traditional custom." See Middleton, "Kenya," 351–352.
[30] Berman, *Crisis and Control*, 93.
[31] Derek Peterson, *Creative Writing: Tradition, Book-keeping and the Work of the Imagination in Colonial Kenya* (Portsmouth, NH: Heinemann, 2004).

engaged in the mundane work of assisting British officers in translating quotidian administrative news and directions. But they also occupied significant roles in the legal arena, interpreting for trial participants in the colonial courts and helping British officers convey the underpinnings of colonial law and order at *baraza* – public, village-based meetings.

Indeed, while there was in the late 1920s a debate over whether "laws affecting natives" should be translated into Kiswahili, laws continued to be promulgated and published in English throughout the colonial era. The decision to retain English as the sole language of published law was supported by the Executive, the Governor-in-Council concluding that "general notifications could be best ensured by District Officers explaining to barazas, in the local vernacular, the principal provisions of enactments affecting natives." The chief native commissioner thus concurred that "Senior commissioners should direct that short lectures on the main Ordinances which affect natives should be given by District Officers at the conclusion of Barazas, Council Meetings and other suitable occasions."[32] Elderly Kamba note that translators generally accompanied district officers to *baraza*, and that during the colonial period dictates and laws were made known via announcements offered by district officers with the assistance of interpreters.[33]

The work of native assessors, in turn, was more complex. The assessor position was not created as part of the system of Indirect Rule in Africa but rather, like so much of the administration of justice in British Africa, had a legal genealogy in Indian codes, which in turn harkened back to the English legal system.[34] Assessors first filled in the gaps in colonial administrative and judicial officials' knowledge on issues of local custom, belief, and practice that emerged in the course of court cases. Second, they assessed the validity of claims made by participants in a case about local law, custom, and practice, and advised British judicial officials accordingly. A distinct system of protocols governed how, why, and about what assessors addressed the courts and how the courts, particularly the justices, were to draw on assessors' knowledge.

Yet, at the same moment, as Ruth Ginio notes, "The ignorance of colonial administrators at all levels regarding local customs denied them the tools to

---

[32] KNA DC/MKS 25/3/2, Memo from Native Affairs Department to all Provincial Commissioners with copies for all District Commissioners, Publication of Laws in Ki-Swahili, 27 October 1927.

[33] W. N., Machakos, September 2004; S. M., Mbooni, September 2004.

[34] John Gray notes that the assessor position in East Africa derived from the Indian Evidence Act and the Indian Code of Criminal Procedure. John Gray, "Opinions of Assessors in Criminal Trials in East Africa as to Native Custom," *Journal of African Law* 2.1 (Spring 1958): 7–8.

examine the assessor's professional capacities."³⁵ Debates over how much legal weight to give assessors' opinions persisted – debates symptomatic of a more generalized colonial conundrum about how much influence could be accorded to local beliefs and practices in the new situation of British rule.

Overall, the activities and status of experts-of-the-local are fuzzier than those of functionaries. There is an absence of easily accessible statutes precisely articulating the duties and backgrounds of translators and assessors and a lack of statistical information about their numbers in Kenya. For example, the minutes of the Kitui Native Council state simply, "After discussion it was decided to appoint 3 elders in each location who could be called upon to act as assessors."³⁶ This inaccessibility of such information renders it easiest to glean what sort of work these men did by examining other types of colonial documents showing them in action. For example, colonial court transcripts show that three or four assessors were regularly present in capital cases, and such documents, detailing questions put to assessors and assessors' replies, highlight the sorts of issues that assessors typically dealt with and point to the degree of influence that their opinions had on British justices' decisions.³⁷

Distinctions in roles and reputations of experts-of-the-local are markedly obscure in the conceptions of elderly Kamba informants. In response to lines of questioning about Kamba people who may have advised on matters of customary law in the colonial courts, the majority of interviewees conflated translators with assessors. Most interviewees answered with a resounding "yes" that they were familiar with such a category of people, and then went on to describe translators, using a Kiswahili-derived title, *mutafuta*, to designate them. Responses such as, "Yes, they were called *mutafuta*. Their work was interpretation, translation. They were young people, not elders," or "Yes, they were called *mutafuta*. They were employed by the Government. The D.C. knew the Swahili speakers and would choose them" are typical. One elderly Kamba man explained their background in more detail, noting,

> Yes, they were interpreters. They were employed by the government and tested by the D.C. for their language skills. They were young people, not *wazee* (elders). They were able to work because they were young. They had no special knowledge of "customary law."

---

³⁵ Ruth Ginio, "Negotiating Legal Authority in French West Africa: The Colonial Administration and African Assessors, 1903–1918," in *Intermediaries*, 121.
³⁶ KNA DC/KTI 2/9/1, Kitui Native Council Minutes (27 August 1928), 180.
³⁷ Ghai and McAuslan, *Public Law*, 168–169. See also, Chapter 6.

And another interviewee explained, "I saw them and they were called translators. I don't know assessors," and proposed, "Maybe the same people were doing both jobs."[38]

Perhaps the language used to describe experts-of-the-local did not sufficiently differentiate translators and assessors as to render them distinct in the recollections of ordinary Kamba people. The Kiswahili verb *kutafuta* can be variously translated as "to seek," "to look for," "to find," or "to obtain" while the Kikamba prefix *mu-* designates "person." Loosely speaking, a translator and an assessor were each persons who used specialized knowledge (linguistic or legal) "to seek," "to look for," "to find," or "to obtain" the necessary information for British colonial officers who were trained in Kiswahili but who were not necessarily fluent in local vernaculars or in customary law. At the same moment, this tendency to conflate translators and assessors hints at a locally conceived sociology of colonial power in which ordinary Kamba people did not distinguish sharply between the types and levels of power held by Kamba and British authorities.

The situations described above in many cases produced a real though limited administrative synergy between British and Africans in the employ of the colonial state. But whatever notions of devolving authority and negotiating with custom that British officials were willing to consider, they were in no way willing to entertain ceding the primacy of British power. Overall, British colonial cosmology asserted that the purpose of colonial government was to guide and urge (or to direct and propel) Africans along a development continuum. As a result, the administrative system theorized as *Indirect* Rule actually ended up being much more direct in practice.

Commentary from the Kenya Governor's Office on the 1927 Kenya Native Affairs Department Annual Report takes in some of the dilemmas and debates concerning just how direct (or not) British administration should be. It reads,

> In 1911 Sir Percy Girouard wrote (Cmd. 5467, pp. 39 and 47) in speaking of the detribalization of the native in the then East Africa Protectorate:
>
> "There are not lacking those who favour direct British rule; but if we allow the tribal authority to be ignored or broken, it will mean that we, who numerically form a small minority, shall be obliged to deal with a rabble.... There could only be one end to such a policy, and that would be eventual conflict with the rabble."

---

[38] M. K., Tawa, September 2004; E. M. M., Tawa, September 2004; P. K.M, Welfare, September 2004; W. N., Machakos, 2004.

> It is generally admitted that the system of direct rule through British Officers is the simplest and, for the time, the most efficient method of administering primitive tribes in the early stages of development, but the great defects of that system in Africa, which Sir Percy Girouard feared, are now recognised even, I understand, by French authorities. These defects – the evasion of the task of political education, the stultification of the normal progress of native society – when a native people demand a greater voice in the control of their own affairs will be found to have stemmed the growth of the tribe, if indeed they have not destroyed its roots.[39]

Such issues remained largely unresolved throughout the colonial period, and in the years leading up to and after World War II a range of novel and shifting circumstances led to a clamor from a variety of corners for changes in the ways that colonial administration and authority operated. At the same time, shifts in both British and African attitudes toward administration led to the problems presciently stated by Girouard.

ANTHROPOLOGY IN ACTION

An array of dilemmas and demands concerning the supernatural emerged in the decade before World War II and were leveled more strongly in the postwar period.[40] Rather than constituting a dramatic rupture with the past, approaches to administration in this period can be read in many ways as expansions or calcifications of preexisting methods and mindsets. The postwar period was viewed by many inside and outside the colonial administration as ripe with opportunities to reassert control over the colonies through the development of social welfare projects. In the decade immediately preceding and subsequent to World War II, knowledge-for-policy/practice continued to form an important element of the colonial administrative paradigm.

Whereas earlier colonial authorities had sought to make their subjects "knowable" in order to facilitate the establishment of workable administration, during the 1940s and 1950s British officials sought knowledge of colonial communities in order to reinforce existing administrative authority and to smooth the progress of various colonial development schemas. Such knowledge continued to be produced by the "men-on-the-spot" but

---

[39] PRO CO 533/382/13, Native Affairs Department Annual Report, 1927, comments on report from the Office of the Governor of Kenya's Office, April 1929.
[40] G. Gordon Brown and Bruce Hutt, *Anthropology in Action: An Experiment in the Iringa Province of the Tanganyika Territory* (London: Humphrey Milton, 1935).

was also subject to a cadre of professionals charged with formally putting "anthropology in action."[41]

Yet, at the same moment, such schemas and administrative approaches indicated a shift in how colonial authorities were coming to regard African people. While earlier colonial officials regarded Africans largely through the framework of tribe, this attitude was already shifting by the 1930s. And, after the broad participation of African people in the Allies' World War II efforts, authorities in the metropole began to conceive of African people as bearing more individualized subjectivities (and related potentials), albeit highly limited ones.[42]

The movement toward reinvigorated professionalism and formalized anthropology occurred in various permutations over a lengthy period, and moves in these directions had begun by the 1930s. The report of the East Africa Commission argued that "anthropology should be considered as a subject having the most important applications in the sphere of administration in our tropical possessions, and should not be regarded as a study of purely academic interest," and subsequently proposed that "increased efforts should be made to encourage administrative officers, either by special grants or otherwise, to undergo a course of training in modern methods of anthropology and to carry out scientific investigations."[43] Similarly, as explained by a Colonial Office memo entitled "Anthropological Work in East Africa," "It is obvious that successful anthropological investigations must depend to a large extent on the qualities possessed by the individual investigator, and the opportunities afforded to him for study."[44]

One approach, for example, was to enhance pre-career and in-service training throughout the ranks of the colonial administration, in part through programs like the Oxford University Summer School, begun in 1937–1938 in collaboration with the Department of African Linguistics at the School for Oriental and African Studies in London, and also through the Tropical African Services Course, attended by all candidates selected

---

[41] By the time such experts were introduced in Africa, cadres of British experts on matters of culture and custom had long formed a key part of the administrative apparatus in colonial India. For example, Nicholas Dirks, "Colonial Histories and Native Informants: Biography of an Archive," in *Orientalism and the Postcolonial Predicament: Perspectives on South Asia*, ed. Carol Breckenridge and Peter van der Veer (Philadelphia: University of Pennsylvania Press, 1993), 279–313.

[42] Cooper, *Decolonization*.

[43] "Report of the East Africa Commission," Cmd. 2387. Cited in PRO CO 822/21/2, Anthropological Research.

[44] PRO CO 822/21/2, "Anthropological Work in East Africa, 1929."

for appointment to the administrative services in tropical Africa.⁴⁵ And while from the start of the colonial era, officers had been encouraged to familiarize themselves with their counterparts' anthro-administrative writings like Hobley's texts, later on they received more guidance on "doing" anthropology themselves. For example, Machakos District files included a pamphlet entitled "Introductory Questions on African Ethnology."⁴⁶ And in the late 1920s, famed anthropologist and London School of Economics professor Bronislaw Malinowski, writing on the "demand-supply of anthro," put "colonial administrators" first on the list of those "responsible for the development of backward peoples in Africa and elsewhere" and whose work "necessitates the study of primitive cultures through scientific anthropology."⁴⁷

Yet at the same time authorities in the metropole and abroad aimed to enhance the anthro-administrative competencies of the "men-on-the-spot" and considered how to create a body of anthro-administrative best practices, they recognized the limits that workload and environment placed on colonial administrators. Hailey neatly summarized such limits:

> The administrative officer works ... under certain disadvantages. His relations with Africans are apt to be coloured by the fact that he represents the government ... almost everywhere in Africa the present conditions involve a pressure of work which leaves little leisure for detached study ... he is often compelled to confine himself to the more immediate and obvious aspects of the subject into which he is inquiring, unable to consider its wider relations in the social or economic life of the community.⁴⁸

Such limits together with the need for more systematized information for colonial development projects provided an important impetus for the training of anthropological fieldworkers to do research across British Africa in the service of the state. Anthropologists studied at many of the same institutions that provided pre- and in-service training to administrators,

---

[45] Ibid. The Tropical African Services Course included units on "African Arts and Industries" and "the Material Culture of Africa" as well as anthropology.
[46] See George Foucart, "Introductory Questions on African Ethnology." This pamphlet offers a range of guiding questions concerning issues like local legal systems. Included in KNA MAA 7/602.
[47] LSE MALINOWSKI/9/2, "Demand-Supply of Anthro," n.d. Johnstone (Jomo) Kenyatta's *Facing Mount Kenya* is an outgrowth of his studies with Malinowski at the London School of Economics. Louis Leakey's time at the London School of Economics as Malinowski's student overlapped with Kenyatta's tenure. Jomo Kenyatta, *Facing Mount Kenya: The Tribal Life of the Gikuyu*, intro., Bronislaw Malinowski (London: Secker and Warburton, 1938).
[48] Hailey, *An African Survey*, 47–48.

often working on theses linking administrative and anthropological concerns. For example, in the mid-1930s Malinowski supervised a thesis on "crime amongst natives" in Kenya, Southern Rhodesia, and South Africa, which dealt in detail with the dilemmas that witchcraft beliefs and practices posed for administration, particularly the administration of justice and the maintenance of law and order.[49]

Hailey again offered a summary, describing the function and expertise of the professional anthropologist vis-à-vis colonial administration. He explained,

> The professional anthropologist should ... be able to provide a more complete picture of native society and, in areas where native institutions are the least understood he is likely to be of great assistance in providing the government with the knowledge which must form the basis of administrative policy. In general, it may be said that governments are likely to derive the greatest advantage from inquiries undertaken by anthropologists in association with their own technical or administrative officers.[50]

Neither the colonial administrator with his more casual skills nor the professional anthropologist with his formalized training was to work in isolation in the colonial context. Rather, the administrator and the anthropologist were to collaborate in support of a colonial research-policy network bringing administrative concerns and social science research into conversation in order to facilitate effective colonial policy making and implementation. To this end, in the mid-1940s, the Colonial Development and Welfare Act established the position of government sociologist.[51] In Kenya, the government sociologist's role was shaped through joint efforts of the noted anthropologist Isaac Schapera and members of the colonial administration, in particular the Office of the Chief Native Commissioner in Nairobi.

In the mid-1940s, as part of a broader Colonial Social Science Research program into the "problems of African sociology in Kenya, Tanganyika and Uganda," Schapera produced a monograph on field research needs and priorities. He was also responsible for supervising anthropological

---

[49] LSE MALINOWSKI/10/10, "Labour and the Criminal Law," no author, annotated by Malinowski circa 1934, 25–28.

[50] Hailey, *An African Survey*, 47–48.

[51] KNA MAA 7/602. The Colonial Development and Welfare Act (1946) supported the position of government sociologist in part through the provision of research grants. PRO CO 927/65/2, "Social Science Research in the Colonies." See also, J. P. Moffet, "Government Sociologists in Tanganyika. A Government View," *Journal of African Administration* 4.3 (July 1952): 100–103.

fieldworkers serving as government sociologists across Kenya.[52] For example, in instructions to his student U. P. Mayer, the government sociologist working in Western Kenya, Schapera offered guidance about the general terms of Mayer's study and passed along the chief native commissioner's request for a "more detailed enquiry into the Kisii and into topics that are of more direct importance to the Government," many of which had to do with Kisii political organization.[53] In turn, Schapera's memo to the chief native commissioner enjoined the administration to promote collaboration between administrative officers and government sociologists "noting that sociologists should be invited to attend meetings of 'district teams,' official *barazas*, etc. in order to become familiar with the practical problems of district administration and developmental work."[54]

Both professional anthropologists and anthropologically inclined administrators worked in the field in Ukambani to record a range of data and hypotheses about Kamba communities, particularly in regard to their relations with the state.[55] For example, in a 1947 reply to the chief native commissioner, the provincial commissioner of Central Province proposed that a research priority in Machakos should be devising how to facilitate a "welding" of Akamba associations like Akamba Union and Kilungu Youths "into some sort of efficient organization which could serve as the basis for social service and welfare."[56] In identifying Kamba organizations as objects of official anthropological inquiry, the memo presaged Mau Mau-era concern over the politicization of Kamba associations and hinted at the anthro-administrative lens that would be focused sharply on Ukambani in the mid-1950s.

[52] KNA MAA 2/5/17. The study was published in 1949. Isaac Schapera, *Some Problems of Anthropological Research in the Kenya Colony* (London: Oxford University Press, 1949). Published for the International Africa Institute. Schapera's work was carried out in part in connection with the East African Institute of Social Research at Makerere in Uganda. His program was described in a 1947 memo from the Chief Native Commissioner to all Provincial Commissioners with sufficient enclosures for all District Officers. It was duly circulated from the Provincial Commissioner of Central Province to the District Commissioners of Thika, Kitui, Machakos, Nairobi, and Kiambu. See KNA VQ/16/25; Central Province. Anthropology. See also, Schapera's, "Anthropology and the Administrator," *Journal of African Administration* 3.3 (July 1951): 128–135.

[53] KNA MAA 2/5/17, Note of Instruction for Dr. U. P. Mayer, Government Sociologist, n.d.

[54] KNA MAA 2/5/17, Memo from Isaac Schapera to the Chief Native Commissioner, Sociologists Posted to Kenya, 10 February 1947.

[55] For example, W. E. H. Stanner, "Report by Dr. W. E. H. Stanner on 'The Kitui Akamba.' A Critical Study of British Administration." Included in KNA VQ/16/25. Stanner was a student of Marjory Perham.

[56] KNA MAA 2/5/17, Memo from the Provincial Commissioner, Central Province, to the Chief Native Commissioner, Sociological Research, 15 May 1947.

OF WITCHES AND BUREAUCRATS

From the earliest days of colonial administration in Ukambani, the reports of British authorities attended strongly to Kamba witchcraft, in particular to *uoi*. Witchcraft emerges from these reports as both a descriptor and an analytic. On one hand, such references served to describe the perpetual insecurity of the supernatural situation in Ukambani and to show how such cyclical unease was related to local patterns of power and "native mentalities." On the other hand, witchcraft worked as an analytic, a tool not only for describing contexts in Ukambani but also for obliquely explaining some of the ways in which local beliefs and practices impeded efficient administration.

Throughout the colonial period, administrative discourse figured witchcraft as both a means to power and a way-of-being-in-the-world. In each of these intertwined incarnations, witchcraft was treated as an impediment to colonial rule. Indeed most colonial officials in Kenya (and the metropole) would likely have registered an annual report's contention that witchcraft was "the most serious handicap to Administration" in Ukambani as neither hyperbolic nor unexpected.[57]

In administrative discourse, witchcraft stood for the overall sociopolitical and supernatural situations with which colonial officials – both British and African – had to contend. At the same moment, discussions of witchcraft offered ways of understanding how such supernatural insecurity did work, stripping functionaries of their will and ability to perform their duties and supplanting administrative authority with a witchcraft-centered variety. As a district officer complained in an annual report,

> Headmen and elders fear to do their work because some one might make 'Mchawi' against them; any death that is not absolutely accounted for is put down to witchcraft and it is impossible to convince them of the contrary even if one is oneself convinced there is nothing in it.[58]

Similarly, another report describing the poor performance records of headmen and Native Councils in Ukambani proposed that "the fear of witchcraft has a lot to do with the question" of Kamba elders' extreme

---

[57] KNA DC/MKS 1/3/6, Kitui District Annual Report 1916, 73. Indeed, the minutes of an early 1950s Colonial Social Science Research Committee on Law and Land Tenure meeting stipulate that in "view of the conflict of English and customary legal conceptions," that "a comparative study of witchcraft in native customary law and in Colonial Statutory law" be listed as one of five prospective projects of "primary importance." PRO CO 901/40, Colonial Social Science Research Council Committee on Law and Land Tenure, Minutes of the Second Meeting, 5 July. (No year listed.)

[58] KNA DC/MKS 1/3/6, Kitui District Annual Report 1916, 73.

conservatism and the passive aggression of the Headmen who "prefer[red] to do nothing and merely [said] that the Elders will not obey them."[59]

Reports and record books also figured witchcraft as a more abstract barrier to effective administration. According to colonial accounts, not only did witchcraft beliefs and practices impede the will and efficacy of functionaries but they also colored the way ordinary Kamba people conceived of being-in-the-world, diminishing their sense of their own agency in regard to their circumstances, and by extension, the success of the colonial administration in propelling them along the continuum of colonial development. One colonial official succinctly summarized,

> All the natives in this reserve are saturated in witchcraft. To suggest to a native that witchcraft is powerless is only to look absurd. They are satisfied of its powers and its results, and this makes it very difficult to get in close.... The only way to gain their confidence at all is to agree that witchcraft exists and has very great power but that white witchcraft can in many cases be proved to have even greater power.... I am convinced that any effort for their betterment cannot get to the core of the problem until they go hand and hand with a trained anthropologist and psychologist.[60]

From the perspective offered above then, witchcraft beliefs and practices constituted an administrative problem that could be best approached through professional and ad hoc anthro-administrative inquiries. Further, by describing all Kamba as imbued with witchcraft, the report rendered Kamba people as administratively intractable.

Dealing with *uoi* and *uwe* was also a project of colonial classification. In the course of creating a networked archive of anthro-administrative knowledge about witchcraft, the colonial state also crafted "categories of dangerous persons" and classifications of perilous practices that generally mirrored Kamba ones.[61] Colonial authorities' writings indicate that they understood that Kamba people figured witchcraft primarily as lethal malfeasance and as located in the bodies of Kamba women. For example, an annual report explained, "The Akamba are very superstitious and firmly believe that certain people, chiefly women, have supernatural power of casting spells with the intent to injure or kill. Any death or accident that they cannot account for is ascribed to witchcraft."[62]

---

[59] KNA DC/MKS 1/3/6, Kitui District Annual Report 1916, 63–64, 5. Complaints about the intractability of various Kamba authorities persisted well into the colonial era. See Tignor, "Colonial Chiefs."
[60] KNA PC/CP/4/2/3, Ukamba Province Annual Report 1932, 40.
[61] Suzette Heald, *Controlling Anger*, 12.
[62] KNA DC/MKS 1/3/6, Kitui District Annual Report 1914–1915, 17.

Echoing this language, a subsequent text noted that the "Akamba are intensely superstitious and firmly believe that certain people (usually women) have the inherited power of bewitching and killing people."[63] And colonial reports about witches also attended to the inherited aspect of Kamba *uoi*, elucidating how "If a woman is a witch she is looked upon with great fear and is avoided, although she is allowed to live in the same village. It is said that all her daughters inherit the fascination."[64]

Following Kamba people, British officials recognized a distinction, albeit it an oft-times fuzzy and incompletely understood one, between black magic and white magic, between *uoi* and *uwe*. For example, one Ukambani administrative report explained, "Witchcraft was formerly looked upon from two different points of view. Some witches use their powers for the good of others, they have now been renamed and are called medicine men."[65] Another colonial text proposed, "A witch or a wizard (Mchavi) must not be confused with a medicine man (Mganga) there is no connection."[66]

These statements reflect the general lack of nuance in colonial understandings of *uoi* versus *uwe*. First, it is unclear in the first quotation *who* has reconceptualized "white witchcraft." From the perspective of colonial authorities, did "medicine men" compose a category-of-the-colonizer or a category-of-the-colonized? And the next statement exemplifies the sharp and ultimately artificial distinction drawn between the "*mchawi*" and the "*mganga*." Kamba conceptions take in the gray area in which the practitioner of benevolent witchcraft, the *mu'unde mu'uwe*, must necessarily know the workings of *uoi* and in which also exists the *mu'unde mu'uoi* who is neither a witch by inheritance nor a healer by profession but, instead, a witch-for-hire.

Failures to map the subtleties of *uoi* versus *uwe* and of what lay in between produced confusion among colonial authorities about what the state's stance on white witchcraft should be. In some instances, colonial officials sought clarification from Kamba functionaries. For example, the minutes of an Ukambani *baraza* led by the local chief, Ngovi, noted that when questions about the "position of medicine-men [*sic*]" arose, "it was explained that such people were distinguished from witches and would be allowed to continue."[67] And colonial authorities not only in Kenya but also across the empire attempted to draw a legal distinction between

---

[63] KNA DC/MKS 1/3/6, Kitui District Annual Report 1916, 73.
[64] KNA DC/MKS 1/3/1, Kitui District Quarterly Report 1909, 51.
[65] Ibid.
[66] KNA DC/MKS 1/3/6, Kitui District Annual Report 1914–1915, 15.
[67] KNA DC/MKS 10A/6/1, Native Baraza, Kitui, 1 and 2 January 1915.

witchcraft-for-harm and witchcraft-for-healing in law. But throughout the colonial period, debates and confusion persisted over if and how magic should be allowed to function as a tool of government.

Law provided a primary avenue through which the state sought to discipline and deny witchcraft. In many ways, the terms and themes through which colonial authorities treated African witchcraft are evocative of those located in contemporary language about the history of European witchcraft, discourses that proposed witchcraft as sets of superstitions beyond which Europeans had evolved, thanks in large part to the successes of European judicial systems in legislating witchcraft out of existence.[68] In Kenya (as elsewhere in Africa), colonial administrations developed a series of anti-witchcraft ordinances that criminalized *uoi* and under some readings, *uwe*.

In Kenya, the first Witchcraft Ordinance was debated, revised, and passed by the Legislative Council in 1909.[69] The initial goal of the bill was "to make provision for the punishment of persons practicing or making use of so called witchcraft." In the second reading of the bill, two members of the Legislative Council proposed without success excising the words "supernatural power" from the second section of the bill. In the same meeting, the Crown Advocate successfully moved for the insertion of language protecting African functionaries from prosecution under the ordinance. The new language read,

> No proceedings for an offence under this Ordinance shall be taken against a Chief, Sub-Chief, Headman, or Elder, on account of anything done by such Chief, Sub-Chief, Headman or Elder in exercise of his authority as such, except with the previous sanction of the Governor.[70]

The bill was passed on its third reading in the summer of 1909. As Waller has succinctly summarized, the 1909 legislation established

> three criminal offences; to claim to be a witch or to "pretend to exercise or use any kind of supernatural power, witchcraft, sorcery or enchantment ... for the purposes of gain" (section 2); to advise others on how

---

[68] For example, see the articles in the 1935 special issue of *Africa* on "witchcraft." Especially, G. St. J. Orde Browne, "Witchcraft and British Colonial Law," *Africa: Journal of the International Institute of African Languages and Cultures* 8.4 (1935): 481–487; C. Clifton Roberts, "Witchcraft and Colonial Legislation," *Africa: Journal of the International Institute of African Languages and Cultures* 8.4. (1935): 488–503.

[69] PRO CO 544/2, East Africa Protectorate Legislative Council Minutes, Meetings held 1st March 1909, 18th May 1909, and 5th July 1909.

[70] Ibid. The two members, J. H. Wilson and Captain H. H. Cowie, were settlers.

to use witchcraft or to supply them with the "pretended means of witchcraft" (section 3); and to use such advice or means to "injure any person or property" (section 4).[71]

Punishment varied from terms of imprisonment between one year and ten years.

The evidentiary demands of the 1909 ordinance proved unwieldy, and the 1918 revision of the ordinance repealed section two which stipulated that the offense of "witchcraft" entailed "gain" and substituted instead the following language:

> Any person who holds himself out to be a witch doctor able to cause fear, annoyance, or injury to another in mind, person, or property or who pretends to exercise any kind of supernatural power, witchcraft, sorcery or enchantment calculated to cause such fear, annoyance or injury shall be guilty of an offence and shall be liable to imprisonment of either description for a term not exceeding one year.

Further, the 1918 ordinance struck from section four of the original ordinance the words "to injure any person or property" and substituted the language "to cause fear, annoyance or injury in mind, person, or property to any person."[72] The new language thus shifted the heart of the "witchcraft" offense from material gain to pretense to "supernatural" power and the production of psychological and/or physical harm through such pretense.

The core remained the same in the 1925 ordinance, but fresh language entailed provisions shaping the legality and illegality of witchcraft accusations and roles of functionaries and British authorities in dealing with them. First, the new language made accusing a person of "being a witch or with practicing witchcraft" a crime punishable by fine or imprisonment unless the accusation "was made to a district commissioner, a police officer, an official headman or any other person in authority." Further, the new terms of the ordinance made a headman's failure to report the "practice or pretended practice of witchcraft by any person" to the district commissioner a crime of omission, punishable by fine or imprisonment. Of course, the ordinance also forbade headmen to in any

---

[71] Richard Waller, "Witchcraft and Law in Colonial Kenya," *The Past and Present Society* 180.1 (October 2003): 245. See also, PRO CO 542/2, *Official Gazettes of the East Africa Protectorate*: Witchcraft Ordinance of 1909, 329.

[72] PRO CO 544/12, An Ordinance to Amend the Law Relating to Witchcraft 1918, 190. This language is discussed in more detail in the next section of this chapter.

way allow "witchcraft" or any act that could be considered to counter the provisions of the Witchcraft Ordinance. And the ordinance's new language also rendered employment or solicitation of another "to name or indicate by the use of any non-natural means any person as the perpetrator of any alleged crime or other act complained" a crime punishable by fine or imprisonment.[73]

In sum, additions to the 1925 ordinance carried two basic aims. First was to expand the involvement of functionaries like chiefs and headmen in combating witchcraft-related crimes by assigning them new roles like hearing witchcraft accusations and reporting witchcraft activities in their locations while at the same time criminalizing a willful or indifferent neglect to do so. The additional language also placed more emphasis on the criminality of witchcraft accusations, effectively rendering the activities of diviners as crimes and again blurring the divide between harmful witchcraft and healing witchcraft. Overall, each law in the series of anti-witchcraft ordinances was ineffective in diminishing witchcraft because as elements of an evidentiary based legal system, the ordinances required tangible evidence to prove the perpetration of a crime which was inherently invisible.

The various drawbacks of the ordinances also motivated colonial authorities to employ creative legal and administrative strategies for dealing with witches and witchdoctors that entailed the use of legislation besides the Witchcraft Ordinance. For example, in 1927, the chief native commissioner circulated a memo to all provincial commissioners (with sufficient copies to district commissioners) which explained that he had concluded in consultation with the attorney general that activities such as "claiming to have peculiar powers such as removing witchcraft spells" and "bringing rain or other benefit" could be dealt with under the Vagrancy Amendment Ordinance, 1925.[74]

Colonial authorities also employed the 1909 Removal of Natives Ordinance in dealing with witches and witchdoctors, who were generally brought to their attention by functionaries whose work was the first to

---

[73] PRO CO 542/19, An Ordinance to Consolidate and Amend the Law Relating to Witchcraft 1925, 1131. The Witchcraft Ordinance of 1925 and the Witchcraft Ordinance (revised) of 1981, the law contra witchcraft currently on the books, are in language and substance practically identical. See "The Witchcraft Ordinance (No. 23 of 1925)" and "the Witchcraft Act (Chapter 67, 1981)." Papers contained in KNA AG 1/610 show colonial authorities' long-term attempts to hammer out the semantics and practicalities of "witchcraft."

[74] KNA DC/MKS 25/3/2. See also, the attorney general's opinion in the same file in which he reiterates that "Witchcraft is not recognized by the law as fact."

be disrupted by witchcraft and similar activities.[75] For example, the 1915 Machakos District Political Record Book explained,

> The Elders of Nzauwi having complained against an old man Nzuma wa Kaluki by name for practising witchcraft, he was ordered to be brought into Machakos to reside here for one month. In addition as security for his future good behaviour, four cows and two bulls are deposited here by him to remain for one year.[76]

Such an order to reside by the administrative *boma* was not unusual. For instance, an administrator's note on "Akamba Witch Doctors Security" listed the names of the eleven witchdoctors who had been ordered to reside at the *boma* and who had supplied cows as collateral.[77] Another report indicated that the detention of three "witchdoctors" had had an "extremely salutary" effect that is there had been "no cases of witchcraft reported from the area from which these men came during the past year."[78]

In many instances, deportation or arrest was carried out as much for the good of the alleged witch or witchdoctor as it was for the good of the local community since witchcraft accusations very often resulted in violence against the alleged witch or witchdoctor. As one annual report explained, "Baiting of alleged witches is common."[79] Perhaps with such occurrences in mind, the chief justice of the Supreme Court of Kenya wrote to the governor, proposing the creation of a location exclusively for "witch doctors."[80] Overall, the ultimate inutility of the ordinances dissuaded many colonial authorities from aggressively prosecuting witchcraft in their districts or led them to approach witchcraft through other legal means. At the same time, the ordinances' inutility also encouraged the persistence of local forms of justice for dealing with witches that in turn produced damaged or dead bodies that the state could not ignore.

---

[75] KNA DC/KTI 2/9/1, Kitui Native Council Minutes, 27 August 1928, 158. See also, J. B. Ojwang, "Kenya: Preventative Detention in Context," in *Preventative Detention and Security Law: A Comparative Study*, ed. Andrew Harding and John Hatchard (Norwell, MA: Kluwer Academic Publishers, 1993): 105–107.

[76] KNA DC/MKS 4/6, Machakos District Political Record Book 1915, 79.

[77] KNA DC/MKS 4/1, Machakos District Political Record Book, Vol. I (up to 1910), 26.

[78] KNA PC/CP/4/2/3, Ukamba Province Annual Report 1928, 21–22.

[79] KNA DC/MKS 1/3/12, Kitui District Annual Report 1927, 5.

[80] KNA PC/NZA/2/5/20, Letter from the Chief Justice of the Supreme Court of Kenya to the Governor of Kenya, 25 March 1925. The file also includes a note from Chief Native Commissioner to the Senior Commissioner, Nyanza, regarding the feasibility of special locations for witchdoctors, 12 April 1925.

The "Cosmology" of the Colonial State

In Ukambani, the persistent existence of a parallel judicial system for dealing with witches – *king'ole* – posed a significant challenge to the state's ability to maintain order and to its avowed monopoly on juridical violence. As was the case with *uoi* and *uwe*, state authorities evidenced a familiarity with Kamba *king'ole* that took in the practice's basic elements but less so its nuances. For example, a special report on "Birth, Marriage and Death among the Wakamba," which constituted part of a Machakos District Political Record Book, noted that "When people die while more or less young it is often put down to socery [*sic*]. Anybody can bewitch another ... women more so than men, therefore a woman may by common consent of several villages be put to death as a witch."[81] While this report is correct in assertion about the prevalence of Kamba women's witchcraft, its assertion that *king'ole* must be sanctioned by several villages is incorrect.

Another administrative text explained simply, "A witch if proved to be using her powers for evil purposes is done to death."[82] And, as in other contexts, functionaries often filled in gaps in British administrators' knowledge regarding witchcraft. Bringing together Kamba cosmology and colonial bureaucratic procedure, the local chief reiterated at an Ukambani *baraza* "that witch-craft was inherited and that the councils had to consider the parents of the accused when enquiring into a case."[83]

Colonial authorities were in some instances confused about the obsolescence or persistence of *king'ole*. Some reports – even those dating from the opening years of the colonial era – figure *king'ole* as extinct even though witchcraft beliefs and practices were unabated. For example, a 1909 quarterly report proposed that "In old times a supposed witch was stoned to death by the Village (Kinyola),"[84] while six years later another administrative text stipulated that "In the old days these people were dealt with by 'Kingole' (lynch law) but, of course, that is now obsolete."[85] Such reports also contended that the removal of the witch along with the entire village constituted the contemporary approach to recidivist witches. The first author argued, "At present day when a Village thinks that a witch is present the rest of the inhabitants leave the Village to the supposed witch."[86] The second attended to the place of colonial bureaucracy

---

[81] KNA DC/MKS 4/3, Machakos District Political Record Book, Volume up to 1910. See J. Horman, "Birth, Marriage, and Death among the Wakamba," circa 1910.
[82] KNA DC/MKS 1/3/1, Kitui District Quarterly Report 1909, 73.
[83] KNA DC/MKS 10 A/6/1, Native Baraza, Kitui, 1 and 2 January 1915.
[84] KNA DC/MKS 1/3/1, Kitui District Quarterly Report 1909, 37.
[85] KNA DC/MKS1/3/6, Kitui District Annual Report 1914–1915, 14.
[86] KNA DC/MKS 1/3/1, Kitui District Quarterly Report 1909, 37.

in witchcraft management, explaining, "People have been instructed to report any case and if no satisfactory evidence can be obtained the accused is removed to another Location and kept under observation."[87] The first report offers a scenario that does not accord with ethnographic evidence about *king'ole*. The second constitutes a narrative of best practice, a story of how proper administration should proceed rather than a strict depiction of how policy and practice were actually implemented.

Such misunderstandings of witchcraft management were likely a function of the relative sparseness of evidence about *king'ole* available to British officers, even those with a semi-professional anthropological bent. As noted, the deliberations of a *king'ole* were not part of Kamba public culture even if the spectacular discipline meted out by the *king'ole* was. And *king'ole* justice was banned under colonial law. Thus, the officer writing that Kamba "females who are said to have inherited the power of casting spells without using any paraphernalia" was probably closest to the realities of witchcraft management in Ukambani when he added, "It is certain that some of these women are killed according to the ancient custom but it is very difficult to find out about these murders and we do not get many convictions."[88]

Even if reports about the exercise of *king'ole* per se were not especially common, the dead bodies of witches regularly turned up in the Ukambani bush and thus in official, administrative writings on the province's sociopolitical situation. Such documents consistently reference violence against witches and attend to the inefficacy of the Witchcraft Ordinances as a witchcraft management tool. Reports with statements such as follows were not unusual: "Numerous women and a few men have been accused of being witches or wizards and with having killed people but except in one case (an attempt to poison) no evidence could be obtained to support a conviction under the Witchcraft Ordinance."[89] And a district officer's frustrated remark was typical: "Complaints against witches are very common but I have only obtained one conviction which passed the High Court and after frequently arresting people and having to release them I now do not take up the cases at all." [90]

Such administrative writings also registered Kamba people's complaints about the inutility of colonial law and a concomitant wish to return to the more efficient methods of *king'ole* justice. For example,

---

[87] KNA DC/MKS 1/3/6, Kitui District Annual Report 1914–1915, 14–15.
[88] KNA DC/MKS 1/3/7, Kitui Annual Report 1917–1918, n.p.
[89] KNA DC/MKS 1/3/6, Kitui District Annual Report 1914–1915, 17.
[90] KNA DC/MKS 1/3/6, Kitui District Annual Report 1916, 74, 15.

one administrative text explained, "The Akamba, with some reason, say we prevent them from killing the Witch (which after all was our ancestor's practice some hundred of years ago) but do not substitute an effective remedy."[91] Another noted that "Headmen repeatedly ask if they can revert to the old custom of 'Kingoli' (beating to death) as they say that in the old days that did finish a case while the Government's way generally results in the accused getting off."[92]

But even while colonial and Kamba authorities may have at some moments shared a frustration with the violence produced by witchcraft, and British officers harbored a certain sympathy for the perspective of local functionaries, the Indian Penal Code, and its successor the Kenya Penal Code, rendered the management of witchcraft and particularly the killings of (alleged) witches the sole purview of the state. And the corpus of case law that emerged from the murder trials in which alleged witches were the victims served to reinforce the jurisdiction of the state and to suppress claims to a parallel, local system of justice. Overall, a district officer's simple lament, "There is a real fear of Witches and the question has yet to be solved by the Administration," neatly summed up the supernatural state of colonial Kenya.[93] The next chapter investigates the most high-profile witch-murder case of the colonial era, the Wakamba Witch Trials.

---

[91] KNA DC/MKS 1/3/6, Kitui District Annual Report 1917, 142.
[92] KNA DC/MKS 1/3/6, Kitui District Annual Report 1916, 74.
[93] KNA DC/MKS 1/3/6, Kitui District Annual Report 1917, 142.

5

The Wakamba Witch Trials

A Witch-Murder in 1930s Kenya

Throughout the colonial era, the "supernatural" state of Kenya was one of conflicting codes and contested justice. The contentious nature of justice, law, and order in Kenya emerges in high relief in cases of witch-killing. In the course of investigating and adjudicating such cases, state authorities aimed simultaneously to discipline and deny local "witchcraft" practices and beliefs while African actors asserted the efficacy and legitimacy of their communities' approaches to witchcraft.

Accordingly, this chapter analyzes the most high profile witch-killing case in colonial Kenya – that of Mwaiki, a Kamba woman killed in 1931 by a group of men from her community who believed her to have bewitched a neighbor woman. Mwaiki's case, officially known as *Rex v. Kumwaka s/o of Mulumbi and 69 Others*, achieved international recognition when it was tried in the Supreme Court of Kenya and sixty of the seventy defendants were sentenced to death. These sentences were upheld by the Court of Appeal for Eastern Africa and ultimately commuted by the Governor of Kenya.[1] *Rex v. Kumwaka* brought to bear imperial anthro-administrative networks of knowledge about witchcraft and engendered vociferous debates in Kenya and the metropole about what made British justice in the African Empire.

Despite the empire-wide furor that *Rex v. Kumwaka* produced, the case is overwhelmingly neglected by the limited secondary literature on

---

[1] *Rex v. Kumwaka s/o Mulumbi and 69 others*. Law Reports of Kenya: Containing Cases Determined by the Supreme Court, Kenya Colony and Protectorate and by the Court of Appeal for Eastern Africa and by the Judicial Committee of the Privy Council on Appeal from that Court. Volume XIV 1932 (Nairobi: Government Printer, 1932), 137–139. Hereafter, 14 L.R.K. (1932). See also, PRO CO 533/420/8, Wakamba Witch Trial.

Ukambani.[2] The absence of *Rex v. Kumwaka* from Kamba historiography is remarkable because of the relative ease with which a straightforward narrative of the case can be assembled from Ukambani district and provincial reports, judgments and judicial decisions, Colonial Office correspondence, press reports from across East Africa and Britain, and paperwork generated by organs of civil society.[3] These discursive remains bring to light broad colonial networks or "circuits" of knowledge and power,[4] indicating how the archive was a "living" and usable entity for its colonial compilers.[5]

The scant historical and historiographical accounts that do touch on *Rex v. Kumwaka* have simply summarized the case, treating it as an element of broader Kamba institutions like *king'ole* or as part of wider discussions about law in the empire.[6] Yet the case speaks to more complicated concerns than such accounts suggest, particularly when the documentary record is read in conversation with ethnographic sources. It demonstrates how important categories like custom, crime, victim, expertise, and "modernity" were not clearly defined and hegemonically employed by the state. Rather, the meanings of such categories were up for grabs and their uses contested in colonial Kenya.

ASSEMBLING THE FACTS OF THE CASE

The documentary sources enumerated earlier enable the assembly of the facts of the case as articulated in colonial discursive spaces. According to the report of District Officer Brumage, two Wakamba men, Kumwaka and Mnyoki, arrived at the administrative *boma* in Machakos during late 1931 to report the death of Mwaiki d/o Mboloi. Brumage explained that Kumwaka believed that Mwaiki had bewitched his wife, rendering her mute. After organizing a group of young Wakamba men, Kumwaka then "seized Mwaiki and took her to his hut." Mwaiki then said that she had "removed part of the spell." Subsequently, "the patient recovered to some

---

[2] See Chapters 1 and 2.
[3] Regrettably, the trial transcripts and assorted court documents pertaining to *Rex v. Kumwaka* are lost. A fire at the Secretariat in Nairobi in 1939 destroyed many important records.
[4] Stoler and Cooper, "Beyond Metropole," 28.
[5] Ann Laura Stoler, "Colonial Archives and the Arts of Governance: On the Content in the Form," in *Refiguring the Archive*, ed. Carolyn Hamilton, Verne Harris, Jane Taylor, Michele Pickover, Graeme Reid, and Rezia Shah (Cape Town: David Philips Publishers, 2002), 83–128.
[6] KNA PC/CP/4/2/3, Ukamba Province Annual Report 1931. See also, Penwill, *Kamba Customary*; Munro, *Colonial Rule*; Waller, "Witchcraft and the Law."

extent and was able to speak." Mwaiki ran away from Kumwaka's hut in the night, and was "chased" by Kumwaka and his group who "beat her with thin sticks until they killed her." Kumwaka and Mnyoki, Mwaiki's son, attempted to report the "murder" to their headman, Nzioki. Finding the headman not at home, Kumwaka and Mnyoki spoke with the headman's retainer and returned to the "scene of the crime." The pair reported the murder in Machakos, and they were then sent home to collect the rest of Kumwaka's group. The young men whom Kumwaka had organized earlier "gave themselves up without assistance and came singing into Machakos like a gang of porters."[7] Such were the circumstances that led to *Rex v. Kumwaka*.

As a capital case, *Rex v. Kumwaka* was tried in the Kenya Supreme Court. The prosecution presented its case first, developing its arguments around Mnyoki's testimony that he had been present in the deceased's hut when a group of men came to take her away and that he had told the group that he would "carry the matter to court" if they beat or killed his mother. He heard his mother declare, "I am not a witch" as one of the men grabbed her by the wrist and made her stand. Mnyoki fell back asleep while his mother was taken away from the hut and did not awaken until he heard screams which caused him to leave his hut and witness a woman running from a group of men who were all wielding sticks.[8]

Mnyoki claimed that "he did not actually see them beat her, but they were running on all sides of her, and then he saw the woman fall to the ground and remain there." The men circling the woman then left her, and sat down some distance away. Mnyoki explained that he "visited some elders, and sent them to look at the body of the deceased." He himself also viewed Mwaiki and observed that she was dead. Mnyoki confronted one of the accused who said simply "What can I do?" Mnyoki then went with Kumwaka to the local headman and later to Machakos to report the killing. Mnyoki testified that "The man who went with him was the man who had caught hold of his mother's wrist – he admitted that it was through him that she had met her death."[9] Under cross-examination, Mnyoki claimed that he "knew people regarded his mother as a witch" but that he had never seen her practice "witchcraft" nor had he "heard of spells cast by her over the first accused's wife."[10]

---

[7] KNA DC/MKS 4/9, "Nzavi Murder Case. Machakos Criminal Case No.* 576/31. Rex versus Kumwaka s/o Mulumbi and 70 others," 125. Hereafter, "Nzavi Murder."
[8] "A Strange Setting for a Murder Trial," *East African Standard (EAS)*, 2 February 1932.
[9] Ibid.
[10] Ibid.

Mwaiki's brother also testified for the prosecution, claiming that he too had been in the hut when the deceased was taken away and that he had also warned the men that there would be trouble if his sister were hurt.[11] A third witness testified that he had seen the body of the deceased but was not yet old enough to touch it. He also explained, "Only when a person was really dead was the body put out in the bush, unless the death took place from sickness when it was burned. This body was not buried because the woman was killed."[12]

The defense opened its case with a lengthy statement by Kumwaka and testimony from the other sixty-nine defendants that they had participated in the killing because Kumwaka had summoned them. When Chief Justice Jacob Barth asked Kumwaka why he had killed Mwaiki, Kumwaka replied, "She was a witch."[13] Later, Kumwaka's statement made in a lower court was read. According to the statement, trouble had come to pass because the deceased had placed a spell on Kumwaka's wife. Kumwaka testified that Mwaiki had threatened to put a spell on his wife that rendered her mute because she would not "go to" Mnyoki. Kumwaka pointed out, "My wife fell sick the same day" that Mwaiki had threatened to bewitch her.[14]

Kumwaka claimed that Mnyoki agreed to join him in "tak[ing] responsibility for the punishment to be given" to Mwaiki for bewitching Kumwaka's wife. The pair led a large party of young men collected by Kumwaka to a place that Mwaiki frequented and seized Mwaiki there. Mnyoki took the load his mother was carrying while she was taken to Kumwaka's hut where she was to remove the spell she had placed on Kumwaka's wife. "At the third cock-crow," sounds of Mwaiki fleeing the hut awoke the group. They overtook her and beat her, but she "ran on until she neared her own village where she collapsed and died." Kumwaka stated that the body was removed a hundred yards because "it is not a good thing for young men to look on a deceased person."[15] On the trial's second day, Kumwaka reiterated his testimony but added that Mwaiki had removed "only half the spell" before she ran away. Kumwaka also claimed that upon overtaking Mwaiki, he and his comrades had implored her to return to Kumwaka's hut and remove the second half of the spell. When Mwaiki refused, the men beat her with small sticks as she walked along. After awhile Mwaiki sat down, and the men asked Kumwaka to get her some water. She

[11] Ibid.
[12] Ibid.
[13] Ibid.
[14] Ibid.
[15] Ibid.

died during his absence. The native assessors rested the blame for the death with Kumwaka, stating that he had "no right to summon the other accused, a number of whom were young men and did only what they were told."[16]

On 6 February 1932 the chief justice handed down death sentences for the seventy accused. The appeal period was set at thirty days, and the chief justice recommended the guilty parties to the governor's clemency. In the meantime, *Rex v. Kumwaka* and its relationship to British "justice" became the topic of questions in the House of Commons and also the subject of various reports and correspondence in newspapers in Britain and abroad. A few weeks later, the Court of Appeal for Eastern Africa met in Entebbe, Uganda, and dismissed the appeal lodged by Black and Varma, advocates for Kumwaka and his cohort, further fanning the flames of contention about the case.[17] On 2 April 1932 the Governor-in-Council commuted the death sentences handed down by the Supreme Court, sentencing the group to varying terms of hard labor.[18] Ultimately, *Rex v. Kumwaka* spurred the Colonial Office to generate an extensive report, entitled *Inquiry into the Administration of Justice in Criminal Matters Affecting Natives in Kenya, Tanganyika, and Uganda*, and prompted sharper attention within the courts and case law to the complicated legal issues tied up in witch-killing cases.

At first glance, the facts of the case assembled from the archive place the primacy of colonial rule at the center of *Rex v. Kumwaka* and assert the hegemony of colonial authority. Yet the fact that the case exists in the archive at all points to a rupture in colonial control. Accordingly, the following sections reexamine the facts of the case with an anthropological eye, working to "unravel" colonial discourse through attentiveness to the "logics" through which state actors heard and read argumentation and to the local "logics" that precipitated and were deployed to justify Mwaiki's killing.[19]

COURT NARRATIVES AND COMPETING CODES

As Ranajit Guha notes, judicial discourse works by "trapping crime in its specificity, by reducing its range of signification to a set of narrowly

---

[16] "The Wakamba Murder Trial," *EAS*, 3 February 1932.
[17] No information beyond that contained in the *Kumwaka* texts is available about Black. A Judicial Department file offers limited information on Varma. See KNA AP/1/1579, *Mukhi Ram Varma*, 1929–1932.
[18] "Wakamba Witch Case," *EAS*, 2 April 1932.
[19] Ibid., 17.

defined legalities, and by assimilating it to the existing order as one of its negative determinants."[20] Colonial judicial discourse in *Rex v. Kumwaka* belongs to a broader legal "genre" concerned with narrowing, condensing, and controlling the terms and circumstances of the case. It shifted the focus of the case away from Mwaiki's alleged misdeeds and toward her death, effectively transforming the messy story of witchcraft presented by the accused into a legally usable narrative of murder.

A summary section from the *Law Reports of Kenya* succinctly narrates the events of *Rex v. Kumwaka* as assembled by the courts.

> The first accused (Kumwaka) summoned the rest of the accused and brought them to the vicinity of the hut in which was his wife, the woman believed to have been bewitched. Next, the witch, the deceased, was seized and brought to the sick woman's hut and ordered to remove the spell. The accused allege that she removed half the spell during the night. Early in the morning, the witch was detected running away. All accused ran after her and beat her with the thin sticks referred to above. As a result of the beating the witch was killed. On perusing the evidence we entertain no doubt that she died, and died as a result of the beatings administered.[21]

Overall, judicial discourse compresses written records of oral speech to assert further the courts' authority and produces a syllogism of guilt.[22] The courts concluded that (1) the belief in witchcraft is not reasonable, (2) fear of witchcraft is not a basis for self-defense, and (3) the government does not tolerate the killing of witches. The courts' narration of the case through the genre of legalese thus strips the story of Mwaiki's killing of its dramaturgic elements, instead setting up the courts' control over an orderly narrative expressed in matter-of-fact language and with categories of deliberated ambiguity.[23]

When read in isolation, documents surrounding the case of *Rex v. Kumwaka* therefore offer a simple juridical narrative in which the witch-killing clearly indicates the contravention of colonial law. The courts' findings were contoured not only by the evidence presented but

---

[20] Ranajit Guha, "Chandra's Death," in *A Subaltern Studies Reader, 1986–1995*, ed. Ranajit Guha (Minneapolis: University of Minnesota Press, 1997), 38.

[21] 14 L.R.K. (1932), 138. The report on *Rex v. Kumwaka* contained in the *Law Reports of Kenya* is that of the Court of Appeal for Eastern Africa. It concurs with and quotes extensively from the original Supreme Court of Kenya judgment among other legal sources.

[22] Carlo Ginzburg, *The Cheese and the Worms: The Cosmos of a Sixteenth Century Miller*, trans. John Tedeschi and Anne C. Tedeschi (Baltimore: Johns Hopkins University Press, 1980).

[23] Guha, "Chandra's Death," 38.

also by the law-as-written, judicial precedent, and anthro-administrative understandings that shaped the ways in which evidence was assimilated. But ethnographic sources suggest a competing judicial story in which the witch-killing points to the *maintenance* of local law. Read in conversation, these varied sources foreground some of the ways Mwaiki's death was a nexus in which juridical codes collided, in which judicial settings were contested, and in which the meanings of victim and perpetrator, of crime and custom, of murder and justice emerged at odds.[24]

As noted, the Kenya Penal Code rendered witchcraft a crime. But so did the *local* codes of most ethnic groups in Kenya. While the Witchcraft Ordinance demanded an untenable level of evidence to prove a crime that was intrinsically invisible, local laws were simpler and clearer, relying on consensus and confession rather than complicated issues of burden-of-proof in order to convict and contain. Local codes about witchcraft were directed at dealing with damage to the *bewitched*. Colonial laws, in contrast, were interested primarily in the death of the witch and the accusations that had led to his or her killing.

While witchcraft was a crime that colonial authorities could and often did overlook, a dead body was evidence of the sort of *public* disorder and challenge to state authority that could not be ignored. Indeed, although colonial sources refer to Mwaiki categorically and without explanation as "the witch," the courts were interested in her only *after* her death. From the colonial standpoint, Mwaiki was the foremost victim in the case of *Rex v. Kumwaka*.

The status of the other woman involved in the case, Kumwaka's wife, was more ambivalent, however. Purported to be a victim of witchcraft, Kumwaka's wife was injured by an act that colonial law simultaneously denied and banned. After being harmed through a type of embodied *uoi* called *ndia*, which produces "dumbness" in its objects, Kumwaka's wife experienced a second silencing in the colonial courts. In the available documents, her name is never mentioned and there is no evidence that she was called as a witness in a case of murder that was committed seemingly on her behalf. From the colonial legal perspective, witchcraft did not create an accessible body of evidence as Mwaiki's corpse did.

Further, in the eyes of the courts, Kumwaka and his cohort were both culpable for Mwaiki's death and victims of their own misguided ideas about witchcraft. Sir Charles Griffin, chief justice of the Court of Appeal for Eastern Africa, wrote, "It is widely known, and as appears from the

---

[24] Cohen and Odhiambo, *Burying SM*, 11, 13.

evidence in this case the fact was present to the mind of the first accused that the Government does not tolerate the killing of witches." But he also acknowledged that "The belief in witchcraft is, of course, widespread and deeply ingrained in the native character."[25] From the courts' perspective, the Kamba men's witchcraft beliefs led them to produce a corpse when they should have produced a magistrate.

In the Kamba perspective, in contrast, the bewitched body of Kumwaka's wife evidenced of the sort of *public* danger that could not be ignored. *Uoi* constituted the crime demanding recompense that spilled into retribution. Kumwaka's (sickened and muted) wife was the foremost victim in the story from the standpoint of Kumwaka and his cohort, while Mwaiki's corpse, in turn, indicated that a risk to the community had been resolved.

Though documents surrounding Mwaiki's death do not reveal or even hint at what Kumwaka's group thought of the court's judgment, reading them in conversation with other sources remarking on the inefficacy and inutility of the witchcraft ordinances suggests that the Kamba men also likely saw themselves as the victims of misguidedness – that of a legal system that held that the diffuse dangers posed by witchcraft could be dealt with by colonial law when what they really demanded was the corpse of the *mu'unde m'uoi*. As a present-day informant suggested, "The *serikali ya ukoloni* did not know about *uoi*. They did not know enough to make laws about it."[26]

Both the Kenya Penal Code and Kamba codes of justice contained sets of consequences for causing the death of another person. The penal code differentiated among types of killing, largely according to the presence or absence of "malice aforethought." According to the penal code, all killings committed with "malice aforethought" were automatically murder, and murder was always a capital crime.[27] The penal code also included different legal consequences for other types of killing.

Kamba codes, in turn, were compensatory. As Penwill explained in his notable treatise, *Kamba Customary Law*, "Kamba law does not distinguish between murder, manslaughter, or a death caused by accident. The blood price is payable in each case."[28] Further, the gender and generation

---

[25] 14 L.R.K. (1932), 139.
[26] P. M., Kilungu, August 2004.
[27] Penal Code of Kenya (1930): Division IV – Offences Against the Person, Chapter XIX Murder and Manslaughter. Jomo Kenyatta University Library (University of Nairobi) Afr. Docs. J 750.155.P4 1930.
[28] D. J. Penwill, *Kamba Customary*, 81.

of the victim, rather than the motive of the killer, determined the compensation. For example, an administrative report explained, "murder and accidents causing death are dealt with by the Akamba as one," adding that the compensation for the death of a man was twice that of a woman.[29] Lindblom noted similarly, "No consideration is paid to the motive for a crime or to the way in which it was committed, but only to the result. The damage is just the same if a person has, for instance, been killed accidentally or murdered."[30]

Both the Kenya Penal Code and Kamba law employed judicial killing. Judicial killing was a regular punishment in the colonial courts, driven by colonial policies that regarded most killing as murder, and all murder as a capital crime. Local law employed judicial killing differently and less often.[31] Kamba law stipulated that the *king'ole* execute only serial malefactors whose consistent misdeeds could no longer be dealt with through compensatory means – for example, the recidivist *uoi* of an unrepentant *mu'unde m'uoi*.

Tied to perceptions about the embodied nature of Kamba women's *uoi*, precolonial and colonial-era cases of witchcraft were frequently resolved by destroying, or at least, harming the body of the *mu'unde m'uoi*. One colonial report starkly related a case of lethal violence against two alleged witches contemporaneous with *Rex v. Kumwaka*. The families of a woman whose cause of death had been diagnosed by a "witch-doctor" as "witchcraft," seized "with the consent of all concerned" the two women alleged to have perpetrated the "witchcraft" and "put one in a house, setting fire to it." The other woman was "spreadeagled on the ground ... tied to stakes" while a "fire was lit between her legs, and lighting brands were inserted in her vagina."[32] Similarly, Mwaiki's beaten body demonstrated to Kumwaka and his cohort that they had administered the requisite punishment for repeat *uoi*: *king'ole*.

Both within the colonial courts and local spaces of justice, the treatment of Mwaiki's death was informed by judicial precedents having to do with "witchcraft," or *uoi* and murder. A wider understanding of precedent – one which considers it as a body of past actions and behaviors that is well known, well understood, and collectively considered by authorities in decision making targeted toward maintaining social order – suggests

---

[29] KNA DC/MKS 1/3/2, Kitui District Quarterly Report 1910, 10.
[30] Lindblom, *The Akamba*, 161.
[31] Stacey Hynd, "Killing the Condemned: The Practice and Process of Capital Punishment in British Africa, 1900–1950s," *Journal of African History* 49.3 (2008): 403–418.
[32] KNA PC/CP/4/2/3, Ukamba Province Annual Report 1932, 41.

that Kamba codes and colonial law *each* drew on precedent in managing witchcraft and killing. Yet, notions of precedent too were at odds.

In the Kamba context, consistent *king'ole* action against a recidivist *mu'unde m'uoi* composed a sort of judicial precedent. But *king'ole* action was in turn driven by the precedent that the *mu'unde m'uoi* had established through his or her own behavior. Had the *mu'unde m'uoi* killed regularly? Refuse to reverse *uoi*? Ignored the *king'ole*'s warnings? If such was the case, precedent indicated that the *king'ole* was within its rights, or even obligated, to kill the *mu'unde m'uoi*. If it was not the case, past precedent prescribed a range of cleansing activities, most often an oath, to get the *mu'unde m'uoi* to cease and reverse his or her work.[33]

Though jurisprudence in *Rex v. Kumwaka* does not cite earlier cases of witch-killing that passed through East Africa's highest courts, a review of these cases shows that there was *not* precedent in the colonial courts for treating the alleged witchcraft of the deceased as mitigation for murder. There was, however, precedent for dismissing defense claims that witch-killing was a realization of customary law.

The highest profile witch-killing case in the era before *Rex v. Kumwaka* was *Rex v. Karoga wa Kithenhi* (1914) in which a Kikuyu *kiama* or council of elders, tried, sentenced, and burned to death two alleged witchdoctors with the sanction and participation of their chief. During the Supreme Court trial, solicitors for the *kiama* members raised a three-pronged defense: (1) members of the *kiama* had not been instructed as to the limits of their jurisdiction under the Native Tribunal Rules, 1911; (2) they acted on the advice of their chief; and (3) in doing so, they were justified in exercising their "ancient customary jurisdiction to sentence witchdoctors to death." Unsurprisingly, this defense failed on the grounds that under colonial law the *kiama* no longer had the authority to exercise customary forms of justice.[34]

In *Rex v. Kumwaka*, the courts regarded defense claims about customary justice having been exercised via *king'ole* with the same sort of skepticism that their predecessors had applied to the activities of the *kiama*. Acknowledging *king'ole*, but denying its legitimacy, Chief Justice Griffin argued instead that "no belief could well be more mischievous

---

[33] J. K. S., Kilungu, September 2004; M. W., Imani, September 2004.

[34] *Rex v. Karoga wa Kithenhi and 53 others*. Law Reports of Kenya: Containing Cases Determined by the Supreme Court, Kenya Colony and Protectorate and by the Court of Appeal for Eastern Africa and by the Judicial Committee of the Privy Council on Appeal from that Court. Volume V 1913–1914 (Nairobi: Government Printer, 1914). Hereafter, 5 L.R.K. (1913–1914), 50–53.

or fraught with greater danger to public peace and tranquility" than the belief that "an aggrieved party could take the law into his own hands."[35] As state authority is in part retrenched by dismissing the claims of competing sources of power, the courts mobilized expert knowledge to dismiss the arguments that the Kamba men voiced about their authority over Mwaiki's death.[36] The mobilization of expertise, in turn, entailed various strategies of translation.[37]

First, colonial experts on *king'ole* sought to translate the practice into more familiar terms, setting up equivalencies between it and other better known "barbaric," customary practices in the British Empire. For example, early colonial officials described *king'ole* as a "dreaded secret society" whose tactics were "as cruel as the practice of *suttee* in India."[38] This equation with *suttee*, or "widow burning," would have carried a double resonance in early 1930s Kenya as liberal members of Parliament and church leaders had set up an equivalency between the Indian practice and female genital cutting during the Kenyan Female Circumcision Controversy, which reached its zenith shortly before Mwaiki's case.[39] Thus, colonial expert opinion discounted *king'ole*, suggesting that a practice as "cruel" as *suttee* and excision could not possibly be part of a legitimate legal institution.

Also, native assessors argued during the trial that Kumwaka had "had no right to summon the other accused" because rather than being Kumwaka's peers they were mainly "young men [who] did only what they were told."[40] Colonial ethnographic sources and present-day informants insist that a *king'ole* must be composed of *atumia*, or elders, each with the knowledge and experience to participate in making life-and-death decisions. According to the expert opinion of the assessors, the inappropriate age-group composition of the *king'ole* that killed Mwaiki rendered the *king'ole* illegitimate in the eyes of the courts and according to local law.

A Machakos District Annual Report echoed and elaborated this opinion, adding that not only had the *king'ole* been inappropriately composed, but that it had acted without customary due process. It explained,

---

[35] 14 L.R.K. (1932), 139.
[36] Timothy Mitchell, "The Limits of the State: Beyond Statist Approaches and Their Critics," *American Political Science Review* 85.1 (March, 1991): 77–96.
[37] Cohen and Odhiambo, *Burying SM*, 48–49.
[38] Munro, *Colonial Rule*, 56.
[39] Susan Pedersen, "National Bodies and Unspeakable Acts: The Sexual Politics of Colonial Policy-making," *Journal of Modern History* 63 (1991): 647–680.
[40] "The Wakamba Murder Trial," *EAS*, 3 February 1932.

According to the *Kinyole* law, however, elaborate proceedings which must be sanctioned and directed by the Elders are necessary before the community may act.... [O]nly a section of the community i.e. a number of relations and friends of certain "bewitched" individuals – acted on the spur of the moment without customary sanction.[41]

Finally, the provincial commissioner offered a similar, two-point opinion. First, he suggested that *king'ole* entailed specific processes and sanctions that had not been followed. Second, in an opinion reminiscent of that made by the appellate court in *Rex v. Karoga*, he argued that the colonial government's co-option of the local tribunals had stripped these bodies of their power to sanction *king'ole*. He wrote,

> Under [*king'ole*], persons accused of witchcraft could be killed with impunity, but only after the Nzama or Tribunal had given its consent. The procedure was elaborate and clearly defined.... (See Lindblom's work on the Wakamba). As the Nzama are now a body carrying out the functions of the Government, its permission in this case could not, of course, be obtained.[42]

In sum, according to the expertise mobilized by the colonial courts, the *king'ole* that killed Mwaiki was illegitimate for the following reasons: (1) it was another example of a "cruel" local custom, (2) it was composed of youth rather than elders, (3) it had acted without due process, and (4) the authority of the colonial government superseded that of the *nzama* in matters of judicial killing.

The courts' conclusions, not merely about *king'ole*, but also about witchcraft more generally, engaged larger imperial networks which brought together anthropological, administrative, and judicial knowledge about witchcraft and which formed part of an empire-wide debate over British justice and customary law.[43] Drawing on their knowledge gleaned through participation in these networks and debates, it was both easy and logical for the justices of both the Kenya Supreme Court and the

---

[41] KNA DC/MKS 1/1/24, Machakos District Annual Report 1931, 33–34.
[42] KNA PC/CP/4/2/3, Ukamba Province Report 1931, 31–32.
[43] For example, an article entitled "Witchcraft and Its Effect on Crime in East Africa," which addressed some of the ways in which investigation and prosecution of crimes related to "witchcraft" constituted a significant stumbling block to the administration of justice in East Africa, was published in the *Police Journal and Quarterly Review for Police Forces in the Empire* in 1929. See F. Peacock, "Witchcraft and Its Effect on Crime in East Africa," *Police Journal and Quarterly Review for Police Forces in the Empire* (1929): 121–131. I am grateful to Cedric Barnes for introducing me to the Cambridge University Commonwealth Collection.

Court of Appeal for Eastern Africa to perceive the culture of Kumwaka and Mwaiki's community as necessarily shot through with witchcraft. In producing their verdicts, justices functioned not only as legal authorities but also as "anthropologists" in robes and wigs, both drawing on existing knowledge about witchcraft and mobilizing it to ask more questions and form further conclusions.[44]

Overall, for colonial officials and Kamba authorities, Mwaiki's killing signaled competing moments at which social control had been lost due to witchcraft, to *uoi*. And the goal of each legal system was to right a respective perceived wrong, be it the killing of a witch or the recidivist practice of *uoi*. For the colonial courts, Mwaiki's death, and the legal proceedings it necessitated, also presented an opportunity to reassert the authority of the state, in large part through the dismissal of the competing Kamba code, *king'ole*. But alternatively, a simultaneous attention to the Kamba codes at work in Mwaiki's death reveals the edifice of colonial law to be just that, an elaborately constructed front. The rules and norms that provided the *structure* of law and order within Kamba communities sprang from local sources and undergirded a parallel judicial system and juridical code, existing outside of, but along with, the colonial.

JUDICIAL SETTINGS AND PUBLICS

Categorizing "native murders," Hobley explained the mechanisms by which cases like *Rex v. Kumwaka* penetrated official colonial consciousness and the paths that such cases generally followed. He noted,

> Murder cases in native areas come first of all before the Commissioner of the district, who is an officer with an understanding of his people and deliberate misinterpretation or misrepresentation would have little chance. In the bigger townships and in settled areas, murder cases are in the early stage, dealt with by Resident Magistrates. If the accused is committed for trial, the case goes to the Supreme Court where the judge sits with native assessors selected from one of the Native tribunals, men who are accustomed to weigh evidence; a counsel for the defence is also engaged and for whose enquiries adequate time [is] given. Finally and perhaps most important, every capital sentence is then considered by the Executive Council, upon which sit men who have deep sympathy with the natives and that Council is ready, invariably, to give full weight to

---

[44] Carlo Ginzburg, *Clues, Myths, and the Historical Method*, trans. John Tedeschi and Anne C. Tedeschi (Baltimore: Johns Hopkins University Press, 1992).

the extenuating circumstances, e.g. beliefs in witchcraft, undue provocation, etc. In many cases it makes recommendations of clemency and in such cases a commutation of the sentence by the Governor follows.[45]

Indeed, following the trajectory of Mwaiki's death exclusively through colonial documentation establishes a linear path up the hierarchy of the colonial administrative and legal system, from the headman to the district officers to the Supreme Court to the Court of Appeal to the Governor-in-Council. Tracing this path creates a simultaneously limited and undifferentiated notion of the "publics" that the courts sought to address, most directly that of a monolithic African "other" and more tangentially that of a colonial community concerned that the courts carry out the letter of the law.[46] But applying additional strategies of reading to these documents and engaging with other sources expands the scope of "judicial settings" and "publics."

A judicial setting is not exclusively the building in which a trial is held but also encompasses the varied literal and figurative spaces in which legal processes are carried out. Within different judicial settings, officials aim not simply to speak to, but also to constitute, various publics under their authority. Mwaiki's killing was both dealt with in judicial settings and carried out in a judicial setting. Further, her body – and responses to it – spoke to and delineated a range of publics.

At first glance, the colonial legal setting of *Rex v. Kumwaka* and the publics that the courts addressed appear self-evident. According to colonial law, the fact of the corpse rendered the Supreme Court of Kenya and the Court of Appeal for Eastern Africa the appropriate legal settings for the trial and appeal of *Rex v. Kumwaka*. The unprecedented number of defendants, however, necessitated a shift in location. The drama of the Supreme Court trial was thus highlighted and played out in its relocation to the theater of the Railway Social Institute. As a reporter for the *East African Standard* described,

> The setting of the Court was distinctly strange, His Honour the Chief Justice occupying the stage amidst bizarre surroundings, an askari occupying the orchestra pit and counsel, accused, witnesses and the public being accommodated in the body of the hall ... the court looked like a setting for a modern mystery play, but the principle characters, the 70 accused men were not on the center stage.[47]

---

[45] Hobley, *Bantu Beliefs*, 309.
[46] Cohen and Odhiambo, *Burying SM*, 50.
[47] "A Strange Setting for a Murder Trial," *EAS*, 2 February 1932.

The judicial assessments offered in the settings of the courts during the trial and appeals proceedings addressed and delineated with varying degrees of specificity four primary publics: (1) the defendants, (2) the court room audience, (3) Africans *writ large*, and (4) colonialists in general. These assessments, reinforced by the authority of the legal settings in which they were presented, spoke directly to the crime at hand and also contained a sub-text of assurance that colonial justice was being readily and appropriately meted out. The legal settings of the courts, and the publics to whom the justices spoke, were all concerned with Mwaiki *after* her death. The spaces of the courts offered plainly bounded legal settings for dealing with a clear-cut crime while simultaneously speaking to publics constituted vaguely enough to receive the courts' messages. Overall, the "judicial 'theatre of death,'" Hynd writes, "had many audiences to impress – metropolitan, official, settler, and African – many of whom had differing attitudes towards its enactment."[48]

As a parallel code of justice existed alongside the colonial legal system, so did alternative legal settings and the additional publics they involved. The legal settings of *king'ole* justice were serialized, but scattered, and the publics they incorporated were diversely constituted. The first legal setting was the meeting of the *atumia* held to discuss the *mu'unde m'uoi*. A more specific conference of the *king'ole* council constituted the next legal setting. The third legal setting was the primary homestead of the family of the *mu'unde m'uoi* where the *king'ole* conferred with relatives about their plans for her. The home of the *mu'unde m'uoi*, where the *king'ole* confronted the *mu'unde m'uoi* and demanded *uoi* be undone, was the fourth legal setting. For a repentant *mu'unde m'uoi*, the home of the victim where he or she undid *uoi* and/or a public space in which cleansing transpired constituted additional legal settings. But for a *mu'unde m'uoi* like Mwaiki who would not or could not undo *uoi*, the bush, like that in which Mwaiki died, constituted the ultimate legal setting for the exercise of local justice.

Within these judicial settings, a number of publics interacted and were constituted. Unlike the more bounded proceedings of the colonial legal system, *king'ole* justice involved and addressed various members of the community in proceedings noted above. These steps and settings were both didactic – that is, providing a spectacular lesson about the appropriate treatment of social malefactors – and compensatory, paying back the individuals harmed by the *mu'unde m'uoi* and the community in

---

[48] Hynd, "Killing," 404.

general whose collective equilibrium had been upset by having a recidivist *mu'unde m'uoi* in their midst. The spaces of local justice offered a series of legal settings for dealing with a clear-cut crime, while simultaneously speaking to publics constituted diversely enough to participate in different elements of *king'ole* justice.

These competing legal settings, the colonial courts versus the *king'ole*, opened a third legal setting, one in which heated debates over the efficacy of colonial law in the face of a witch-killing were carried out. *Rex v. Kumwaka* spilled outside the colonial courts and engaged an additional public, a British metropolitan public composed of intellectuals, journalists, politicians, and human rights activists concerned with debating British justice in regard to African mentalities. The discussions of this metropolitan public countered and contested the claims about the efficiency and hegemony of colonial justice.

These debates reflect some of the ways in which courtroom contests produce "tradition" and "modernity."[49] On the one hand, the courts sought to reinforce their authority by couching their assessment of *Rex v. Kumwaka* in terms of the modern, the rational, the here-and-now. In referring to the assault on Mwaiki as part of "an *old* Kamba custom," the chief justice dismissed the coevalness of Kamba codes.

On the other hand, the opinions offered by members of the metropolitan public responding to and contesting the courts' claims articulated issues of tradition and modernity differently. British critics condemned the death sentences as unfair given the sway that traditional beliefs in witchcraft and in the justice of witch-killing held over Kamba minds. For example, Labour MP Morgan Jones demanded of Secretary of State for the Colonies Cunliffe-Lister whether he would "take steps to ensure that these sentences for a crime due to ignorance and superstition are not carried out."[50]

Parties interested in the *Kumwaka* case and appeals process also queried the real function and flexibility of a modern legal system. British authorities in the metropole and in Kenya were for the most part inclined to promote the primacy of the law-as-written, to uphold colonial legal hierarchies, to promote administrative power through law, and to allow little wiggle room for negotiation with local custom outside the civil arena. Indeed, Cunliffe-Lister responded shortly to the member's question, asserting that his information regarding the case did not exceed that available through press reports and restated the Supreme Court's

---

[49] Cohen and Odhiambo, *Burying SM*, 59–62.
[50] House of Commons Debates 10 February 1932. Vol. 261. 857–858.

assertion "that there was no alternative to finding the prisoners guilty of murder."[51] Overall, he aimed to make it "clear that the decision as to the exercise of the Royal Prerogative of Mercy rests constitutionally with the Governor of Kenya alone."[52]

This view is also reflected strongly in letters from Acting Attorney General of Kenya T. D. H. Bruce to the colonial secretary. Attending to Morgan Jones's question and Cunliffe-Lister's reply, Bruce's writings highlighted continued colonial and metropolitan concerns about following the law to the letter in the case of *Rex v. Kumwaka*. Bruce wrote that he had read, "a question has been asked in the House of Commons about this case and that the Secretary of State answered that he was asking the Governor for full particulars." Bruce argued that "the greatest care should be exercised to follow the normal procedure in this case unless there are the strongest reasons, of which I am not aware, to the contrary." If the governor of Kenya suggested quelling questions around *Rex v. Kumwaka* by giving a recommendation before the appeal had been lodged and considered, Bruce wrote that he would "advise His Excellency that this case should not be considered in Executive Council until the full expiration of thirty days allowed for appeal to the Court of Appeal for Eastern Africa."[53]

The reasons for following standard procedure in the case of *Rex v. Kumwaka*, Bruce explained, were manifold. First, Bruce referred to the law-as-written. He wrote,

> With the greatest respect I would submit that the true meaning of Article 42 of the Royal Instructions dated 11th September, 1920, read, as it must be, in conjunction with the East Africa (Court of Appeal) Order in Council, 1921, is that the Report of the Judges shall be taken into consideration at the first meeting of the Executive Council which may be held conveniently after the *final* condemnation of the convict.

If the governor and the Executive Council "consider[ed] the case before the appeal was decided," a continuous conflict between the executive and the judiciary would necessarily ensue. Bruce explained how such a conflict could potentially play out. He theorized that "When a sentence of

---

[51] Ibid.
[52] PRO CO 533/420/8, personal letter from Philip Cunliffe-Lister in reply to Geoffrey Dawson, Esq. concerning a report in *The Times of London* about the death sentences on "sixty Kenya natives for the murder of a 'witch,'" 31 March 1932.
[53] KNA AG 34/549, letter from T. D. H. Bruce to the Colonial Secretary, 2 December 1931.

death was quashed on appeal, any commutation which the Governor in Council might have advised would fall to the ground, and where the Executive Council confirmed the death sentence the conviction for murder might be quashed by the Court of Appeal, thus bringing the Executive Council into conflict with the judiciary."

Bruce also appealed to precedent and procedure. He noted first that "the practice hitherto has invariably been for the Executive Council to take no action until the convict has had the opportunity of his appeal being heard by the Court of Appeal for Eastern Africa." In order to clarify procedure, Bruce enclosed a copy of a letter by Sir R. W. Hamilton, formerly chief justice and then undersecretary of state for the Colonies, to the chairman of the Prisons Board that provided "instructions as to the procedure to be followed in informing illiterate natives convicted of murder of their right of appeal." Bruce noted that according to practice, "the prison officials not only tell them [natives] of their right of appeal, but inform them that they would be wise to appeal as the appeal can do no harm and might result in an acquittal." He restated his opinion that deviation from the standard appeals procedure could potentially create a conflict between the executive and judiciary elements of the colonial government. Bruce wrote,

> In this case, therefore, if the Executive Council considered the case before the time of appeal had expired and commuted the sentence as suggested by His Honour the Chief Justice, it is a practical certainty that some or all of them would lodge an appeal against their conviction for murder, and it is quite possible that, when the appeals come on, the Court of Appeal might quash the conviction for murder or reduce the conviction for murder or reduce the conviction to one of say grievous harm, and sentence the convicts to a milder sentence than that which the Executive Council had already imposed in commutation of the death sentence. In either event it appears to me that His Excellency the Governor in Council would stultify themselves [sic], and the executive would come in conflict with the judiciary which, in my view, is a most undesirable state of affairs.

Noting that commuting the death sentences in Executive Council before the Court of Appeal for Eastern Africa had ruled would effectively "deprive" Kumwaka and his cohort of their "right of appeal against their conviction for murder," Bruce reiterated that "some or all" of Kumwaka's group "will in any event appeal against the conviction for murder whatever the commutation might be." Overall, in Bruce's opinion the law concerning the appeals process needed to be followed to the letter. Attention to procedure and precedent in the case of *Rex v. Kumwaka* was "quite a proper practice" and the one most likely to ensure that, "so far as is ever possible, complete justice shall be done."[54]

But views like those expressed by Cunliffe-Lister and Bruce were hardly uncontested. Another credentialed and vocal camp queried the function and flexibility of a modern legal system, asking instead if it was the role of the legal system to administer harsh punishments for violations of British law, in effect "frighten[ing] the natives out of certain harmful and superstitious beliefs?"[55] Or, they demanded, was it to revise a body of law "unsuited ... to the peculiar needs of primitive people"[56] and to deal with local beliefs "sympathetically and not scornfully, [but] scientifically?"[57] Such questions emanated from a broad range of people and institutions – even from Buckingham Palace – and flooded into the Colonial Office.[58]

Individual members of the clergy like the Reverend H. D. Hooper as well as religious and human rights organizations like the Anti-Slavery and Aborigines Protection Society, the Secretary for Catholic Crusade, the Church Missionary Society, and the London Group on African Affairs wrote to the Colonial Office and to colonial authorities in Kenya.[59] Letters also came from the members of the legal profession and from journalists. Written in the period before the Governor-in-Council's clemency decision, these letters condemned the death sentences handed down in *Rex v. Kumwaka* and upheld by the appellate court. They also queried what truly constituted "justice" in colonial settings like Kenya. In the opinions of these writers, colonial law was neither hegemonic nor unequivocally appropriate and applicable.

---

[54] Ibid.
[55] PRO CO 533/420/8, letter from W. B. Stevenson to undisclosed recipients titled "Death Sentence on Sixty Africans," 6 February 1932. For figures on death sentences in Kenya see the Judicial Department Annual Report 1932 for Kenya. PRO CO 544/38, Annual Report on the Social and Economic Progress of the People of the Kenya Colony 1932.
[56] "The Wakamba Witch Case," *EAS*, 31 March 1932.
[57] Frank Melland, "A Shadow over Africa: The Terrors of Witchcraft, Law and Belief," *Times of London (ToL)*, 13 April 1932.
[58] PRO CO 533/420/8, memo exchanged between Assistant Undersecretary of State for the Colonies Cecil Bottomley and Philip Cunliffe-Lister, 31 March 1932. White Kenyan expatriates also took a lively interest in the case, exhibiting perspectives similar to those expressed by metropolitan Britons. See the letters contained in the newspaper for expatriates, *East Africa*, from late winter and early spring of 1932. For example, Edward A. Bell, "The Kenya Witch Murder Trial," *East Africa*, 24 March 1932.
[59] Colonial Office Registers of Correspondence located at the Public Record Office give lists of correspondence concerning *Rex v. Kumwaka* that the Colonial Office and Government House, Nairobi, received and to which the institutions responded. Unfortunately, the overwhelming majority of this correspondence was destroyed under statute. PRO CO 628/27, Kenya Registers of Correspondence 1932.

For example, the London Group on African Affairs, an organization that described itself as being "founded on the principles and policies of the South African Joint Councils of Europeans and Africans to assist in the improvement of race relationships in Africa," initiated a telegram campaign to ask Governor Joseph Byrne to "exercise his right to prevent the execution of 60 natives in Kenya." In the course of this campaign, Fredrick Livie-Noble, secretary of the London Group on African Affairs, wrote to a host of intellectuals and authorities on Kenya such as Julian Huxley, Lloyd George, Lord Lugard, Lord Passfield (Sidney Webb), Mrs. Sidney Webb, Dr. Drummond Shields, Bertrand Russell, Lord Parmoor, J. A. Hobson, and J. H. Driberg, asking them to lend their names to a telegram entreating Byrne to employ his prerogative of mercy.[60] Kumwaka and his cohort, Livie-Noble argued, "have been legally condemned to death for an act which neither they nor their tribe hold reprehensible."[61]

Correspondence between Livie-Noble and Lord Parmoor concerning the case and campaign called into question the efficacy of British law when applied to "natives."

Parmoor wrote to Livie-Noble,

> In my view the death sentence should not have been pronounced in such a case which is far removed from the ordinary factors in a murder case, under the principles of British Law. I think that the death sentence should have been commuted to a shorter period of imprisonment on two grounds: (1) to emphasise the distinction between murder as ordinarily understood in British criminal law, and in a witchery case in East Africa. (2) That imprisonment is much more trying than it would be to an Englishman in England, and may well result in the death of a number of natives concerned unless special care is taken.... To pass sentence of death on such a case is calculated to make the natives distrust the ... application of British justice.[62]

Livie-Noble responded in a similar vein,

> My own feeling very strongly is that the original sentence justifiable as it undoubtedly is in English law should never have been passed; and the whole incident calls for the early consideration of a much larger question – how far are British legal systems and codes applicable to African

---

[60] RHL Mss. Afr. s. 1427, proposed telegram from Frederick Livie-Noble to Governor of Kenya Joseph Byrne, n.d., 116.

[61] RHL Mss. Afr. s. 1427, letter from Frederick Livie-Noble to various recipients (see footnote 59), 1 April 1932, 115. The Anti-Slavery and Aborigines Protection Society produced correspondence in the same vein. See RHL Mss. Brit. Emp. s. 19.

[62] RHL Mss. Afr. s. 1427, letter from Lord Parmoor to Frederick Livie-Noble, 4 April 1932.

communities which we govern? If this unfortunate case causes the more fundamental question to be considered, then some good will have been served.[63]

Letters also came from those affiliated with the academy like Glasgow University professor W. B. Stevenson who questioned the efficacy of British law and its application in the colonies and raised questions about the ways in which "natives" would interpret the verdict. In a letter to Member of Parliament John Buchanan and to unknown recipients, Stevenson expressed his "astonishment" and "indignation" over the verdict in *Rex v. Kumwaka*, arguing that the sentence itself was an "outrage" and that it was "hardly credible that the sentence should be carried out."[64] The sentence, Stevenson asserted, was outrageous because of the context of the crime. He maintained that the "cause of the murder should also be taken into account." He explained,

> The murderers were, from their point of view, administering justice – extirpating from their midst a pernicious and evil power. Even had the murder been the work of only two or three, its motive would have been a good reason for mitigation of the extreme penalty. How much more when, as the numbers involved show, the act was done in full accordance with the general sense of right and justice as a whole tribe or locality?

Overall, Stevenson asserted, "Even half a dozen executions would be too much in such a country for such an offence."[65]

Stevenson was also concerned with the ways in which the verdict would affect the reception of British justice among colonized peoples. The sentence, he explained, showed "great ignorance of the response it will evoke amongst the native population of Kenya Province." "Natives," Stevenson argued, "will suppose that such a sentence is merely part of a scheme for destroying them in order to get possession of their land. Besides they know that when a black man is killed by a white man even one execution does not take place." The sentence, he added,

> may be intended to frighten the natives out of certain harmful and superstitious beliefs and practices. Whatever its influence in this direction

---

[63] RHL Mss. Afr. S. 1427, letter from Frederick Live-Noble to Lord Parmoor, 17 April 1932, 118.
[64] PRO CO 533/420/8, letters from W. B. Stevenson to John Buchanan and unnamed others, 6 February 1932.
[65] PRO CO 533/420/8, letter from W. B. Stevenson to undisclosed recipients titled "Death Sentence on Sixty Africans," n.d.

it will certainly confirm the native peoples in their conviction that the white men's government is unjust.⁶⁶

British concern over the verdict was reiterated in Kenya shortly before the governor's decision by an *East African Standard* editorial and in a letter to the editor by Sir Fiennes Barrett-Lennard, chief justice of Jamaica and a former member of the High Court of Uganda and of the Court of Appeal for Eastern Africa. The suitability of British law in the context of colonial Kenya concerned the editors of the *East African Standard*. They noted that under the "law as it is today" the Supreme Court could "not avoid imposing" the death sentence. However, the editors asserted that the existing law was "unsuited ... to the peculiar needs of primitive people." While the murder of a "witch" was a "crime" from the perspective of the Supreme Court, the editors wrote, in the minds of the Wakamba men sentenced to death, witch-murder was "not easily if at all distinguishable from a responsibility imposed by beliefs and tribal custom." The editors enjoined the governor to make his decision regarding the appeal quickly for the sake of justice and for the benefit of the imprisoned Wakamba awaiting news of their fate. "No human being," the editorial stated, "whatever his mental capacity can be indifferent to his position in such circumstances, and no civilized machinery of justice is intended to prolong that condition if swift and definite action can be taken."⁶⁷

While many of Sir Fiennes Barrett-Lennard's opinions mirrored those of the editors of the *East African Standard*, his letter also introduced concerns about the case in light of Britain's historical treatment of its own "witches" and about the verdict's impact on British prestige.⁶⁸ "Witchcraft," Barrett-Lennard pointed out in an evolutionist vein, was a "terror common to all humanity." Though he had "never heard an Englishman admit belief in it [witchcraft]," Barrett-Leonard noted the last person to be publicly called a witch in Britain had been "cruelly murdered" in Ireland a mere forty years before *Rex v. Kumwaka*.⁶⁹ He foregrounded the fact that

> down to the 18th century, witchcraft in Europe was rated by Europeans as a capital crime. Witches were tortured on the Continent of Europe in

---

⁶⁶ Ibid.
⁶⁷ "The Wakamba Witch Case," *EAS*, 31 March 1932.
⁶⁸ Fiennes Barrett-Lennard, "The Wakamba Witch Case: Views of a Colonial Judge," *EAS*, 31 March 1932.
⁶⁹ This reference to a recent *Irish* witch-murder might be intended to point to primitivity within Great Britain's own bounds as well as to the history of witchcraft beliefs and practices in Great Britain.

order to induce confessions. We hanged them. A great Chief Justice was threatened with a motion of censure in the House of Commons because he ridiculed witchcraft. He won. We turned witches into rogues and vagabonds and such is the legal description of them today.[70]

In Barrett-Lennard's estimation, though two centuries earlier British conceptions of witchcraft had been similar to those of the contemporary Kamba, British mentality and law had evolved to the point where witchcraft no longer posed any significant threat to the social order.

Barrett-Lennard also referenced the history of British treatments of witch-murder in Africa. Recalling his tenure on the High Court of Uganda, Barrett-Lennard wrote that the Ugandan murderer of a "witchdoctor" had received "a long sentence of rigorous imprisonment" rather than a death sentence because the members of the court "knew him to be very primitive and in constant dread of occult experiences." Following his own encounters with Africans' "primitive" beliefs in witchcraft and his knowledge of the history of "witchcraft" in Britain, Barrett-Lennard argued that the death sentences in *Rex v. Kumwaka* were inappropriate and failed to serve justice. He wrote,

> In view of the condition of the Akamba and in view of our very history, the death sentences on 60 of them were cruel mockeries, forced on the Chief Justice by a code of the local adaptors which (1) forgot that the laws exist for the people and not the people for the laws; or (2) disliked giving essential powers to the Courts. The Penal Code in India does give them a discretion though a limited one.

Finally, Barrett-Lennard acknowledged that though the chief justice of Kenya "felt constrained to pass" the verdict in *Rex v. Kumwaka*, the "trial in the Ukamba witch case ... is very injurious to British prestige" because "no Court ought to be under the duty of ordering a punishment destined never to be carried into effect." He entreated colonial authorities in Kenya to keep in mind that Supreme Court verdicts needed to "command confidence and respect." This would be impossible if the court had "blindly to register sentences only suitable for the advanced races of the world in many instances."[71]

---

[70] Barrett-Lennard is referring to the historic shift in the legal treatment of witchcraft in Britain. See Martin Chancock, *Law, Custom, and Social Order*, 94. Chanock writes, "Seventeenth-century legislation punished people for being witches – i.e. for possessing the power of witchcraft. The 1736 Vagrancy Act and later the Vagrancy Act of 1824 abandoned this and henceforth punishment was to be for the pretence of possessing this power. The earlier law aimed at the practice of a real power, the later at a practice of a pretended one."

[71] Barrett-Lennard, "The Wakamba."

Overall, the editors of the *East African Standard* and Barrett-Lennard shared similar attitudes regarding the outcome of the Wakamba Witch Trial. They were concerned with the meting out of justice. Though the editors and Barrett-Lennard believed the British should take into account the "primitive" Kamba mentality in which witchcraft constituted a material threat, they also saw the Kamba worldview as something which could ultimately be shed in much the same way that the British cast off their own superstitions after two hundred years of "progress." Equally as important if not more so, Barrett-Lennard and the editors saw justice as ineluctably granted *to* the Kamba *by* the British.

THE CONCLUSION OF MWAIKI'S CASE?

After the rejection of the appeal lodged in the Court of Appeal for Eastern Africa by solicitors for Kumwaka and his cohort, the case was referred to the Governor-in-Council with the justices' recommendation for clemency, which the governor granted. The sixty death sentences were commuted to varying periods of hard labor on 2 April 1932.[72]

Through these results, the neat colonial narrative situating the successful exercise of colonial control at the center of Mwaiki's case was concluded. Nonetheless, irresolvable questions linger about how *Rex v. Kumwaka* has been figured in Ukambani.

First, how did African publics regard the case and its outcomes? Absent from colonial sources is any trace of the reactions of colonial subjects to whom the efforts of the colonial courts were ostensibly directed. As Lauren Benton writes, "Colonial powers sometimes sent messages through legal institutions that were simply not received."[73]

Second, has *Rex v. Kumwaka* been an active location of memory?[74] Present-day informants who recall other contemporary events and speak readily about *uoi* and *uwe* evidence a reluctance or inability to speak about

---

[72] "Wakamba Witch Case," EAS, 2 April 1932. Indeed the governor had been planning to commute the sentence all along but had been constrained by procedure. In a mid-February telegram to the Colonial Office marked private and personal, the governor messaged, "You need not have any anxiety over the Wakamba murder case. The Chief Justice has already recommended commutation in each case. Intend to act on his advice but until Appealable [sic] time has expired it is not possible for me in Executive Council to exercise prerogative of mercy." PRO CO 533/420/8, telegram from Governor of Kenya Joseph Byrne to the Colonial Office, n.d.

[73] Lauren Benton, *Law and Colonial Cultures: Legal Regimes in World History, 1400–1900* (Cambridge: Cambridge University Press, 2002), 16.

[74] Nora, "Between Memory and History."

the case. Indeed, it is impossible to know at what juncture the story of the Wakamba Witch Trials disappeared or to what degree it was ever present in Kamba popular knowledge at all. Yet this silence still speaks, suggesting that in many ways certain colonial efforts at control mattered mostly to colonial actors and spoke primarily to colonial audiences. It raises the question of how many more witches who died in less spectacular circumstances than did Mwaiki are buried inside and outside the archival field.

Such silence also poses the issue of what kind of work the case ultimately did. *Rex v. Kumwaka* is cited in most subsequent cases of witch-killings to come through the courts in the pre-independence period and in many postcolonial cases as well. And, the case was integrated into larger discussions about the appropriate relations between legal and anthro-administrative practices in the empire. Nonetheless, the persistence of witch-killing cases up to the present day suggests that *Rex v. Kumwaka* was ultimately unknown or unimportant to the very people it was meant to address.

RESONANCES AND RAMIFICATIONS

In the aftermath of the commutation, debates about witchcraft and British justice continued to rage in the fora mentioned earlier. Notably, former anthro-administrator Frank Melland and Lord Frederick Lugard engaged in a spirited conversation in the pages of the *Times of London* about the problem of witchcraft in Africa generally, and the issue of witch-murder in particular. Melland's and Lugard's writings exemplify two central, competing schools of thought about the challenges witchcraft posed to justice, law, and order that persisted throughout the remainder of the colonial era. Drawing on his personal experience, an impassioned Melland argued for a didactic, largely educative, approach to eradicating witchcraft and critiqued the ways in which colonial approaches had been imagined and implemented. The phlegmatic Lugard, in contrast, argued for the primacy of British law and for deterrence through state-sponsored juridical killing.[75]

Melland pointed out that the sheer number of witch-murders in Africa was a problem in and of itself. He noted that while cases like *Rex v. Kumwaka* or the "Mwanalesa Baptism Murders" that he had dealt with in Rhodesia attracted attention because of the numbers involved, "the cases which reach the Courts are an infinitesimal percentage of the cases of

---

[75] See also, Hynd, "Imperial Gallows," 99–100.

witch-killing that occur."⁷⁶ The frequency of witch-murders was, Melland wrote, a result of the African mind-set in which "witchcraft was a terrible reality" and "an everlasting obsession to the 126 million African Natives." Witch-murders were also ubiquitous because, Melland argued, killing was the only means by which Africans could ensure "public welfare," as destroying witchcraft was linked strongly to destroying the body of the witch. Colonial authority, he asserted, failed to offer viable solutions to any of these issues.⁷⁷

In Melland's estimation, two key changes were needed to remedy witch-killing in Africa: a shift in colonial law and a shift in African mind-sets. Colonial law was a failure, he explained, because it "stereotype[d] an attitude that was preposterous to the natives" and forced colonial authorities – both white and black – into "persecuting those who are fighting what they believe to be the most evil and unnatural curse that afflicts man-kind." The problem of witchcraft, he argued, would not be eradicated by "*force majeure*"; rather, altering the law to recognize the reality of witchcraft would be the first step in the eradication of witchcraft. Ultimately, Melland maintained, witchcraft eradication was a job for "anthropologists and psychologists rather than lawyers."⁷⁸

Lugard countered Melland's point that colonial governments failed to adequately consider witchcraft, locating responsibility for dealing with witchcraft broadly in the "men-on-the-spot" like Melland himself and in the justices sitting on the benches of colonial courts.⁷⁹ "So far as my experience goes," Lugard wrote, "the reality of the belief is fully admitted," and consequently, "the accused is assured of a sympathetic hearing before any body of English gentlemen." Echoing the appellate court in *Kumwaka*, Lugard argued that the colonial administration of justice should be primarily deterrent, with elements of didacticism, in matters of witch-killing. He maintained, "the fact that participation involves liability to the death sentence ... is to some extent a deterrent if – as it should be – the fact is widely known."⁸⁰ Overall, Lugard and Melland both took the view that evolution of attitudes and actions toward witchcraft – be they African or colonial – could be hoped for, but not counted upon.

---

⁷⁶ Melland, "A Shadow over Africa." On Mwanalesa, see Karen E. Fields, *Revival and Rebellion in Colonial Central Africa* (Princeton: Princeton University Press, 1985).
⁷⁷ Melland, "A Shadow over Africa."
⁷⁸ Ibid.
⁷⁹ Sir Frederick Lugard, letter to the editor, "Witchcraft in Africa: Credulity and Crime, Lord Lugard's View," *ToL*, 20 April 1932.
⁸⁰ Ibid.

Clearly, furor surrounding *Rex v. Kumwaka* was not the first instance in which colonial authorities had confronted the constitution of British justice in the empire, particularly in the criminal realm.[81] Up to the *Kumwaka* period, the state had made adjustments to the administration of criminal justice, either through the introduction of new legislation or through the refinement of laws already on the books. Many of these adjustments spoke to important issues in witchcraft-related cases. For example, the Collective Punishment Ordinance (1909), which allowed the levying of fines on "all the natives" of a given "community" if they "*or any of them* had colluded with or harboured criminals, suppressed or combined to suppress evidence," had been used to deal with witch-killings.[82] As an Ukambani annual report notes, "In one case during the years a fine of Rs. 5,000/ was imposed on a sub-Location for killing a so-called Witch."[83]

Also, in the early years of the colonial period, "The Penal Code Ordinance" was passed to amend the law relating to the sentencing of young persons, that is, persons under the age of sixteen, who had been convicted of offenses punishable by death. The second section of the ordinance stipulated:

> No sentence of death shall be pronounced on or recorded against a young person, but in lieu thereof the Court shall sentence the young person to be detained during His Majesty's pleasure and, if so sentenced, the young person shall be liable to be detained in such place and under such conditions as the Governor may direct whilst so shall be deemed to be in legal custody.[84]

Nine of the youngest members of Kumwaka's cohort benefited from this law, which made it legally untenable for the court to sentence them to death for their culpability in Mwaiki's murder.

In 1933, however, the piecemeal approach of alternately adding and amending criminal legislation was temporarily jettisoned in favor of a full-on systematized inquiry into British justice led by the Colonial Office. The Commission of Inquiry into the Administration of Justice in Kenya, Uganda and the Tanganyika Territory in Criminal Matters

---

[81] For a basic outline of colonial-era concerns, see, C. Clifton Roberts, "African Natives under the English System of Penal Law," *Journal of Comparative Legislation and International Law Third Series* 15.4 (1933): 169–175.

[82] W. McGregor Ross, *Kenya from Within: A Short Political History* (London: George Allen and Unwin 1927), 435. Italics in the original.

[83] KNA DC/MKS 1/3/6, Kitui District Annual Report 1917, 142.

[84] PRO CO 542/2, Ordinance No. 10 of 1909, 1 August 1909, 329.

Affecting Natives, called in shorthand, "the Bushe Commission" because it was directed by the Colonial Office Legal Adviser H. Grattan Bushe, was established to address the problems of administering criminal law in the empire.[85] Witnesses were pulled from all ranks of the colonial governmental apparatus and even included a number of African functionaries. While the Bushe Commission covered topics as far-ranging as "bail" and "stock-theft," "witchcraft" beliefs and practices, particularly as they precipitated murders and assaults, were key foci of a variety of witnesses' testimony. As with *Rex v. Kumwaka*, the issue of witchcraft offered avenues into broader problems like African mentalities and degrees of murder.

The Bushe Commission both emerged from and was constitutive of imperial networks of knowledge about law and anthro-administration and the challenges that witchcraft beliefs and practices posed. *Rex v. Kumwaka* was consistently referenced in discussions surrounding the commission and by those testifying during the inquiry. For example, a 1932 high-level Colonial Office circular memo on the possibility of establishing a commission to address "what extent English law procedure was suitable for natives," also mentioned that "the witch case in Kenya" had produced suggestions to the League of Nations that they "set up an investigation into the relation of native customary law and the law of the Protecting power." The memo also proposed that the Colonial Office work with the British representative to the International Law Association who had suggested clarifying the aims of the potential Colonial Office inquiry in order to "quash the proposal about the League of Nations" and thus "have the great advantage of being first in the field."[86]

In the early spring of 1933, the Bushe Commission was put in motion and witnesses and information were solicited through imperial networks. In Kenya, for example, anthro-administrative knowledge was gathered through the orders contained in a circular from the Office of the Chief Native Commissioner and reinforced via a memo from the Native Affairs Department to all provincial commissioners entreating the commissioners to submit a memorandum for the Bushe Commission's consideration.[87]

---

[85] *The Commission of Inquiry into the Administration of Justice in Kenya, Uganda and the Tanganyika Territory in Criminal Matters Affecting Natives*. Cmd. 4623. (London: His Majesty's Stationery Office, 1934). Hereafter, Bushe Commission. See also, Morris and Read, *Indirect Rule*, 90–94.

[86] PRO CO 822/44/10, memo to Sir Cecil Bottomley from Colonial Office authority, 6 May 1932.

[87] KNA VQ/10/11, circular from A. de V. Wade, Chief Native Commissioner to all Provincial Commissioners with sufficient copies for District Commissioners, 23 January 1933;

The original circular stipulated that the secretary of state had proposed that questions of reference be

> to enquire into the administration of the criminal law in Kenya, Uganda and Tanganyika Territory in relation to procedure and practice of: (a) the Courts (and other Native Courts), and (b) the Police Authorities, and to consider whether in regard to the procedure or practice of such Courts or Authorities any alterations are desirable, (a) in the case of natives, and (b) generally.[88]

Provincial and district officers from across Kenya responded to the chief native commissioner's request with varying degrees of specificity. The colonial authorities from Kenya who were actually called upon to testify before the commission established many of the themes of the inquiry and their perspectives attracted significant notice in both East Africa and the metropole. In many instances these officials directly addressed the challenges that witchcraft posed not only for the administration but also for the definition of British justice in the empire.

Generally speaking, the testimony by British authorities in the Kenya administration evidenced more sympathy for the sway that witchcraft beliefs held over local mentalities and the implications this influence held for colonial order than did texts like political and district record books and annual reports. Nonetheless, the sorts of concerns expressed by the administrators of the 1930s had been presaged in a 1921 memo from the district commissioner's office, Nyeri, to the Native Punishment Commission. The office wrote,

> A deliberate, brutal, calculated murder is a very rare occurrence among any native tribes of which I have had experience, such murders as are committed being almost invariably the result of some impulse, or if deliberate are prompted by racial antagonism or by the workings of witchcraft. A native acting under the influence of witchcraft, although not legally insane, is scarcely compos mentis and would seem to be a fit subject for compassion.[89]

KNA VQ/10/11, memo from H. H. Low, Department of Native Affairs, to Provincial Commissioners, Nyanza, Kikuyu, Nzoia, Coast, Masai, Rift Valley, Ukamba, N.F.P., Turkana, 21 February 1933.

[88] KNA VQ/10/11, circular from A. de V. Wade, Chief Native Commissioner to all Provincial Commissioners with sufficient copies for District Commissioners, 23 January 1933.

[89] KNA PC/CP 6/4/3, memo from the District Commissioner's Office to the Native Punishment Commission with a copy to the Senior Commissioner Nyeri, 13 October 1921. The Native Punishment Commission did not attend to issues of witchcraft in any substantive way.

In the course of broader discussions about whether murder charges should be differentiated by degree, a number of Kenya administrators testifying before the Bushe Commission argued for treating a belief in the witchcraft of the deceased as an extenuating, if not mitigating, circumstance in murder cases. The testimony offered by Chief Native Commissioner Armigel de Vins Wade typifies many of the perspectives provided by members of the Kenyan administrative apparatus and is worth quoting at length. Speaking on the different "categories" of murder present in the colony, the chief native commissioner argued,

> The next category are [sic] cases of murders that are committed through witchcraft. These cases are generally merely acts of self-defence. The murdered, or murderers, knows quite definitely in his own mind, it is not merely fear with him, it is definite, absolute knowledge, that he is going to be bewitched and killed if he does not take action, and putting to death the witch or witch doctor is an act of self-defence and from their point of view is no more blameworthy than a man shooting an armed marauder who is aiming a revolver at him. In these cases I personally would like it to be made possible that the murderer should not even be sentenced to death. I think that deterrent aspect is quite different in witchcraft cases from cases of vendetta or tribal custom. If a man kills a witch doctor from no other motive than self-defence, I think that he will continue to do so quite irrespective of what the penalty will be if he is found out. A particular case of which I know that you have heard is the Wakamba case. In that case as the law is at present I understand the judge had no alternative whatever, but to sentence them to death and I believe I am right in saying that the appeal also had no alternative in dismissing the appeal.[90]

Perhaps such perspectives were more sympathetic because they were presented in the aftermath of *Rex v. Kumwaka* or maybe the less subtle approach present in district and provincial records was a function of the relatively strict content in the form of such documents.[91] Whatever their ultimate origin, opinions like that of the chief native commissioner attended to local rationalities and to the strength of witchcraft beliefs. Following the self-defense argument offered and struck down in *Rex v. Kumwaka*, de Vins Wade's testimony moves beyond the recognition of the affective basis of self-defense – the element of fear – to the local logics incumbent in killing a witch or witchdoctor. Yet at the same moment

---

[90] Bushe Commission, 13.
[91] Hayden White, *The Content of the Form: Narrative Discourse and Historical Representation* (Baltimore: Johns Hopkins University Press, 1987).

that officials like de Vins Wade realized that colonial codes failed both to discipline and deny witchcraft, they also continued to support the ultimate primacy of the colonial legal system and to understand the constraints of the law-as-written.

The opinions of judicial officials, in turn, adhered even more closely to the importance of upholding unreconstructed British justice. For example, echoing the trope of discipline and denial located in the Witchcraft Ordinance, the chief justice of Kenya, Jacob Barth, even argued before the Bushe Commission that the Witchcraft Ordinance realistically offered "the native a chance of prosecuting people who practice these alleged supernatural powers."[92]

Ultimately, neither *Rex v. Kumwaka* nor the Bushe Commission produced any changes in the law as written regarding witchcraft or legally complicated the charge of murder. The issue of what constituted British justice in the empire remained unresolved. The varied and competing positions taken in the course of *Rex v. Kumwaka* and the Bushe Commission point not to the easy restoration of colonial order but instead to the fissures and fractures in the edifice of colonial control. Nonetheless, the empire-wide debates about witchcraft carried out in the early 1930s opened the door a bit wider for the courts to *tacitly* consider witchcraft as a mitigating or extenuating circumstance in murder cases. The next chapter investigates how the Colonial Office and colonial jurisprudence approached claims about the role of witchcraft in the commission of crimes.

---

[92] Bushe Commission, 33–34.

6

Witchcraft, Murder, and Death Sentences after *Rex v. Kumwaka*

Yes, she believes that the deceased had bewitched her two children.[1]

In colonial Kenya, procedure in murder cases dictated that each prisoner remanded on a capital charge undergo a standardized medical examination by the medical officer in charge of the Nairobi jail. This examination was directed toward ascertaining the prisoner's physical and psychological health prior to appeals proceedings in the Court of Appeal for Eastern Africa. Information concerning physical and psychological states provided additional layers of evidence upon which the advocates and justices could draw in formulating arguments and decisions about the culpability of the prisoner. The beginning quotation represents a typical answer to a standard question on the medical officer's examination form, "Does the question of witchcraft arise?" The inclusion of such a question points not only to the prevalence of witch-killings in colonial Kenya but also to broader imperial concerns with witchcraft and murder.

By the late 1930s, a nexus of juridical and administrative circumstances underscored the importance of considering witchcraft as a mitigating circumstance in capital cases. First, *Rex v. Kumwaka* remained a benchmark in adjudicating capital cases in which the witchcraft of the deceased was posed as mitigation. Case law suggests that justices in the East African colonies were increasingly considering witch-murder cases referentially rather than on a case-by-case basis. Further, jurisprudence from the post-*Kumwaka* period shows how witchcraft cases emerged as central to the

---

[1] KNA MLA 1/117, "Medical Report upon Prisoner Remanded on a Capital Charge," 2 August 1941.

development ideas of what a made a "reasonable" African and to elaboration of the key legal principle of "grave and sudden provocation."

While jurisprudence in witchcraft-related cases constituted one element of colonial networks of knowledge about witchcraft, Colonial Office debates circulating among authorities in the metropole and those in the colonies formed another. Metropolitan interest in witchcraft did not expire after *Rex v. Kumwaka* or even after the Bushe Commission, in large part because officials from across the empire consistently sought Colonial Office advice on how to manage the challenges to law and order caused by witchcraft in their respective colonies. In turn, through debates and dialogues among colonial and metropolitan officials, witchcraft was made to speak to a range of broader issues concerning British justice in colonial contexts.

Yet at the same moment, witch-murder cases not only reflect governmental disorder but also highlight distress and drama in individual lives. As David Pratten writes about a spate of occult-centered killings in Nigeria, "A paradox of the murders, therefore, is the way in which some of the most mysterious and secretive events in colonial Nigerian history reveal rarely glimpsed intimacies of human life."[2] The assorted records pertaining to cases of witch-murder offer local perspectives on the production and uses of knowledge about witchcraft (and witches). They can be read as a variety of court-contoured field notes, demonstrating how witchcraft worked in the lives of the accused and their circles of intimates and acquaintances.

Accordingly, this chapter traces the production and circulation of knowledge about witchcraft and capital crimes in three interpenetrated arenas: imperial discourse, colonial jurisprudence, and local belief. It delineates the broad contours of imperial discourse and colonial jurisprudence pertaining to witch-murders from the late 1930s forward, demonstrating how the production of witchcraft as a colonial category provided grounds for (tacit) considerations about the relevance to and operation of local beliefs in regard to capital crimes. Parsing the cases of three witch-murders in which the courts respectively concurred with, contested, and contradicted claims about the witchcraft of the deceased as a mitigating circumstance, this chapter shows how knowledge and debates about witchcraft were brought to bear in the post-*Kumwaka* era.

---

[2] David Pratten, *The Man Leopard Murders: History and Society in Colonial Nigeria* (Bloomington: Indiana University Press, 2007), 25.

WITCHCRAFT AS AN EMPIRE-WIDE CONCERN

As myriad documents indicate, in the era after *Rex v. Kumwaka*, colonial authorities in Africa and in the metropole variously figured witchcraft as a problem on which the authority of British justice across the empire significantly hinged. Administrators in the colonies queried metropolitan officials about revised policies and principles that could be applied to witchcraft-related cases on an empire-wide basis. Discourse flowing in and out of the Colonial Office attended to queries about subjects as diverse as the role of the courts, the functions of native assessors, and the consideration of native mentalities. Colonial Office authorities, in turn, typically replied to the queries of their colleagues in Africa by underscoring both the value of local expertise and the primacy of British law in dealing with the thorny challenges that witchcraft beliefs and practices posed to law and order.

Colonial Office correspondence from 1932 reflects these different strains and demonstrates how in the midst of the furor over *Rex v. Kumwaka*, the questions of what made British justice in an imperial setting, and how witchcraft should be engaged (or not) by colonial legal systems, emanated from colonies besides Kenya. For example, the governor of Tanganyika wrote to the secretary of state for the Colonies noting, "witchcraft is almost universal in local feeling here," and that as such, the Executive Council had been considering the "question of the infliction of the death penalty in cases where a native has been convicted of murder committed as the result of a belief in witchcraft." He neatly laid out the "divergent schools of thought" on the issue; the first, the exaction of the death penalty was not "good policy," and the second, the exaction of the death penalty "will gradually inspire the conviction in the native mind that the Government so abhors murder that it does not regard even a belief in witchcraft as condoning the offence in any way." The governor archly explained that he and the Executive Council were in "unanimous" agreement with the second view, noting that "no doubt" should be left in "the native mind about official unbelief in the power and practices of witchcraft," and that as such, "habitually" waiving the "legal penalty for murder" would frustrate that aim.[3]

The governor's missive prompted strong, diverse reactions in the Colonial Office. For example, engaging the network of knowledge about witchcraft, one Colonial Office official exclaimed that by the governor's

---

[3] PRO CO 691/126/10, letter from Sir George Stewart Symes, Governor of Tanganyika, to Sir Philip Cunliffe-Lister, Secretary of State for the Colonies, 27 October 1932.

logic, "Then the 60 Wakamba should have been hanged!" and directed his colleagues to the Colonial Office dossier on *Rex v. Kumwaka*.[4] Another argued that it was the "man-on-the-spot," not the man in the metropole, who was best equipped to deal with the extent of witchcraft beliefs and the "precise effect that punitive measures would have on them."[5] Yet another suggested that deeper anthropological knowledge, perhaps produced by an institution like the International Institute for African Languages and Culture, "would help the Administrator to deal with the whole question of witchcraft and prevent popular beliefs and sanctions from getting into conflict with the laws of the country."[6] Such broad, unresolved debates, in turn, gave rise to more questions about the permutations of African witchcraft and British justice.

In subsequent Colonial Office correspondence, witchcraft emerged as a touchstone in debates over larger issues of "custom." In a 1937 file, tellingly entitled "Remission of Sentences Passed on Natives Convicted of Murder Committed in Pursuance of Tribal Custom," witchcraft was used analytically and referentially to deal with the question of how "tribal custom" should be considered in murder cases. The discussion centered on a request from the governor of Northern Rhodesia for the Colonial Office's advice on a policy under consideration in his Executive Council to remit life sentences in cases of murder perpetrated in the course of following "tribal custom."[7] His question was initially spurred by a case in which a baby who had cut its upper teeth first was killed according to "native custom." Colonial Office authorities commenting on the governor's query, returned to the colonial archive on witchcraft, following circuits of earlier opinions in which the question of witchcraft as a mitigating factor in murder cases had been debated. The first writer cited the 1932 Tanganyika documents addressed earlier. He wrote,

> Of the various files dealing with the commutations of death sentence that I have been through, 31276/32 Tanganyika is the most interesting and the most relevant.... Briefly, the question dealt with by the Governor

---

[4] PRO CO 691/126/10, unsigned comment, 25 November 1932.
[5] PRO CO 691/126/10, comment by A. Fiddian, 7 December 1932. Neither the ranks of the "men-on-the-spot" nor of those in the metropole were particularly plentiful. As Berman notes, "the small staff of administrative class officials at the Colonial Office (less than thirty-five in 1929 and fewer than fifty ten years later) was not expected or even able to superintend all policy developments in every colony." Berman, *Control and Crisis*, 76.
[6] PRO CO 691/126/10, comment by H. Vischer, 5 December 1932.
[7] PRO CO 847/7/7, circular memo by Sir Hubert Winthrop Young, Governor of Northern Rhodesia, 2 November 1936.

of Tanganyika is the infliction of the death penalty in cases of murder committed as a result of belief in witchcraft, and his conclusion, supported by the unanimous opinion of the Executive Council, is that, by exacting the death penalty for murder committed on account of belief in witchcraft, a conviction will gradually be established in the Native mind that Government so abhors murder that it does not regard even a belief in witchcraft as condoning the offence in any way, and that consequently, cases of murder inspired by witchcraft will gradually diminish and eventually disappear altogether, to the inestimable advantage of the Native population as a whole.[8]

His colleague, in turn, quoted the Tanganyika file concurring with its legal view that "so long as the law remains as it is, the legal penalty for murder should not be habitually waived in cases where the offence is prompted by a belief in witchcraft."[9] The Tanganyika file and subsequent citations of it reinforced the legal perspective articulated in *Rex v. Kumwaka* that "witchcraft" should be neither completely discounted nor taken as an excuse, an attitude followed in witchcraft-related murder cases throughout the remainder of the colonial period.

Yet at the same moment, Colonial Office opinions, including those discussed here, attended strongly to the relevance of the local expertise in such cases. For instance, the first writer concluded that questions of custom and of its relationship to British justice "can be far better decided by those who are in daily contact with the Natives concerned,"[10] while his colleague concurred that "local knowledge must count for everything" in such matters.[11] And another Colonial Office official added, "It is difficult, I should think, to lay down any ground rule ... in crimes prompted by strong native beliefs and customs. Circumstances are sometimes very extenuating."[12] Such commentary highlighted the need for expert knowledge, not simply in the law, but also for expertise in local social situations and relationships pertaining to witchcraft-related cases. From the perspective of many colonial writers, the highly contingent character of such cases was central, and most officials concurred that they could not be dealt with effectively through an invariable formula of rules and regulations.

Responding comprehensively to the governor's request, Josiah Flood, a Colonial Office legal expert, emphasized the peril of a fixed policy

---

[8] PRO CO 847/7/7, comment by Smith, 23 March 1937.
[9] PRO CO 847/7/7, comment by Davies, 21 April 1937.
[10] PRO CO 847/7/7, comment by Smith, 23 March 1937.
[11] PRO CO 847/7/7, comment by Davies, 21 April 1937.
[12] PRO CO 847/7/7, comment by Calder, 11 May 1937.

concerning witch-murders, reiterated the importance of local expertise, laid out the politics of death penalty commutations, suggested how witchcraft beliefs might be manipulated or fabricated as defense strategies, and underscored some of the ways in which British law was at odds with African attitudes about justice. He wrote,

> There can be no general principle and it would be very unsafe to attempt to lay down any rules from here. The Governor of each place must be guided by his own discretion and his knowledge of the circumstances, gathered as it will be gathered, from advice given by his senior and experienced officers.... It is however another story when it comes to trying to lay down rules about exercising prerogative in cases of witchcraft. If you exercise prerogative as a general rule, you are doing what Sir Grattan Bushe described as "bringing the solemn death penalty into disrepute." Then it will be argued that it does not matter whether a man is sentenced to death in a witchcraft case or not because he is bound to get off. It follows also that however much you may feel for the accused, yet if he is found guilty in the eyes of the law, then in order to keep up the respect for the death sentence if clemency is exercised, the sentence should usually be commuted to something pretty substantial such as ten years.... Still, the law being the law and murder being murder I would not advise that the law in regard to the illicit taking of life should be altered as to remove witchcraft cases from the category of unlawful killing. If you did, then the defence of witchcraft would be easy to raise in any case of a native murder and, perjury being an offence which is not well understood and is so easily practiced, it would be easy to disguise the most cold-blooded and willful murder as almost a ritual observance. Also, we do wish to do away with the idea of killing for witchcraft. I am not such a fool as to assert that there is nothing in "witchcraft," nor would I endorse the view that witchcraft murders are instances of childish barbarisms, and that the only way to stop it is to convict a murderer and let the law take its course. Such a line ... might prevent cases being reported, but it would not do anything to do away with the belief in witchcraft and it would only drive the whole thing underground.[13]

Overall, Colonial Office dossiers underscore how the problems of culpability and commutation, of belief and fabrication, of local and legal expertise, of colonial penal codes and imperial prestige, permeated debates about imperial justice, law, and order. These debates about witchcraft were themselves part of a process for producing order and usable knowledge out of the chaos of crime. In the service of such ends, a referential body of legal opinion about witchcraft and capital crimes was generated in East Africa's highest courts from the late 1930s onward.

[13] PRO CO 847/7/7, comment by Flood, 13 May 1937.

WITCHCRAFT IN THE COURTS AND ON THE BOOKS

From the late 1930s forward, numerous witchcraft-related murder cases similar to *Rex v. Kumwaka* regularly came through the individual Supreme and High Courts and through the Court of Appeal for Eastern Africa and were increasingly recorded in the digests of these bodies. Unlike the judgments and decisions predating *Kumwaka*, later judicial texts were highly referential, working in particular to elaborate "grave and sudden provocation" and to grapple with the issue of "reasonableness" in regard to defense claims that the witchcraft of the deceased counted as mitigation.[14] Overall, they turned on the same question that plagued colonial officials in Africa and the metropole: When, if ever, was the witchcraft of the deceased sufficient to commute a capital sentence?

The witch-murder cases recorded in the Court of Appeal for Eastern Africa digests from the late 1930s forward were appeals from death sentences for murders in which the appellants claimed that they had killed the deceased after coming to believe that the deceased had somehow practiced witchcraft against them or members of their families. The appeals were made on the grounds that the witchcraft of the deceased had constituted "grave and sudden provocation," a legally mitigating condition capable of reducing sentences of murder to ones of manslaughter or even lesser charges. For example, in *Rex v. Kimutai arap Mursoi* (1939) the appellant argued that he had killed the deceased because he believed the deceased was a "wizard" who had laid a spell on the appellant's child.[15] In the 1941 case, *Fabiano Kinene s/o Mukye, Seperiano Kiwanuka s/o Kintu, Albert Iseja s/o Kintu*, the appellants argued that the "witchcraft" of the deceased had driven them to kill him by inserting twenty green bananas into his anus after they had encountered the deceased crawling naked around their compound.[16]

In deciding these cases, the court debated the constitutive elements of "grave and sudden provocation," and turned to the precedent established

---

[14] Unfortunately, none of the sets of digests held at the School for Oriental and African Studies Library, the University of Nairobi Law Library, and the Kenya National Archives is complete.

[15] *Rex v. Kimutai arap Mursoi*. Law Reports Containing the Decisions of the Court of Appeal for Eastern Africa, Volume VI 1939 (Nairobi: Government Printer, 1940), 117. Hereafter, 6 E.A.C.A. (1939).

[16] *Fabiano Kinene s/o Mukye, Seperiano Kiwanuka s/o Kintu, Albert Iseja s/o Kintu*. Law Reports Containing the Decisions of the Court of Appeal for Eastern Africa, Volume VIII 1941 (Nairobi: Government Printer), 96–102. Hereafter 8 E.A.C.A. (1941). See also, Luongo, "Motive Rather than Means."

by the decision in *Rex v. Kumwaka*. The following paragraph from *Kumwaka* emerged as a veritable "go-to" passage in adjudicating witch-murder appeals. The passage reads as follows:

> The plea has frequently been put forward in murder cases that the deceased had bewitched or threatened to bewitch the accused, and that plea has been consistently rejected except in cases where the accused has been put in such fear of immediate danger to his own life that the defence of grave and sudden provocation has been held proved.[17]

In *Kimutai arap Mursoi*, the appellate court dismissed the appeal on the grounds of the *Kumwaka* passage cited here.[18] The murder convictions were reduced to manslaughter in *Fabiano Kinene s/o Mukye and Others*, the court relying there on *Kumwaka* and *Kimutai arap Mursoi* to reach the decision that "grave and sudden provocation" had been held proved.[19]

But while straightforward in their rejection or acceptance of the appeals, the decisions in these cases also complicated "grave and sudden provocation," parsing it and reading it in conversation with other legal conditions and circumstances present in the cases such as the appellant's "real but mistaken belief" in witchcraft. *Fabiano Kinene s/o Mukye and Others* involved the most complex analysis and came to be cited in almost all subsequent witch-murder cases. While addressing "grave and sudden provocation," the decision also focused on questions of "malice aforethought," on the veracity and reasonableness of the appellants' witchcraft beliefs, and on native mentalities more generally. First, the court concurred with the original High Court of Uganda judgment that the statements of Fabiano and his cohort demonstrated that they had killed the deceased with "malice aforethought." Second, the court drew on the opinions of assessors and on general attitudes about native mentalities and witchcraft in deciding that Fabiano and the other appellants did hold a "real but mistaken belief" in the witchcraft of the deceased. The decision explained,

> With their strong suspicions of his past history they would need very little to convince them and the sensitiveness of the African mind in this respect is shown by the evidence of the Muruka chief Fenekansi that "if in the night I saw a man naked crawling in my compound I would think he was a witch doctor actually practising witchcraft."[20]

[17] 14 L.R.K. (1932), 139.
[18] 6 E.A.C.A. (1939), 117.
[19] 8 E.A.C.A. (1941), 101.
[20] 8 E.A.C.A. (1941), 100–101.

Yet drawing on the opinions in *Kumwaka* and *Kimutai arap Mursoi*, the court concluded that the appellants' belief in witchcraft, while introducing the *possibility* of a defense of "grave and sudden provocation," did not alone constitute sufficient grounds to prove "grave and sudden provocation." *Fabiano* critiqued the notion of "fear" and added that witchcraft could also be regarded as inducement to the sort of *anger* that was construed as part of the "heat of passion" according to the Uganda Penal Code section dealing with "provocation." The justice explained the principle generally and in regard to the circumstances of *Fabiano*. He wrote,

> In our opinion the principle in those cases [*Kumwaka, etc.*] is stated somewhat too narrowly and perhaps not altogether accurately, in that the words "in the heat of passion" used in s. 198 of the Penal Code (Uganda) are more properly referable to the emotion of anger than to that of fear. We think that if the facts proved establish that the victim was performing in the actual presence of the accused some act which the accused did genuinely believe, and which an ordinary person of the community to which the accused belongs would genuinely believe, to be an act of witchcraft against him or another person under his immediate care (which would be a criminal offence under the Criminal Law (witchcraft) Ordinance of Uganda and similar legislation in other East African territories) he might be angered to such an extent as to be deprived of the power of self-control and induced to assault the person doing the act of witchcraft. And if this be the case a defence of grave and sudden provocation is open to him. It must always be a question of fact as to whether he is in all the circumstances of the particular case acting in the great of passion caused by grave and sudden provocation and of course on such an issue he must be given the benefit of any reasonable doubt. We think it not unreasonable to say that in the present case the accused persons, when they seized the deceased in the compound and proceeded to kill him, may have been so acting.[21]

The above passage thus weaves together two important ideas. First, it argues that more than one affective state, "anger" as well as "fear," is sufficient to induce the immediate and overwhelming passion that was an ineluctable constituent element of "provocation." Second, it attends to native mentalities regarding the question of witchcraft, identifying a standard of reasonableness, which takes in local mind-sets and mores, but which also designates witchcraft as it is extrapolated in *colonial* law.

Ultimately, the murder conviction was reduced to one of manslaughter, and the decision explained how the elements of "grave and sudden

[21] Ibid., 102.

provocation" were present in the case. The "highly suspicious actions of the deceased," crawling naked around the compound at night, could be reasonably considered fear and/or anger-inducing behavior according to local standards and also an offense according to colonial anti-witchcraft legislation. Thus, the behavior of the deceased constituted an "immediate provocative act" in the eyes of the court. Also, the decision emphasized the issue of the time between the "provocative act" and the killing of the deceased, noting how Fabiano and his cohort had almost instantly attacked the deceased upon finding him crawling naked in their space. From the court's perspective then, the killing had been an immediate response to "grave and sudden provocation." Nonetheless, the decision concluded by reiterating that despite the decision in *Fabiano*, the justices "in no way mean[t] to suggest that we believe witchcraft per se will constitute a circumstance of excuse of mitigation for killing a person believed to be a witch or wizard when there is no immediate provocative act."[22]

The decision in *Fabiano* became a key referent in witch-murder cases from the early 1940s onward in much the same way that the decision in *Kumwaka* was central in the previous decade. Subsequent judgments and decisions in individual Supreme and High Courts and in the Court of Appeal for Eastern Africa also asserted the principle articulated in *Fabiano* that a proven belief in the witchcraft of the deceased alone could not reduce a conviction of murder. Referencing each other as well as *Fabiano* and other earlier cases, a number of these decisions also aimed to refine the element of "reasonableness" in regard to appellants' beliefs in the "witchcraft" of the deceased. For example, the 1949 case, *Petero Wabwire s/o Malemo*, was an appeal from a murder conviction in which the appellant asserted that he had killed his wife because she possessed substances or "medicine" whose origin she refused to disclose and he therefore believed that she had been practicing witchcraft against him.[23] Citing *Fabiano*, the decision reiterated that "in order to succeed on the plea of legal provocation, the facts proved must 'establish that the victim was performing in the actual presence of the accused some act which the accused did genuinely believe, and which an ordinary person of the community to which the accused person belongs, would genuinely believe

---

[22] Ibid., 101–102.
[23] *Rex v. Petero Wabwire s/o Malemo*. Law Reports Containing the Decisions of the Court of Appeal for Eastern Africa and the Judicial Committee of the Privy Council on Appeal from that Court, Volume XVI 1949 (Nairobi: Government Printer, 1949), 131–134. Hereafter, 16 E.A.C.A. (1949).

to be an act of witchcraft.'"[24] The appeal was dismissed on the grounds that the actions of the deceased would not have been construed as witchcraft by a "reasonable" member of the community and that the deceased had not performed the alleged "provocative" act in the presence of the appellant.[25]

In these cases, the court was restrained by the law from considering witchcraft as a defense without attaching it to another legal category, most often "grave and sudden provocation." But an attention to witchcraft enabled the court to distinguish killings in retribution for witchcraft from killings for more mundane or mercenary reasons. These cases both followed and reinforced the precedent of recommendation to the governor's clemency, a practice that often resulted in the reduction of capital sentences. Overall, the circumstances of the cases discussed here are very similar to those experienced by Weyulo, Maganyo, and Charo Hinzano, whose cases were not recorded in the digests but can be extracted from the archives.

WHEN THE QUESTION OF WITCHCRAFT AROSE

This section excavates three witch-murder cases culled from Kenya's Ministry of Legal Affairs dossiers. As much as any murder can be "typical," the circumstances of these cases conform to those in numerous, scattered records of witch-murders from throughout Kenya and across British Africa more generally. The basic contours of the cases are as follows. In 1941, Weyulo binti Kakonzi, a young Kamba woman from Kitui District, was tried in the Supreme Court of Kenya for killing her father-in-law, Kathanja wa Ithuko, with a *panga*. The defense argued that Kathanja had killed one of Weyulo's children and sickened another with witchcraft and threatened to kill Weyulo through witchcraft as well. A year earlier, a Luo man in Nyanza Province, Oyugi s/o Ouku, died of spear wounds in the stomach inflicted in the course of an attack by his neighbor, Maganyo s/o Ochiel. Maganyo, the defense asserted, had killed Oyugi because the latter had killed his children with witchcraft and had been found mixing more lethal "medicines" outside of Maganyo's door. Finally, in 1941, Mdago wa Randu, a Giriama man from Kilifi District, died of neck wounds at the hands of his wife's lover, Charo Hinzano. The defense claimed that Charo Hinzano had killed Mdago because Mdago

[24] 16 E.A.C.A. (1949), 134.
[25] Ibid.

had first threatened to kill him by witchcraft. Reading these witch-murders closely foregrounds how the courts mobilized complicated narrative protocols and a phalanx of expertise in order to assess witchcraft claims like those made by Weyulo, Maganyo, and Charo Hinzano.[26]

As Hynd reminds us, capital cases involved "real bodily violation, real pain, real death."[27] The work of the courts then was to transform messy, intimate stories of witchcraft-related killings into ordered, usable narratives of witch-murder. Such narratives served to determine the culpability of the accused and the consequences of the crime. These narratives aimed also to reinforce the power of the state, controlling the flow of information and the terms of expression surrounding witchcraft and wider, important (and contested) issues like order, law, custom, and justice.

Making usable narratives demanded a wide range of knowledge – not simply about the operation and intricacies of law and governance but, perhaps even more important, about local social situations and the notions of "reasonableness" that informed them. To glean this knowledge, the courts relied on widely differentiated categories of witnesses to offer broadly defined types of knowledge and expertise. Control over the delineation of information and expertise facilitated the courts' efforts to "discipline and exploit the multivocality of cases" and to order the ambiguities of "witchcraft."[28]

At the most immediate level, cases like those of Weyulo, Maganyo, and Charo Hinzano occurred in the specific contexts of individual *communities* thus necessitating that the courts enlist local witnesses who could elucidate and establish the exigencies of this context. In the large majority of cases, the witness pool was constituted by the family members, friends, and neighbors of the deceased or the accused.[29] It was not unusual for witnesses to be affines of both the deceased and the accused. These witnesses introduced their intimate knowledge of the social worlds that they

---

[26] KNA MLA 1/117, *Rex v. Weyulo binti Kakonzi* 1941. And KNA MLA 1/63, *Rex v. Maganyo s/o Ochiel* 1940. Also, KNA MLA 1/113, *Rex v. Charo Hinzano* 1941. Unfortunately, a fire in the Secretariat in Nairobi in 1939 destroyed a vast array of government documents.

[27] Hynd, "Imperial Gallows," 2.

[28] Cohen and Odhiambo, *Burying SM*, 96; Jonathan Sadowsky, *Imperial Bedlam: Institutions of Madness in Colonial Southwest Nigeria* (Berkeley: University of California Press, 1999), 37.

[29] In many instances, "witchcraft" can be read as a variety of domestic violence. See Katherine Luongo, "Domestic Dramas and Occult Acts: Witchcraft and Violence in the Arena of the Intimate," in *Domestic Violence and the Law in Colonial and Postcolonial Africa*, ed. Emily S. Burrill, Richard L. Roberts, and Elizabeth Thornberry (Athens: Ohio University Press, 2010), 179–200.

had inhabited together with the accused and the deceased into the space of the courts.

Witness speech was rendered "good testimony" by the kinds of questions the courts asked, which, in turn, demanded the sorts of responses that met with the courts' expectations of credibility and use value. Although trial transcripts do not list the questions being asked by the courts, the sorts of testimony that witnesses offered hint at the types of questions that might have been asked. The courts' investigative modes were meant to elucidate the general facts of the case and to answer the questions "Who?" "What?" "When?" "Where?" "Why?" and "How?" in such a way that they developed a body of information ordered according to colonial categories that the courts could use in determining degrees of culpability and appropriate consequences.

Content and form determined the usability and intelligibility of testimony. First, good testimony was expressed in linear narratives that aided in ordering the events and circumstances of the case. These narratives assembled relations of cause and effect in witch-murder cases. Good testimony also provided relevant and usable details – without extraneous information. It provided particular information about time and space, attending to problems of provocation and premeditation. Good testimony discussed weapons and wounds, again speaking to intention and planning. And it noted the affective language surrounding the killings, speaking to issues of motive.

For example, the testimony of Anyango given in the Supreme Court trial of Maganyo s/o Ochiel illustrates many of the attributes of good testimony. Termed by the courts "an old woman, concise and credible," Anyango provided testimony that conformed to the colonial legal standards of intelligibility and usefulness. She testified,

> I am the Aunt of the accused. About the beginning of August there was a quarrel between accused and my husband. I was present at the quarrel.... Oyugi went to milk the cattle and closed the gate of the cattle boma. The cattle strayed outside and ate the grass off the roof. Oyugi asked accused why he allowed the cattle to stray outside and eat grass off the roof. Accused abused deceased by his mother's "anus." He said "Your mother's cunt" and deceased replied "The same to you." Oyugi raised his rungu first and then accused raised his rungu. Oyugi did nothing with his rungu. Accused didn't do anything. No blows were then struck at that time.... Nyakembo along with Nyangori arrived. This is Nyakembo (brought into Court). He separated them. Nyamkembo led his father Oyugi to my hut. Nyangori took accused to his own house. Later he (accused) returned with his spear, to the door of my hut. Oyugi and myself

were at the door together. Accused came to door and told Oyugi "I can stab you." Accused stabbed Oyugi in left side of the body. Went in about height of waist, about halfway between front of hip and navel. It came out on right hand side. This is the spear the accused used.... He stabbed, withdrew, dropped it down and ran away. He threw it, then caught hold of it again and withdrew it. Shortly afterwards Oyugi died.[30]

Adhering to the contours of good testimony, Anyango's "concise and credible" statements remade an affective drama into an orderly narrative that could be assessed by the courts.

In addressing witchcraft specifically, the testimony of affines and associates alternately redefined the deceased as the initial aggressor in the story of a witchcraft killing or as the victim in a narrative of witch-murder. Testimony typically followed in one of two routes. First, witness testimony worked to define the deceased by what he or she was *not* – a witch. By defining the deceased as "not-a-witch," witness testimony in turn served to break down the accused's own claims about the provocative witchcraft of the deceased. In the second case, by naming the deceased as a witch, witness testimony spoke to issues of motive and provocation. Testimony supporting the notion that the deceased was a witch could work to reinforce the accused's claims regarding witchcraft as a provocation to the killing.

For example, the statement of the deceased's son in *Maganyo* worked to counter Maganyo's claims about the witchcraft of the deceased. The deceased's son testified, "My father was never called a wizard by anybody. Yes, I heard accused charge deceased with being a wizard on that day. Accused abused him saying 'You wizard'. He did not say deceased had bewitched his child. I never heard my father admit his powers."[31]

Testimony about witchcraft in *Weyulo*, in contrast, defined the deceased *as* a witch, initially seeming to support the defendant's contentions. A relative of the defendant and the deceased stated,

> Yes, we knew that Kathanja (deceased) possessed witchcraft charms. Yes I believe in witchcraft. Our tribe is afraid of witchcraft.... When Kathanja dies no one will inherit his witchcraft powers, Yes we believe that if the wizard is killed the child will recover from sickness and the child has recovered. I won't dispute that accused may have believed that deceased had cast a spell on the children.[32]

[30] KNA MLA 1/63, testimony of Anyango w/o Oyugi, 2 October 1940, 2. "*Rungu*" is the Kiswahili word for "knobkerry."
[31] KNA MLA 1/63, testimony of Nyangori s/o Ochiel, 2 October 1940, 3–4.
[32] KNA MLA 1/117, testimony of Musembi wa Mutaba, 11 August 1941, 3.

But further testimony, making use of the witness's knowledge of the general tenets of witchcraft within the tribe nevertheless suggested that Weyulo's assertion that Kathanja had bewitched her children was unreasonable. Musembi wa Mutaba added, "We were not afraid of him [Kathanja] because he was a relative of ours. People who were not his friends feared him."[33] Despite identifying the deceased as a "witch," witness testimony still worked in this case to break down the accused's claims about the witchcraft of the deceased.

The accused were also allowed to speak – directly or through their advocates – thus establishing additional layers of context and culpability in their cases. Conforming to the courts' standards of intelligibility and usefulness, the testimony of the accused shared many of the organizational characteristics of witness testimony. Yet it also entailed dramaturgics absent from the testimony of witnesses, a deeper attention to the interior life – the affect and beliefs – of the accused.

In general, the testimony of the accused worked to reorient attention away from the murder that the accused was alleged to have perpetrated. It focused on the earlier killings that the deceased was alleged to have carried out using witchcraft methods and means. Weyulo's speech, for example, most closely attended to the standards of good testimony that framed that of witnesses. She stated,

> Kathanja was my husband's father. I killed him because he had bewitched my children. He told me he had done so and next day one child died. I greatly upset [sic]. The second child got very ill and I killed him that day. I believed that my turn would be next and I believed that if I killed him I would save my child's life and my own. I believed that if Kathanja died his spells would die with him.... It was very few days not a month before I killed him that he told me he would finish the children first and then myself.[34]

Weyulo's testimony followed a linear narrative that ordered the events of the case. It referenced her relationship with the deceased and established a cause-and-effect explanation for his killing. But at the same time, Weyulo's testimony contained a dramaturgical flair lacking in the witness testimony about her case. It referenced the degree of her emotions and set up a metanarrative in which her killing of Kathanja was posed as a (heroic) story in which Weyulo not only "saved" her child's life and her own, but rid the community of a malfeasant presence because "if Kathanja

---

[33] Ibid.
[34] KNA MLA 1/117, testimony of Weyulo binti Kakonzi, 11 August 1941, 5.

died his spells would die with him."³⁵ At the same moment, time, a key category in what made good testimony, worked *against* Weyulo, demonstrating that she did not act out of *immediate* fear for her own life or as the result of a passion which had not had time to cool.³⁶

Maganyo's testimony to the Supreme Court also included many of the characteristics of good testimony. He stated,

> Yes, I stabbed Oyugi at the door of my hut. He came to bewitch me.... He was praying with a charm that I might die. No I was not afraid. I recognized his voice and I said "This man is a wizard and he is going to kill me." I went outside and saw he had some roots and ashes. He was stirring ashes and roots, so I told him you have threatened to kill me and now you have come. Then Nyangori arrived and deceased lifted up his stick and said to me "I will kill you today." Then I said deceased has already killed my child; he troubled me and bewitched me and I had sickness in the stomach and now he has raised his stick and threatened to kill me. Then I seized hold of my spear – deceased started to run – I stabbed him but I don't know where he fell. I counted 2 things he had done to me and I counted myself a dead man. When I saw the ashes, that was the end....
>
> I know people know he is a witch but they won't come here. I have no witnesses.... I cannot call anyone because only I have been bewitched. No one will come here and say deceased is a witch on my behalf....
>
> I realized my story is totally different to the Crown witnesses evidence.... I know my Advocate did not ask any questions of Nyangori bearing out my story.³⁷

Maganyo's testimony also established a linear narrative. It was specific and consistent in the details of the verbal exchanges that transpired between Maganyo and the deceased. In drawing attention to the specifics of Oyugi's witchcraft paraphernalia, Maganyo's testimony sought to (re)establish the logic in Maganyo's witchcraft beliefs.

At the same time, Maganyo's testimony also demonstrated an awareness of the court's workings and expectations. Recognizing that the court would require witnesses to corroborate his allegations of Oyugi's witchcraft, Maganyo explained why he had no witnesses to call. His testimony also suggested an understanding that the court and its experts worked to shape the stories that the accused told. He located the blame for the discrepancies in his story in his advocate's failure to ask the appropriate questions. A member of the Colonial Office Prisons Commission, reporting about his tour of East Africa in 1939, noted, "I regret to say that I

---

³⁵ Ibid.
³⁶ Ibid.
³⁷ KNA MLA 1/63, testimony of Maganyo s/o Ochiel, 2 October 1940, 4.

found in a number of instances that the counsel assigned to the Defence had taken their duties so lightly that they had never visited the prisoner and had indeed never seen him until he arrived at the Court to stand trial for his life"; therefore, this accusation was likely not misplaced.[38] Finally, while the category of time worked *for* Maganyo, suggesting the immediacy of his response to Oyugi's threats, his statements about affect – that he was "not afraid" – worked against his case, suggesting that his attack on Oyugi was not driven by passion or fear for his own life.

It was not a requirement that the accused speak for themselves. Charo Hinzano, for one, declined to testify. His advocate, C. A. Patel, was charged instead with telling Charo Hinzano's story. He stated,

> Defence of accused is in statement in Lower Court – he admitted he killed the deceased – allegation of witchcraft in statement. No reason to disbelieve accused's statement – If he was put in such immediate fear of danger to his own life, then he would not be guilty of murder. It is manslaughter because of provocation and immediate danger to his life. Mdago, he says, he would look for medicine with which to bewitch him.[39]

In the advocate's rendering, Charo Hinzano's story was framed by judicial categories and told in legal language. The advocate's speech posed reasons for reducing the charges of murder to manslaughter. Rather than being a narrativization of the events surrounding Mdago's death, the advocate's telling instead offered a syllogism: Charo Hinzano alleged bewitchment by Mdago. Bewitchment creates fear and provocation. Fear and provocation reduce murder to manslaughter. Thus, Charo Hinzano was guilty of manslaughter instead of murder.

Even after witnesses and the accused had testified, the question of how witchcraft, and "reasonable" responses to it, were ordinarily imagined and acted upon in local communities remained somewhat oblique for the courts. As such, the legal system developed a coterie of advisory experts, that is, native assessors, to determine local standards of "reasonableness" in regard to witchcraft and to assess the actions of the accused according to these standards. Native assessors' work entailed occupying a middling intellectual space in which they moved consistently between their own knowledge of the local and the courts' protocols.

The opinions of assessors were not narrative evaluations of the case but instead offered sets of answers to the courts' specific queries. Their

---

[38] PRO CO 822/96/4, letter from Alexander Paterson, Prison Commission, to Sir Grattan Bushe, Colonial Office Legal Advisor, 15 September 1939.
[39] KNA MLA 1/113, statement of C. A. Patel, 24 June 1941, 5.

opinions were further framed by the courts' instructions in the meanings and uses of particular judicial categories – for example, "malice aforethought" and manslaughter – and by examples and explanations of judicial precedent. Embedded in these questions and instructions were the courts' expectations of what made "reasonableness" and good practice in relation to witchcraft. For example, documents from Weyulo's case illustrate the interaction of the courts and native assessors. Notes for an address to the assessors read as follows:

> Murder manslaughter and malice aforethought explained. Onus thus on the prosecution to prove guilt beyond a reasonable doubt. Decision in Rex. versus Kimutai arap Mursoi 1939 VI E.A.C.A. 117 and Rex v. Mawala binti Nyangweza Criminal Appeal No. 61 of 1940 explained. Defence of provocation explained. Accused must be given benefit of the doubt if case as a whole raises a reasonable doubt as to whether there was such provocation as to reduce crime to manslaughter.[40]

Contained in these short notes is a great deal of information about the categories and concepts through which the courts directed the opinions of native assessors. They point to the important judicial concepts according to which the justices would ultimately rule and to the concepts available to the defense. The notes also identify precedent in earlier witch-murder cases. Finally, they address the problem of burden of proof. Overall, the instructions to assessors established a framework through which native assessors were to evaluate the various competing claims about witchcraft, law, and order wrapped up in the case.

Extracts from the assessor's opinions in Weyulo's case, for example, highlight the interplay of court categories and local expertise. The assessors stated,

> *1st Assessor*: I am satisfied that accused killed Kathanja. I believe her story except that I don't believe that Kathanja bewitched her children at all. I accept that she believed it and she believed that her own life was in danger but father-in-laws do not bewitch their sons [sic] wives.
>
> *2nd Assessor*: She killed Kathanja but I don't believe that Kathanja did what she believed he did. She killed Kathanja because she thought he would kill her young child which was ill and then she thought Kathanja would kill her.
>
> *3rd Assessor*: Accused killed Kathanja for nothing although she thought that Kathanja had killed one child and was killing the other one [but

---

[40] KNA MLA 1/117, address to Assessors, 11 August 1941, 5.

this] was not so. She thought her own life was in immediate danger but she killed Kathanja for no reason.[41]

The assessors' opinions referenced expert knowledge of witchcraft to appraise Weyulo's claims about the witchcraft of the deceased. In this way they fleshed out spare legal categories and suggested that Weyulo's actions did not meet local standards of "reasonableness" in regard to witchcraft. Yet no matter how nuanced and responsive the assessors' opinions were, the judgments about what amounted to provocation, what made a "reasonable" man (or woman) in Africa, and what constituted British justice overall in cases of witch-murder rested with the justices of East Africa's highest courts.

EXISTENCE AND BELIEF

As the previous testimony indicates, for many of the people involved, witchcraft-killings were untidy and complicated. But for the justices of the colonial courts, precedent, protocol, and the Penal Code rendered the adjudication of cases of witch-murder relatively straightforward. Indeed, judgments followed a fairly standard structure: statement and assessment of the defense, acknowledgment of the opinions of the assessors, attention to court categories, and reference to precedent.

Though judgments in cases like those of Weyulo, Maganyo, and Charo Hinzano universally denied the *existence* of witchcraft, they assessed the veracity and validity of the accused's witchcraft *beliefs*. As elaborated earlier, the law-as-written constrained justices' ability to consider witchcraft beliefs as mitigation in capital crimes unless another legal category attached. However, the justices' recommendations to the Governor-in-Council ultimately turned on whether the accused had demonstrated his or her beliefs in witchcraft to be sufficiently "real." In the cases of Weyulo, Maganyo, and Charo Hinzano, the judgments of the courts respectively concurred with, contested, and contradicted the accused's claims about witchcraft.

The Supreme Court judgment in Weyulo's case adhered to the typical structure and assessed the validity of Weyulo's claims about witchcraft. Extracts from the judgment in Weyulo's case read,

> The defence is that Kathanja who is proved to be a witch doctor had told the accused about a month before the crime that he had bewitched

---

[41] KNA MLA 1/117, statements of Assessors Nyama wa Mukulu, Kithingu was Mulla, and Ngwatu wa Nzila, 11 August 1941, 6.

her 2 children.... The evidence given by the accused is not corroborated in any way except that one of her children did die about a month before the killing of Kathanja and that when Kathanja was killed her other child was ill. There was no evidence that she told any one of Kathanja's threats and though like the assessors I am satisfied that the accused believed without any justification that Kathanja was responsible for the death of one of her children and for the illness of the other I am not prepared to believe the rest of her evidence except as to the killing. From the way and manner in which accused gave her evidence I believed her story as to Kathanja telling her he had bewitched the children and as to his threatening her life was not true. The fact that a native is not likely to cast spells on his grandchildren strengthens the belief....

Even were I have to believed her evidence as to the threat to her own life or to her belief that her own life was in danger which I did not do I cannot see how she could believe that there was any immediate danger to her own life when she committed the crime as her second child was not yet dead and of course the danger would had been extremely remote at the time of the alleged threat and the killing occurred if not a month at least some days after the alleged threat.

In view of the decision in Rex v. Kumwaka wa Mulumbi and others (14 K.L.R. 137) which was followed in Rex v. Kimutai arap Mursoi (6 E.A.C.A. 117) that this defence "has been consistently rejected except in cases where the accused has been put in such immediate danger to his own life that the defence of grave and sudden provocation has been held proved" I must hold that the defence in this case fails.[42]

The judgment in Weyulo's case summarily reiterated her defense that Kathanja had bewitched her and her children. At the same time, it evaluated the validity of claims about her witchcraft beliefs and the role they played in driving her to kill Kathanja, and found that while Weyulo may have believed herself and her family to be bewitched, this belief was not reasonable. The judgment attended to what would have made Weyulo's claims reasonable in the eyes of the court; the testimony of witnesses who, according to their own observations or at the least to what Weyulo had told them before Kathanja's death, could corroborate Weyulo's claims that Kathanja had threatened her and her family with witchcraft. The justice also attended to performative elements in Weyulo's testimony when assessing her claims about witchcraft, noting that the "way and manner in which she told her story" led him to believe that her story was false. In order to cast Weyulo's claims about Kathanja's witchcraft as invalid, the judgment also drew on the opinions of the assessors, which

---

[42] KNA MLA 1/117, "Judgment," n.d., 6–8.

stipulated that it was unlikely that Kathanja would have bewitched his own grandchildren.

The judgment also read claims about witchcraft against legal categories and in conversation with precedent. Even if the justice had accepted Weyulo's claims about witchcraft as reasonable, her story did not align with the mitigating judicial categories that her advocate had aimed to mobilize. The lag time between Kathanja's alleged threats and Weyulo's attack on him disabled claims that she felt her own life to be in "immediate danger." Similarly, precedent worked to break down Weyulo's claim to witchcraft as a mitigating factor. Weyulo could neither prove that she believed her own life to be in "immediate danger" through Kathanja's witchcraft nor could she establish the circumstances of "grave and sudden provocation" that would reduce her case to manslaughter.

Yet witchcraft still counted in Weyulo's case. Though the justice did not believe that Kathanja had practiced witchcraft against Weyulo – and precedent suggests it would not have mattered all that much if he had – he did concur that Weyulo truly believed that Kathanja had bewitched her family. The court's recognition of what could be legally termed Weyulo's "real but mistaken belief" in Kathanja's witchcraft rendered her case one that could be recommended to the clemency of the Governor-in-Council.

Although the judgment in Maganyo's cases generally followed the structure of that in Weyulo's case, the court contested Maganyo's claims about witchcraft. Extracts read,

> The accused admits that he killed the deceased and his defence is that it was done under grave and sudden provocation and a faint suggestion that he acted in self defence. More strongly put forward is that defence that the deceased was a wizard and that the offence is only manslaughter.
>
> The prosecution witnesses subject to what I say later, say that the killing was nothing to do with the accused's belief that the deceased practiced witchcraft but anger and a quarrel because deceased complained of accused leaving a gate open so that the cattle wandered and ate grass off the roofs....
>
> Accused puts up the 2 defences of provocation and self defence. He destroys the second defence himself when he says in evidence he was not afraid when the deceased came to him just before he (deceased) was killed.
>
> There is a doubt raised by the evidence as a whole whether the accused had in fact an honest and genuine belief that the deceased practiced witchcraft and that the deceased had bewitched his son. The benefit of that doubt must be given to accused.

That is a long way from finding as a fact that the accused was put in immediate fear of danger to his own life or even that he believed himself to be in danger. I am quite convinced that he was not put in any such position such as to amount to grave and sudden provocation and further that he did not believe himself to be in such a position.... The accused was not acting of necessity or to protect his own life.... There is no reasonable doubt that the accused may have killed the deceased because he the accused believed the deceased was in the habit of practicing witchcraft and believed that the deceased had bewitched his dead child.... The element of witchcraft will no doubt receive the attention of the Governor in Council.[43]

In Maganyo's case, the judgment countered claims about witchcraft, suggesting instead that witchcraft operated as a smokescreen for the real motive for the killing – "anger and a quarrel" proceeding from Oyugi's cattle destroying Maganyo's property. Unlike that in Weyulo's case, witness testimony did not bear out Maganyo's contention that Oyugi practiced witchcraft. In Maganyo's case, a more material motive for the killing existed. Further, the judgment also attended to the weakness of the defenses put forward by Maganyo. The intertwined arguments of the defense – that Maganyo feared for his own life and that Oyugi was a witch – faltered on Maganyo's contention that he was *not* afraid of Oyugi.

Yet witchcraft still had sway in Maganyo's case. While the evidence in the case did not establish incontrovertibly that Maganyo had believed that Oyugi had practiced witchcraft against him and killed his child, neither could the evidence prove that Maganyo had *not* believed these things. In such instances, the court noted, the "benefit of the doubt must be given to the accused," and this benefit extended to the consideration of the "element of witchcraft" by the Governor-in-Council.

While judgment in Charo Hinzano's case followed a structure similar to that in the earlier cases, it contradicted Charo Hinzano's claims about witchcraft. Extracts read,

> This is a very clear case of murder. It is not disputed that the accused killed Mdago.... In this statement is an allegation that the husband Mdago had threatened to bewitch the accused after he had received malu from the accused for the latter's adultery with Mdago's wife. There is not a little evidence to support this allegation and I am quite satisfied there is no truth in it whatsoever.... The Assessors are all of the opinion that the accused is guilty of murder and reject as I do the most unconvincing allegation of the threat of witchcraft by Mdago. There is in the case not

[43] KNA MLA 1/63, "Judgment," 5 October 1940, 1–2.

the smallest evidence that the accused was in fear of immediate danger of his life, even if the accused's account be true and I am certain that it is not. There is no element or suggestion of intoxication or insanity in the case and I therefore find the accused guilty of murder as charged.[44]

The justice rejected Charo Hinzano's claims about Mdago's witchcraft, focusing instead on the more plausible motive for the killing – the conflict over the *malu* Charo Hinzano had paid under arbitration for seducing Mdago's wife – and on the absence of evidence to support Charo Hinzano's contentions about witchcraft. The justice noted that his opinion coincided with that of the assessors and indicated that even had Charo Hinzano's claims about witchcraft been true, the argument for *self*-defense was untenable because there was still no evidence that Charo Hinzano had feared for "immediate danger of his own life." Because Charo Hinzano had failed to offer convincing evidence of his belief that the deceased had practiced witchcraft against him or even to establish reasonable doubt that he might have believed in Mdago's witchcraft, the justice read the case as a simple murder and did not recommend Charo Hinzano to the governor's clemency.

Under the Penal Code of Kenya each of the cases amounted to murder. Weyulo was found to have murdered Kathanja; Maganyo to have murdered Ouygi, and Charo Hinzano to have murdered Mdago. Confined by the law that stipulated that murder was necessarily a capital crime, the justices of the Supreme Court of Kenya were bound to sentence each of the accused to death. But judgments in each of the cases reveal the justices *did* consider the existence of "real," or at least plausible, beliefs in witchcraft in their recommendations to the Governor-in-Council. In Weyulo and Maganyo's cases where "real" beliefs in witchcraft were held proved, or at least not *dis*provable, the court recommended clemency.[45] But in Charo Hinzano's case, the justice contradicted the accused's claims about "witchcraft" and treated the case as an ordinary murder.[46]

COMMUTATION AND CLEMENCY

The rooms where the Supreme Court of Kenya sessions were held were not the last judicial spaces in which stories like those of Weyulo,

---

[44] KNA MLA 1/113, "Judgment," 10 July 1941, 1.
[45] KNA MLA 1/117, "Judgment," n.d., 8. And KNA MLA 1/63, "Judgment," 5 October 1940, 2.
[46] KNA MLA 1/113, "Judgment," 10 July 1941, 1.

Maganyo, and Charo Hinzano were told. Rather, it was common for those convicted of murder to appeal to the Court of Appeal for Eastern Africa. Indeed, as a member of the Colonial Office Prisons Commission noted of his visit to East Africa in 1939, "I found that nearly every convicted murderer appealed against the sentence."[47]

Regrettably, complete records of the appeals are not included in the dossiers of Weyulo, Maganyo, and Charles Hinzano. Documents do show, however, that appeals were dismissed in these cases and that justices of the Supreme Court made various recommendations concerning clemency to the governor of Kenya.[48] Extracts from the Supreme Court's recommendations and the appellate court's decisions in the cases of Weyulo, Maganyo, and Charo Hinzano point to how the recommendations varied according to the strength of earlier claims about witchcraft.

> *Weyulo*: The killing in this case was clearly murder but the case may be and probably is judging from the evidence deserving of sympathetic consideration by the Executive.[49]
>
> *Maganyo*: There being this doubt as to what the real motive was I gave the benefit of the doubt to the accused and held that he had an honest and genuine belief that the deceased practiced witchcraft and that the deceased had bewitched his child.
>
> I recommend, following what appears to be the practice, that the sentence of death be not carried out and that substitution therefore of a term of imprisonment by hard labor be imposed.[50]
>
> *Charo Hinzano*: The learned trial Judge and the assessors were unanimous in finding the accused guilty of murder. The evidence supports this finding and the accused admits having decided upon the death of the deceased. On the evidence the case is murder. Appeal dismissed.[51]

These recommendations took in not only earlier judgments, but also attended to another layer of expertise, that of the medical officers who assessed prisoners like Weyulo, Maganyo, and Charo Hinzano remanded to the Nairobi jail on a capital charge. Medical officers assessed the

---

[47] PRO CO 822/96/4, letter from Alexander Paterson, Prison Commission, to Sir Grattan Bushe, Colonial Office Legal Advisor, 15 September 1939.

[48] KNA MLA 1/117, letter from Judge, H. M. Supreme Court, of Kenya to the Governor of Kenya, 2 September 1941; KNA MLA 1/63, letter from Judge, H. M. Supreme Court of Kenya, to Governor of Kenya, 21 November 1940; KNA MLA 1/113, letter from Judge H. M. Supreme Court of Kenya, to the Governor of Kenya, 1 September 1941.

[49] KNA MLA 1/117, Criminal Appeal No. 127 of 1941, 28 August 1941.

[50] KNA MLA 1/63, letter from Judge, H. M. Supreme Court of Kenya, to Governor of Kenya, 21 November 1940.

[51] KNA MLA1/113, Criminal Appeal No. 118 of 1941, 20 August 1941.

physical, physiological, and emotional states of prisoners, and the expert information they produced worked descriptively to broaden the context of cases and analytically to weigh prisoners' claims about the deceased and about themselves. In the case of witch-murderers, it referenced the affective and embodied elements of witchcraft.

In producing reports, medical officers followed questions and recorded information on standard examination forms. These particular forms spoke to issues of the "content of the form" of bureaucratic documents, or the ways in which the structure and protocols of standardized bureaucratic documents in turn shaped particular bodies of information.[52] The questions and categories of such documents reflected not only the types of information that authorities wanted to elicit, but also the sort of information that they expected to be able to obtain. They foregrounded what kinds of information had juridical use-value and helped to delineate what counted as medical "expertise." The reports' questions and categories were functions of larger colonial conversations about the workings of bodies, minds, and emotions.

A report's categories and questions did different kinds of work. Categories like "Personal History" and "Venereal Disease" primarily addressed the condition of the prisoner's body.[53] Questions, treating such topics as mental derangement and appreciation of the crime mainly attended to the prisoner's psychological and emotional states. The space for "recommendations" invited medical officers to use their expertise to summarily assess the information above.

In Weyulo's case, the (categorical) assessment of her body rendered no usable information. Her medical history reported no family history of serious disease, insanity or epilepsy, a similar personal history, and no habits of alcohol, bhang, or tobacco. According to her report, Weyulo's body contained nothing – neither sickness nor substance – to help explain her beliefs and actions.[54] Similarly, Charo Hinzano's report suggested only that he had suffered from venereal disease, but seemingly not a case sufficiently serious to influence his perceptions and behavior.[55]

---

[52] White, *The Content of the Form*.
[53] In addition to standard demographic categories, name, tribe, and so on, the forms contain the following categories: Family History – Father, Living or Dead? Mother, Living or Dead? History of Insanity? History of Epilepsy? Personal History – Previous Diseases? Venereal Diseases? Epilepsy? Insanity? Habits – Alcohol? Bhang? Tobacco?
[54] KNA MLA 1/117, Medical Report upon Prisoner Remanded on a Capital Charge, Nairobi, 2 August 1941, 1–2. Hereafter, "Weyulo Medical Report."
[55] KNA MLA 1/113, Medical Report upon Prisoner Remanded on a Capital Charge, Nairobi, 24 July 1941, 1–2. Hereafter, "Charo Hinzano Medical Report."

The assessment of Maganyo's body, in contrast, worked to shore up the "reasonableness" of his purported beliefs in Oyugi's "witchcraft," the "magical harm" that he perceived as responsible for the death of his child and his own severe stomach pains. Under "Family History" Maganyo's mother's cause of death was listed as "abdominal disease." Maganyo's "Personal History" noted, "He says he has suffered from abdominal pain for a long time." And the report described "numerous scarifications on abdomen, presumably to cure abdominal pain."[56] The assessment of Maganyo's body then, posited a genealogy for and materiality to his contentions about the type of "witchcraft" he believed to have been practiced against him.

The form's questions produced more usable information, querying the extent of the prisoner's "intelligence," "delusions of persecution," beliefs in "witchcraft," and appreciation of the seriousness of the crime. This nexus spoke to the mental and emotional health of the prisoner, working to ascertain evidence of diminished capacity or mistaken belief. The medical officer in charge of the Prison Hospital found Weyulo and Charo Hinzano to be of average intelligence and to show no evidence of mental derangement. Both admitted their crimes and suggested explanations for them. Weyulo felt that "she was compelled to act as she did," while Charo Hinzano stated that he "was not right in his head at the time or he would not have done it." Maganyo did not explain himself in the same way. The medical officer found Maganyo to be unsettled, "intensely suspicious and frightened," and perhaps "feeble-minded" to the point that he was "almost unexaminable mentally."[57]

In each of the cases, of course, the question of witchcraft arose. The information about witchcraft recorded on the forms for Weyulo, Charo Hinzano, and Maganyo simply offered the bare summaries of what they had claimed about "witchcraft" in more detail in various other settings. Only in Maganyo's case were the medical officer's physical findings and the prisoner's assertions in conversation. Of Maganyo, the medical officer noted, "He believes that his child had been killed by witchcraft and that his own abdominal pains were similarly caused by the deceased."[58]

The medical officer's recommendations vary interestingly. In Maganyo's case, the medical officer highlighted the intersection of physical findings and Maganyo's claims about witchcraft noted earlier. He suggested that

---

[56] KNA MLA 1/63, Medical Report upon Prisoner Remanded on a Capital Charge, Nairobi, 15 November 1940, 1–2. Hereafter, "Maganyo Medical Report."
[57] "Weyulo Medical Report," 2. Also "Charo Hinzano Medical Report," 2. And "Maganyo Medical Report," 2.
[58] "Maganyo Medical Report," 2.

"consideration be given to the extensive scarification of the accused's abdomen, as corroborating very clearly his statements in regard to his own illness."[59] In the other cases, the medical officer suggested only that Weyulo's youth be considered – she is listed as between eighteen and twenty years old – and that attention be drawn to the "evidence of witchcraft" mentioned in Charo Hinzano's examination.[60] While certainly unable on their own to confirm or negate a judgment or decision, such findings nonetheless had the potential to influence recommendations regarding clemency that the Supreme Court made to the Governor-in-Council.

MAKING PLEAS

A broad survey of cases including, but exceeding, those discussed in this chapter suggests that the Supreme Court was inclined to recommend clemency in cases in which prisoners like Weyulo, Maganyo, and Charo Hinzano were deemed to have held a real and genuine (though mistaken) belief in the witchcraft of the deceased. Indeed, such recommendations emerge as a strand of governmental good practice in the post-*Kumwaka* period.

Furthermore, prisoners convicted of capital crimes could plead their cases to the Governor-in-Council. The prose of the pleas was governed in varying degrees by judicial protocols. It largely substituted the categories and concepts of the courts for the voices of the imprisoned. A Colonial Office authority shed light on the reasons for this situation and on its potential pitfalls. He explained that the typical prisoner was

> quite incapable of drafting his own appeal, and this duty was thrown on the harassed and overworked Superintendent of the Gaol. As the Superintendent had not seen the depositions in the case, but had only read the finding of the Court, he was really quite incompetent, being no lawyer himself, to do justice to the prisoners, and a great deal of his time was taken up in this task.[61]

Records do not reveal who specifically drafted appeals for the prisoners in the three cases under consideration here. A formulaic approach, perhaps suggesting the writer was a jailer rather than a lawyer, is identifiable in Weyulo and Charo Hinzano's pleas. They pleaded as follows,

> *Weyulo*: I killed Kathanja because he was a well-known witch-doctor and he had bewitched my children. One died and the other was very

---

[59] Ibid., 1.
[60] "Weyulo Medical Report," 2. Also "Charo Hinzano Medical Report," 2.
[61] PRO CO 822/96/4, letter from Alexander Paterson, Prison Commission, to Sir Grattan Bushe, Colonial Office Legal Advisor, 15 September 1939.

seriously ill. It was a very few days before I killed my children. He would kill me. I acted under great provocation, and was very upset when I killed him.[62]

Charo Hinzano: I killed the deceased because the deceased had threatened to kill me by witchcraft. The deceased had killed my mother, wife and two relatives by witchcraft. I reported this matter to the Elders. I admit I committed adultery with the deceased's wife so when the deceased discovered he threatened to kill me by witchcraft. I therefore killed him to save my own life.[63]

Pleas reiterated the circumstances of the case, attending to questions of motivation and procedure. They framed the circumstances of the cases in referring to the sorts of judicial concepts on which legal decisions were based. Weyulo acted therefore "under great provocation," while Charo Hinzano killed Mdago to save his own life. Attending to the recommendations of the courts, the Governor-in-Council commuted Weyulo's sentence to hard labor.[64] Charo Hinzano's death sentence, in turn, was upheld.[65]

Maganyo, in turn, did not offer a plea. A memo from the senior superintendent of the prisons to the chief secretary noted that Maganyo, "owing to his peculiar mental condition," was "unable to file a petition to His Excellency the Governor."[66] Handwritten comments included in the *Maganyo* dossier indicate that he was ultimately certified insane.[67] Overall, the conclusions of these cases underscore that, as Hynd pithily notes, a "problem for the courts was how to determine between the 'mad', the 'bad' and those who thought themselves bewitched."[68]

There is no record of how the results of these cases of witch-murder were apprehended in the communities in which they took place. But stories of witchcraft and killing, which commenced long before the colonial state had any knowledge of them, likely endured in the experience and memory of those who had been directly and tangentially involved, even long after the state had deemed the cases closed. Charo Hinzano left behind his lover. Maganyo likely left the Nairobi jail in the same disturbed state that the medical officer described. It is doubtful that Weyulo

---

[62] KNA MLA 1/117, petition form, 15 August 1941.
[63] KNA MLA 1/113, petition form, 23 August 1941.
[64] KNA MLA 1/117, memo from R. G. Turnball (for the Chief Secretary) to the Honorable Provincial Commissioner, Central Province, Nyeri, 12 December n.d.
[65] KNA MLA 1/113, Executive Council, Criminal Case No. 71/1941, 19 September 1941.
[66] KNA MLA 1/63, memo from B. B. Donald, Senior Supdt. of Prisons to the Hon'ble Chief Secretary, Nairobi, 21 November 1940.
[67] Sadowsky, *Imperial Bedlam*, 37–39.
[68] Hynd, "Imperial Gallows," 106.

had any place to go except back to the village where her in-laws lived. And surely for the families and friends of those killed by Weyulo, Maganyo, and Charo Hinzano, stories of witch-killing retained their proximity and relevance.

Complex legal efforts to manage witchcraft like those mapped out in this chapter persisted into the 1950s. So did debates about the role of local knowledge and the place of metropolitan authorities in dealing with witchcraft and its implications for imperial justice, law, and order. Accordingly, the next chapter addresses how the Kenya administration mobilized colonial officials' local expertise, co-opting Kamba witchcraft and criminalizing another category of Kamba supernatural practice in its efforts to combat the threats to British justice, law, and order posed by the Mau Mau rebellion.

7

The World of Oathing and Witchcraft in Mau Mau–era Machakos

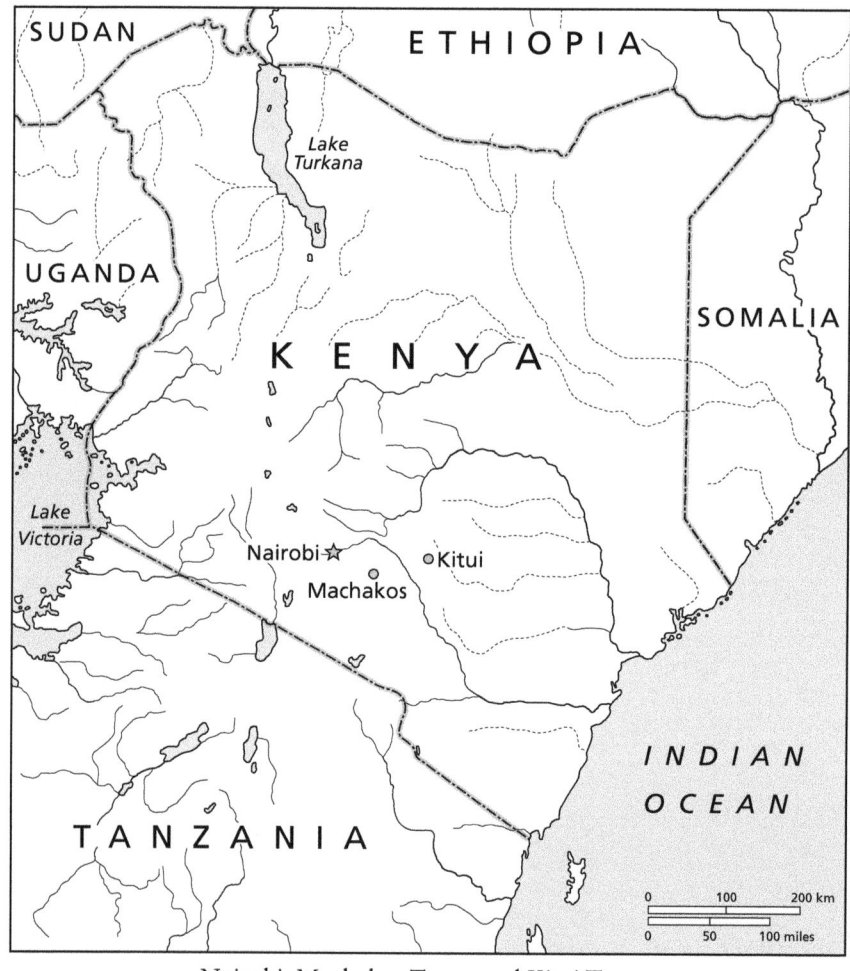

Nairobi, Machakos Town, and Kitui Town.

The colonial state in Kenya confronted the ultimate challenge to its authority during the Mau Mau rebellion. From October 1952 to December 1959, Kenya was officially under a state of emergency resulting from a violent, anti-colonial insurgency conducted by (largely) Kikuyu guerrilla fighters. In much the same way that witchcraft carried multiple meanings, "Mau Mau" came to refer to the insurgent movement itself, to the guerrilla fighters and the rebellion's more passive adherents, and also to the oaths of allegiance that fighters and adherents took, or were forced to take.

The Mau Mau rebellion arose from decades of consistently increasing levels of socioeconomic insecurity and political marginalization experienced by the substantive numbers of Kikuyu squatters in the White Highlands and Kikuyu slum-dwellers in Nairobi, and came to involve members of other tribes, albeit in much smaller numbers. Violence first flared on settler farms in the White Highlands in 1952, and the colonial government moved to squash the spotty insurgency that quickly "transformed into a formidable guerrilla force."[1] Berman explains the state's response to the insurgency:

> With metropolitan political and military backing, the colonial state moved to crush the radical challenge through massive force and the imposition of an extraordinary degree of direct administrative control. At the same time, the Provincial Administration became once more the dominant and most important element of the state apparatus.[2]

With such substantial expenditures of force and intensified administration, the colonial state's efforts to put down Mau Mau were ultimately successful. Talks surrounding the end of the rebellion were held and Kenya became independent in 1963.

In addition to expressing grievances over the depredations and depravations of colonial rule, the Mau Mau rebellion can also be understood as constituting another "critical event" through which violence related to supernatural beliefs and practices challenged the ability of the colonial state to maintain law and order. Mau Mau oathing practices did indeed draw on important elements of local cosmologies. But more important, many colonial authorities preferred to read Mau Mau abstractly as a primarily supernatural situation in which atavistic black magic was an engine and means of anti-colonial resistance rather than as a socioeconomic and political conflict rooted in tangible concerns, the remedying

---

[1] John Lonsdale, "Mau Maus of the Mind: Making Mau Mau and Remaking Kenya," *Journal of African History* 31.3 (1990): 394.
[2] Berman, *Control and Crisis*, 347.

of which would necessitate the relinquishment of a significant degree of colonial privilege and power. This chapter addresses how readings of Mau Mau as a supernatural situation are reflected in the character of colonial administrative policies and practices instituted to "rehabilitate" and "cleanse," or "de-oath," known or suspected Mau Mau adherents.

As part of the administration's efforts to combat Mau Mau in the mid-1950s, the British colonial government instituted de-oathing campaigns in areas surrounding Nairobi in order to cleanse black Kenyans known or supposed to have taken the Mau Mau oath. These campaigns were part of the state's broader strategy of eradication and rehabilitation which entailed tactics like interning black Kenyans in labor camps and removing them to "safe" villages established by the state.[3]

Though Kikuyu from Central Province bore the brunt of these tactics most heavily, other ethnic groups from provinces in proximity to the capital were also targeted. As Ukambani and Central Province bordered each other, and substantial numbers of Kamba worked in Nairobi and regularly returned to rural *mashamba* in Machakos, the colonial state regarded Kamba communities as highly vulnerable to Mau Mau influences and activities. Concerns about Mau Mau among the Kamba also figured in a Colonial Office dossier on the subject of the "Infiltration of Mau Mau into Tribes Other than the Kikuyu in Kenya."[4]

Through its efforts to deal with Mau Mau among the Kamba, the anthropologizing and archiving state produced knowledge about the Kamba supernatural and in doing so purposefully remade that knowledge to suit its own aims. In developing and implementing Mau Mau de-oathing procedures, the state officially bureaucratized the supernatural, integrating supernatural beliefs and practices into its administrative repertoire. In many ways, the "magic" of the colonial state in Ukambani during the Mau Mau era was in its efforts to transform the Kamba quotidian – oathing and witchcraft – into the state-managed exceptional and the state itself into wielder of supernatural power.[5]

A "SHADOW" ACROSS THE DISTRICT: MAU MAU AMONG KAMBA

By 1953, colonial authorities were expressing significant concerns about Mau Mau in regard to Kamba people and places. A secret telegram on

---

[3] Elkins, *Imperial Reckoning*.
[4] PRO CO 822/780, Infiltration of Mau Mau into Tribes Other than the Kikuyu in Kenya, 1954–1955.
[5] Michael Taussig, *The Magic of the State* (New York: Routledge, 1997), 5.

"Kamba infection" sent by the Nairobi government to the secretary of state for the Colonies complaining that "terrorists are making determined efforts to win over as many Kamba as possible by suborning tribesmen in Nairobi in order to spread the disease to the Reserve" was representative of colonial attitudes and tone.[6]

Colonial documents also evidenced a special concern with Mau Mau and Kamba youth in Nairobi, one going so far as to say that the city was to "this District [Machakos] what the forests have been to Kikuyuland," that is, the central site of Mau Mau recruitment, activities and sanctuary.[7] The 1953 Machakos District Annual Report, for example, noted that the year had seen the "conversion of some considerable numbers of young Kamba in Nairobi – especially those employed by E. A. Railways and Harbours and stone quarries – into Mau Mau agents and thugs; from whence attempts were made to inject the leaven of dissatisfaction into the District."[8] Colonial officials' depictions of the sorts of threats to law and order posed by Kamba youth living and laboring in Nairobi and its environs are best encapsulated in a Ministry of African Affairs file entitled, "Akamba in Nairobi," the contents of which were produced by and circulated among the provincial commissioners, district commissioners, and district officers from Kamba locations, and the secretary for African Affairs.[9]

Memos and correspondence in the dossier cast urban Kamba youth at the worst as Mau Mau-supporting "spivs," that is "gangsters," or at the best as highly vulnerable to Mau Mau "contamination" because of their low standard of living and the influences of their equally debased urban Kikuyu counterparts.[10] They also highlighted the large number of Kamba youth in Nairobi (29,000 by the end of 1954) and pointed out that a third had arrived in the city after the commencement of Operation Anvil, the colonial crackdown on Mau Mau put into motion on 24 April 1954.[11] The officer-in-charge of Nairobi Extra-Provincial District (an area taking in market centers on Nairobi's far reaches and the edges of Ukambani) described the Kamba "as the tribe most liable to contamination at the present time [who] should be placed at the head of the

---

[6] PRO CO 822/780, secret telegram from the Officer Administering the Government of Kenya to the Secretary of State for the Colonies, 26 June 1954.
[7] KNA DC/MKS 1/1/31, Machakos District Annual Report 1953, 16.
[8] Ibid.
[9] KNA MAA 7/112, "Akamba in Nairobi," July 1954–February 1955.
[10] KNA DC/MKS 1/1/32, Machakos District Annual Report 1954, 6.
[11] KNA MAA 7/112, memo from Officer-in-Charge, Nairobi Extra-Provincial District, to Secretary for African Affairs with copy to P.C. Southern Province, D.C. Nairobi, D.C. Machakos, 2 December 1954.

danger list."[12] A few months later, a colonial government press handout entitled "Wakamba Vigilance" celebrated the arrest of Kamba youths who had "come from Nairobi and administered the Mau Mau oath to three Wakamba women and two Wakamba men" in a location eighteen miles from Machakos Town.[13] Such administrative discourse illustrates how colonial concerns about Mau Mau and Kamba, especially about urban Kamba youth, also derived from broader empire-wide issues such as detribalization and shifting gender dynamics, and more concrete problems like rural-urban migration and social welfare.[14]

Yet colonial accounts also attended to the historic "loyalty" of Kamba people to the colonial state, particularly that of Kamba who had remained in Ukambani. Weaving together strands of colonial discourses about rapid socioeconomic change and relations between Kamba communities and the colonial government, a mid-1950s Machakos District Annual Report asserted,

> The significant fact about this District, to which everything else must be related if it is to be understood, is that the flood waters of progress and change which are affecting every people in Africa are here running, ever more rapidly, through the channels that are prepared for them – in other words, that there is confidence between the Government and the people. This is the basic reason for the check to Mau Mau from the Kamba as whole, who in matters of security are the first corner stone of the Kenya house.[15]

Kamba people had been regarded by the colonial administration as "the first corner stone" of the colony's security long before Mau Mau, performing military service for Britain during the two world wars and joining the ranks of the colonial police in substantial numbers during the first half of the twentieth century. But the circumstances of Mau Mau provided the Kamba with additional roles in the maintenance of state security. Three thousand "loyal" Kamba were enrolled as anti-Mau Mau "Homeguards" and many more worked in anti-Mau Mau efforts in less formal capacities.[16]

---

[12] Ibid.
[13] PRO CO 822/780, Press Handout No. 1612, "Wakamba Vigilance," 4 January 1955.
[14] For the estimated extent of Mau Mau oathing and activities among Kamba people, see Myles Osborne, "The Kamba and Mau Mau: Ethnicity, Development, and Chieftainship, 1952–1960," *International Journal of African Historical Studies* 43.1 (2010): 66–70.
[15] KNA DC/MKS 1/1/32, Machakos District Annual Report 1954, 7.
[16] Ibid.

Colonial officials read their task regarding the Kamba and Mau Mau as threefold. The first aim was to deal with the Mau Mau threat emanating from Nairobi. The second was to increase the loyalty of urban Kamba and of Kamba remaining in the districts. The third goal was to discipline and rehabilitate known or suspected Kamba Mau Mau.

The first task was to be accomplished by dealing with the conditions through which urban Kamba were thought to be rendered susceptible to Mau Mau. Writing to administrative officers throughout Ukambani, the secretary for African Affairs stipulated that he viewed "the problem of the care of the Kamba in Nairobi as a serious one which should be tackled without delay" and requested a "definite joint plan be now worked out for improved welfare, entertainment, and closer administration of the Kamba in Nairobi."[17]

In reply and with copies to the district commissioners of Kitui and Machakos, the officer-in-charge of Nairobi Extra-Provincial District suggested a complex of social welfare recommendations like "increased education" and "building of a social hall" which echoed those of an earlier meeting of British administrative officers, Kamba chiefs, and district representatives, as well as a range of measures targeted to disciplining the movement, employment, and congregation of urban Kamba. More specifically, the officer recommended measures such as tying residence permits to "accommodation and approved employment," recruiting Kamba only through designated "labour exchanges," "concentrating the higher grade Kamba in a single location," and removing "the numerous Kamba juveniles infesting the city and suburbs."[18]

In pursuing their second goal, colonial officials aimed to put the onus of building and bulwarking the loyalty of Kamba populations on Kamba people themselves. For instance, at a meeting of colonial authorities and Kamba representatives, the "formation of a Society to be named 'The Loyal Akamba Union' (LAU)" was proposed.[19] Indeed, a few days before this meeting, the provincial commissioner (PC), Southern Province, had written to authorities about linking "selected elders" in Machakos and Kitui with a new loyalist party, emphasizing that it should not be seen as

[17] KNA MAA 7/112/1, memo from the Secretary for African Affairs (K. M. Cowley) to the P.C., Southern Province and the Officer-in-Charge, Nairobi Extra-Provincial District, 5 November 1954.
[18] KNA MAA 7/112/1, memo from Officer-in-Charge, Nairobi Extra-Provincial District, to Secretary for African Affairs with cc. to P.C. Southern Province, D.C. Nairobi, D.C. Machakos, 2 December 1954.
[19] KNA MAA 7/112/1, minutes of the Meeting of the Provincial Commissioner Southern Province and the Akamba Elders, 5 July 1954.

"an off-shoot of the Mbagathi screening camp." He also advocated setting up a "Kamba Locational Council" in Nairobi to bring together loyal, urban-dwelling Kamba.[20] A few weeks after the initial planning meeting, the PC realized that the acronym LAU sounded too much like "Mau," and accordingly the organization's name was changed to the Akamba Association (AA).[21]

The use of the (strategic) passive voice in the minutes of the meeting renders unclear the degrees to which the Akamba Association was to be social, political, voluntary, or mandatory. Colonial and Kamba authorities concurred that if such an association was formed, "all Kamba in Nairobi" should be enrolled and that "every Kamba employer in Nairobi should inform LAU." They also raised the issue of using a "loyalty" oath to combat the Mau Mau oath, stipulating that "denouncing Mau Mau by means of an oath" would be a necessary prerequisite for membership in the LAU.[22] Subsequent correspondence reiterated that a central purpose of the new loyalist association was to organize Nairobi Kamba and keep them isolated from Mau Mau. In the same year, the Machakos district commissioner described a revamped Akamba Union (the original organization founded in 1938 was an apolitical burial society), based in Nairobi and Machakos to counter Mau Mau and resolved that any Kamba taking the Mau Mau oath should be stripped of tribal rights.[23]

In addition to fostering (or forcing) loyalty by bringing together and surveilling Kamba people, organizations like the Akamba Association and the Akamba Union were also likely intended as counterpoints to the Ukamba Members Association, the Kamba political association that had emerged strongly during the Destocking Crisis of 1938 and which maintained links with the Kikuyu Central Association. A secret report from Kenya that was circulated in the Colonial Office about Mau Mau among tribes besides the Kikuyu pointed out that the Ukamba Members Association and the Kikuyu Central Association had at one point shared offices in Nairobi, and blamed Paul Ngei, the anti-colonial Kamba "Big Man" detained with Kenyatta and other

[20] KNA MAA 7/112/2, correspondence from Provincial Commissioner, Southern Province, to Officer-in-Charge, Nairobi Extra-Provincial District, 2 July 1954. I am grateful to Timothy Parsons for sharing this information with me.
[21] Ibid.
[22] KNA MAA 7/112/1, minutes of the Meeting of the Provincial Commissioner Southern Province and the Akamba Elders, 5 July 1954.
[23] KNA DC/MKS 1/1/32, Machakos District Annual Report 1954. I am grateful to Timothy Parsons for sharing this information with me.

alleged architects of Mau Mau, with being "mainly responsible for the contamination of the tribe."[24]

Writing to the secretary for African Affairs and to district deputies in Ukambani about "Akamba Affairs" in early 1955, the provincial commissioner, Southern Province, thus reiterated that there was a pressing "need to bring loyal Akamba closer together through the Akamba Association."[25] Colonial officials also suggested adding to the number of Kamba involved in local administration and increasing the level of participation on the ground of existing Kamba (and British) authorities as means for developing and ensuring Kamba loyalty.

The need for closer administration is a theme that runs throughout colonial discourse on Kamba and Mau Mau.[26] The 1953 Machakos District Annual Report noted, for example, that the value of closer administration "cannot be overemphasised."[27] The participation of loyal local authorities in administrative matters, particularly issues pertaining to law and order, was important because colonial authorities regarded areas in which lower members of local administration had gone over to Mau Mau as particularly vulnerable to large-scale Mau Mau penetration. The same report pointed out that "in Mbitini, Mukaa, and Lower Kilungu, one Headman and three Asili took the Mau Mau oath without much force or persuasion being needed; it is only where the lower ranks of the Administration have been contaminated that we have had Mau Mau troubles."[28] And, always concerned with the problem of Mau Mau in Nairobi, the participants in the meeting of colonial and Kamba authorities discussed earlier proposed "more Kamba Chiefs in Nairobi."[29] Overall these varied suggestions for bolstering Kamba loyalty turned on the notion proffered in the 1954 Machakos District Annual Report that "it must be clearly understood that in the long run nobody can keep such

---

[24] PRO CO 822/780, secret report, "The Infiltration of Mau Mau into Tribes Other than the Agikuyu," n.d.

[25] KNA MAA 7/112, correspondence from the Provincial Commissioner, Southern Province to D.C. Machakos and D.C. Kitui with a copy to Secretary for African Affairs, D.C., Narok and D.C., Kajiado, 3 January 1955.

[26] Berman, *Control and Crisis*, 332–333. Also Bruce Berman and John Lonsdale, *Unhappy Valley, Conflict in Kenya and Africa, Book Two: Violence and Ethnicity* (Oxford: James Currey, 1992), 252–253. See also, Carl G. Rosberg and J. C. Nottingham, *The Myth of "Mau Mau": Nationalism in Kenya* (New York: Praeger, 1966).

[27] KNA DC/MKS 1/1/31, Machakos District Annual Report 1953, 18.

[28] Ibid., 17.

[29] KNA MAA 7/112, minutes of the Meeting of the Provincial Commissioner, Southern Province and the Akamba Elders Held at the Provincial Commissioner's Office, Ngong, 5 July 1954.

an insidious, secret, evil as Mau Mau out of an African tribe, save the members of that tribe."[30]

The extent to which the various proposals outlined here were implemented is unclear. The context and idiom of crisis through which British officials were communicating also makes it difficult to judge how serious they were about these various strategies they proposed and the degree to which these proposals constituted another example of colonial narratives of best practice.[31] Nonetheless, the crisis context of Mau Mau also produced very real stakes for British colonial authorities in Kenya and the metropole.

Yet these proposals remain important whether they were implemented or not. As Stoler has argued in the context of colonial Indonesia, it is significant that colonial policies were conceived of at all even if the means to carry them out were not available or if situations shifted before they could be put into in effect because the debates and discourses surrounding such policies highlight the issues that colonial authorities imagined as important.[32] Such policies not only provide keys to colonial imaginations but also give rise to traceable tactics of governance.

What is clear, however, is that extensive coercive and disciplinary measures — the third prong of the colonial strategy for dealing with Mau Mau and the Kamba — were implemented. The Machakos District Annual Report of 1954 emphasized Nairobi as the point of origin of Mau Mau penetration of Kamba people and places, noting that "the threat came to us primarily from Nairobi, and in August of 1953 we had set up our own Investigation Centre" which was run by the district officer and "a local Kamba-speaking farmer."[33] The previous year's report had noted a "screening and investigation team" had been sent from Ukambani to Nairobi and explained that during the later part of the year,

> special arrangements were made both in Nairobi and within the District for screening and cleansing — the "Kithitu" oath proved especially valuable amongst the older men and women. The aim was always to take the initiative to be "one step ahead." The few Kamba oath administrators discovered had case files prepared and forwarded to C.I.D. for speedy hearing at Emergency Assizes.[34]

---

[30] KNA DC/MKS 1/1/32, Machakos District Annual Report 1954, 6.
[31] Dressman, "Theory *into* Practice?"
[32] Stoler, *Along the Archival Grain*, 105–106. See also, William Cunningham Bissell, *Urban Design, Chaos, and Colonial Power in Zanzibar* (Bloomington: Indiana University Press, 2011): 72–74.
[33] KNA DC/MKS 1/1/32, Machakos District Annual Report 1954, 6.
[34] KNA DC/MKS 1/1/31, Machakos District Annual Report 1953, 16.

The language of these reports generates the impression that the discipline directed against Mau Mau and the Kamba was largely bureaucratic, an easy co-option of local custom. Elderly Kamba who experienced the de-oathings or who knew people who did, also described the campaigns as series of orderly steps presided over by administrative authorities and duly recorded by the same. But the coercive nature of the de-oathing campaigns and the fears that the roundups of known/suspected/potential Kamba Mau Mau engendered among ordinary Kamba also emerge from informants' testimony.

The details of the de-oathings are absent from colonial accounts for a number of reasons. In some instances, colonial officials themselves were absent, having put the organization and work of the roundups and cleansings largely in the hands of Kamba functionaries. Also, in certain instances, details of anti-Mau Mau activities were not simply left unsaid but were "unspeakable."[35] For example, in the course of a conversation about such Mau Mau activities in Ukambani, the former district officer stationed at Mbooni in Machakos District during Mau Mau commented that as a young administrator he was appalled when he learned of the anti-Mau Mau activities which had taken place on the ranch of a British farmer whom he did not name. When asked to describe these activities, the ex-officer deemed them "unspeakable" even fifty years later.[36] Overall, outlines, rather than details, of Mau Mau de-oathing programs in Ukambani make up the administrative correspondence and reports cited here because bureaucratic accounts can be by their nature self-sanitizing as the protocols of their production do not necessarily demand detail.[37]

MAU MAU OATHING AND DE-OATHING

The procedures, politics, and presentations of Mau Mau oathing and of concomitant de-oathing activities were debated in a range of colonial documents during the course of the rebellion. In many ways, Mau Mau oathing was mysterious to colonial authorities, and they struggled with defining its origins, its elements, and their meanings. It was neither patently clear to nor easily agreed upon by members of the colonial administration (1) which categories of persons administered the oath, (2) who exactly had taken the oath – voluntarily or otherwise, (3) what

---

[35] Trouillot, *Silencing the Past.*
[36] Interview with John Nottingham conducted by the author, Nairobi, Kenya, July, 2004. Hereafter, Nottingham Interview III.
[37] Bornstein, "How to Read a Page."

precisely oathing entailed, and (4) if the oath was unitary or if different oaths corresponded to varying levels of Mau Mau participation. Indeed, even the term "Mau Mau" was itself obscure. Lonsdale has cogently suggested that it derived from the Kikuyu phrase *kiama kia mau mau*, or "council of greedy eaters," initially used by Kikuyu squatters in the late 1940s to describe the Kikuyu political leadership and later adopted into broad use during the 1950s conflict.[38]

What has been resolved in the intervening five decades since the rebellion is that there were "multiple Mau Maus" and various types of "Mau Mau" oaths whose administration and elaborateness were contingent upon the oath-taker's level of participation and rank within Mau Mau *writ large*. Attention to "multiple Mau Maus" begs the question of whether the administration and components of Mau Mau oaths varied along ethnic lines as well.

Unfortunately, oral evidence about Mau Mau oathing and de-oathing among the Kamba does not shed light upon the specifics of Mau Mau oathing practices in Kamba communities. For example, an informant who described himself as having been "forced" to take the Mau Mau oath explained that he could not talk about the specifics of Mau Mau oathing practices because the oath entailed swearing on pain of death not to disclose its specifics and the de-oathing ceremony he had undergone did not negate this promise. He concluded simply, "I went through the oath and there are some things I can't talk about."[39] Archival and oral evidence does reveal, however, the ways in which Mau Mau cleansing procedures in Ukambani were ethnically specific, drawing upon preexisting Kamba oathing and cleansing protocols and adapting them to the particular context of Mau Mau.

Mau Mau de-oathing was initially developed at the outset of the conflict as a way to combat Mau Mau among the Kikuyu. De-oathing was in significant part an idea of Louis Leakey, the renowned white Kenyan anthropologist, whose expertise and intimacy with Kikuyu culture had been officially recognized by the colonial government long before the outset of Mau Mau. During the early years of Mau Mau, Leakey's research and experience, particularly that related to Kikuyu "magic" and "medicine," informed colonial anti-Mau Mau policies, especially those

---

[38] Berman and Lonsdale, *Unhappy Valley, II*, 426. Also John Lonsdale, "Authority, Gender, and Violence: The War within Mau Mau's Fight for Land and Freedom," in *Mau Mau and Nationhood*, ed. E. S. Atieno Odhiambo and John Lonsdale (Oxford: James Currey, 2003), 58–59.

[39] M. W., Imani, September 2004.

regarding the identification and rehabilitation of Mau Mau participants. What is important to note, as Daniel Branch has explained, is that the "ritual cleansing of oath-takers was rapidly adopted as official policy in mid-1952 as a consequence of Leakey's influence and standing within government circles."[40]

The ideas of British "ethnopsychiatrist" J. C. Carothers were also central to a program of rehabilitation focused in large part upon the cleansing of known and suspected Mau Mau. In a semi-official, but widely circulated report based on two months of work in Kenya, Carothers highlighted various retrogressive and "magical" elements driving the collective "psychosis" of Mau Mau.[41] Both Carothers's and Leakey's work, together with the conclusions drawn by a British political delegation that visited Kenya in the middle of the Emergency, spoke to what has been dubbed "the myth of Mau Mau," or the notion that "Mau Mau was a conspiracy using magic and terror to manipulate the Kikuyu psychologically into a return to savagery."[42]

While Leakey's conceptions of Mau Mau oathing and de-oathing are addressed in his Mau Mau-era monographs and Carothers's attitudes are consolidated in his report, they are also reflected in the Rehabilitation Advisory Committee's 1954 secret dossier entitled "Report on the Sociological Causes Underlying Mau Mau with Some Proposals on the Means of Ending It."[43] Assembled by former administrator T. G. Askwith

---

[40] Daniel Branch, "On Her Majesty's Supernatural Service: Ethnography, Magic and the War against Mau Mau" (unpublished paper, November 2004), 7. See also, Daniel Branch, *Defeating Mau Mau*, 35–46.

[41] J. C. Carothers, *The Psychology of Mau Mau* (Nairobi: Government Printer, 1954), 6–18. In the 1930s, the issue of Africans' "mental aptitudes" was a hot topic in anthropological circles. In the 1930s, Dr. L. H. Gordon, a British psychiatrist, conducted studies on the "mental aptitudes" of Africans using black Kenyans as research subjects. See L. H. Gordon, "The Mental Capacity of the African," *Journal of the African Society* 33.132 (July 1934): 226–243. Gordon's work was met with a call from the International Congress of Anthropological and Ethnological Sciences for further investigation along anthropological lines. See LSE IAI/2, International Institute of African Languages and Cultures Bureau Minutes, 26 October 1934. Gordon's work was sharply criticized by Louis Leakey, Bronislaw Malinowski, and J. H. Oldham, administrative director of the International Institute for African Languages and Culture, for its excessive and outdated focus on cranial capacity. See LSE MALINOWSKI/9/13, letter from Bronislaw Malinowski to the *Times of London*, 8 January 1934. See also, Jock McCollough, *Colonial Psychiatry and "the African Mind"* (Cambridge: Cambridge University Press, 1995).

[42] Berman, *Control and Crisis*, 356.

[43] KNA VP/2/2/21, Report on the Sociological Causes Underlying Mau Mau with Some Proposals on the Means of Ending It.

who was commissioner of Community Development during Mau Mau, the committee also included Harry Thuku and Leakey as members and "was advised by J. C. Carothers."[44] The committee's avowed aim, carried out in a series of ten meetings, was "to inquire into and report on the sociological causes of Mau Mau," the term "sociological" having been "taken to embrace economic, psychological, political, and religious causes in their widest sense."[45] Focusing on Mau Mau oathing among the Kikuyu, the report offered a range of hypotheses about and recommendations for effectively dealing with psychological and/or sociological elements of Mau Mau.

First, the report addressed the character of Mau Mau oathing, reading it as an aberration of "Kikuyuness" and as rejection of Kikuyu tradition. Complementing official colonial discourse (or propaganda) about Mau Mau, the committee members wrote, "it is made plain that the filthy practices of the Mau Mau oath are a complete flouting of all the old traditions" and that the "object must be, and the effect certainly is, to make the initiate feel himself completely cut off from his old associates and loyalties dedicated to a new dispensation." The report also suggested a fluidity to oathing practices, asserting that "the oath became progressively more bestial as the atrocities of Mau Mau increased. It is presumably felt that the more horrible and inhuman the crimes to be performed, the more loathsome and inhuman must be the initiation."[46]

Second, the report advocated and enumerated a "screening" process for identifying Kikuyu who had taken the Mau Mau oath that entailed repeated, public interviews of suspected Mau Mau conducted by teams of screeners led by local headmen. Following the colonial chain of command, the headmen would then advise the district commissioner via the local district officer and chief of the results of the interviews and suggest a course of action as regarded the suspect. The report stipulated that the headman should report "(a) that they are satisfied that the person concerned is not Mau Mau; or (b) that he is a minor offender who should be allowed home on safeguards; or (c) that they recommend a detention order be issued against him."[47] Significantly, the committee also urged that that "parallel steps on the same general lines should be taken in Nairobi and the Rift Valley," and oral and archival evidence indicates that Mau

---

[44] Berman, *Control and Crisis*, 359.
[45] KNA VP/2/2/21, "Introduction," 1.
[46] KNA VP/2/2/21, "Chapter I: Certain Recommendations on Matters of Urgency," 1.
[47] Ibid., 6.

Mau screenings were conducted according to these recommendations in Machakos District as well.[48]

Third, again reflecting dominant colonial discourse, the committee attended to the "psychology" of Mau Mau and the affective states that they thought accompanied Mau Mau oathing and de-oathing, drawing connections among Mau Mau, the supernatural, superstition, disorder, and fear. In a section entitled, "Fear of the Oath," the report suggested that "disillusioned" Mau Mau participants were "afraid to break their oath" and attributed this fear, particularly among "less sophisticated and pagan element ... which forms most of the striking force of Mau Mau," not to an "expectation of Mau Mau vengeance" but rather to a "superstitious dread." The "superstitious awe" with which the average Mau Mau participant regarded oaths – both the Mau Mau oath and the "cleansing" oath – the report posited, had resulted in "instances ... when a man first cleansed has been visibly overjoyed to be rid of his burden."[49] According to the committee members, the disorder of Mau Mau and its remedies were relatable to the affective states – fear, awe, and joy – that each produced.

Fourth, reflecting the strain of colonial discourse that opposed the "pagan" retrogression of Mau Mau to the enlightenment of colonial Christianity, the report employed a Christian idiom to highlight "confession" as the touchstone of the de-oathing of Mau Mau participants and to stress the need for such confessions to be voluntary and sincere. It stipulated,

> The most important and valuable feature in reclaiming a person from Mau Mau is his confession, if freely and voluntarily made in the presence of people who know him well. In many cases if this is followed by a cleansing ceremony properly conducted, this may be of great value in setting a seal of sincerity upon his confession, and also to free his mind and conscience from the oppressing burden of the Mau Mau oath.
>
> It was agreed that a cleansing ceremony was only valuable for a person who believed in it, and while a person might be advised to take it, he should never be forced to do so.[50]

Accordingly, the committee recommended a series of steps reminiscent of Christian adult baptism for the cleansing of confessed Mau Mau

---

[48] Ibid. See also, Berman, *Control and Crisis*, 359–361; Elkins, *Imperial Reckoning*, 62–63; Greet Kershaw, *Mau Mau from Below* (Nairobi: East African Educational Publishers, 1997), 250.
[49] KNA VP/2/2/21, "Chapter I: Certain Recommendations on Matters of Urgency," 3.
[50] Ibid.

participants. They advocated that persons who confessed before colonial authorities to having participated in Mau Mau should then a make a formal and public confession, and be

> cleansed by either a Gutahikio [Kikuyu] Christian or Mohamedan ceremony, after which he should be exhorted to take a Githathi or similar Christian or Mohamedan oath, undertaking never again to participate in the Mau Mau movement.[51]

The report contained a strong emphasis on the importance of keeping screenings and de-oathings local, both in terms of those responsible for overseeing them and in the particular modes cleansings should take. The committee members "generally agreed" that "the degree of utility of the *Guthahiko* ceremony or any other form of cleansing is bound to differ widely according to the individual, the locality, and the social and educational development of the persons concerned." The report advocated a policy in which the details of de-oathing ceremonies "should be left mainly in the hands of the local authorities in any area, subject to the exercise of a benevolent supervision by the provincial and district administration."[52]

The tripartite remedy of screening-confession-cleansing appealed to Europeans as a solution to Mau Mau, and the de-oathing campaign developed in Ukambani followed the lines laid out in the Rehabilitation Advisory Committee's report.[53] In keeping with the committee's recommendations, Mau Mau de-oathing in Machakos District had a local character. Kamba chiefs were appointed specifically to participate in Mau Mau screening and de-oathing activities. Documentary and oral sources indicate that in Mbitini, for example, Simeon Musyoki was appointed chief "to fight the Mau Mau oath."[54]

In Ukambani, Mau Mau cleansing oaths were themselves a form of the well-known and widely respected Kamba oath, *kithitu*. During the rebellion, cleansing *kithitu* were administered by preexisting specialist *kithitu* administrators in Machakos. Screening and de-oathing activities were broadly enforced upon Kamba returning to Machakos from Nairobi or other Kikuyu-heavy areas, reflecting colonial officials' concerns that

---

[51] Ibid., 4.
[52] Ibid.
[53] See Bruce Berman and John Lonsdale, "Louis Leakey's Mau Mau: A Study in the Politics of Knowledge," *History and Anthropology* 5.2 (1991): 142–204. Though by the mid-1950s, "de-oathing" was falling out of favor in Kikuyu areas, it was undertaken in Ukambani.
[54] Nottingham, "Sorcery," 2. P. K. M., Welfare, September 2004.

migrant Kamba workers would have been "infected" by the Mau Mau through their exposure to Kikuyu, and would in turn spread the "contagion" throughout Machakos District. The perceived lethal power of *kithitu* and the existence of recognized specialists at the ready to administer the *kithitu*, together with the oath's flexibility, likely contributed to the selection of *kithitu* as the anti-Mau Mau oath of choice in Ukambani.

According to documentary sources, a "system of confessions and free pardons for those who had merely taken the [Mau Mau] oath and had otherwise not been deeply involved" was developed to deal in part with Mau Mau in Machakos District.[55] Oral sources, in contrast, describe a much more comprehensive and coercive program in which returning Kamba migrants were routinely stopped as they crossed in Ukambani and adult men and women were collected by local Kamba authorities and brought to administrative centers throughout the region where they were subjected to intensive interviewing before being required to undergo anti-Mau Mau *kithitu*.[56]

Yet in Ukambani, colonial concerns with Mau Mau and the supernatural went beyond oathing to include witchcraft as well. Documentary and oral sources indicate that both British and black Kenyan colonial authorities in Kamba areas came to regard supernatural challenges to the state's authority as emanating not only from the activities of Mau Mau insurgents themselves but also from the witches and witchdoctors adhering to the Mau Mau cause and from those *uoi* practitioners taking advantage of the period's instability to practice more broadly and fiercely. Documentary sources suggest that Mau Mau confessions "snowballed," and also that

> in addition to their stories of Mau Mau oathings many of the women concerned began to come out with strange tales of "Witchcraft" practices, producing to the Chief articles which they alleged were in the habit of using to bring about death and injury to others.[57]

Oral sources concerning Mau Mau and *uoi* in Ukambani bleed together even more messily, suggesting that the connections between *uoi* and Mau Mau emerged in even higher relief in the mind-sets and experiences of ordinary Kamba people than they did in the conceptions of colonial authorities. In turn, overlaps in the Kikamba terminology used to describe

---

[55] Nottingham, "Sorcery," 2.
[56] E. M. M., Tawa, September, 2004; M. K., Tawa, September 2004; W. N., Machakos, September 2004.
[57] Nottingham, "Sorcery," 2.

Mau Mau oaths, Kamba oaths to cleanse Mau Mau, and Kamba oaths to cleanse *uoi* further reflect the mixing of Mau Mau and witchcraft in Ukambani, underscoring the characteristics shared both by the oaths and by the types of situations that precipitated their employ.

SORTING THROUGH KITHITU: THE PERCEIVED POWER OF MAU MAU-ERA KAMBA OATHING

In discussing Mau Mau in Machakos, many informants name both the Mau Mau oath and the oath to *cleanse* Mau Mau as "*kithitu cha* Mau Mau" or the "*kithitu* of Mau Mau," and the processes of taking or "eating" the Mau Mau oath *and* the oath to cleanse Mau Mau as *kuusya kithitu*. Significantly, they also refer to the anti-*uoi* cleansing oaths administered by "government witchdoctors" as part of state-sponsored witch-cleansing campaigns aimed to break the ties between Mau Mau and witches and witchdoctors in Machakos as *kithitu cha Mau Mau*.[58] In other instances, informants engage more specific, yet still overlapping terms, citing *ng'ondu*, a type of *kithitu* to counter *uoi*, alternately as an oath used to cleanse Mau Mau and as an oath used to cleanse a *mu'unde m'uoi*.

When analyzed deeply, this terminological overlap can be read as indicative of an imbrication in the conceptual, procedural, and practical elements of Mau Mau oathing, oaths to cleanse Mau Mau, and oaths to cleanse *uoi*. It also points to some of the ways in which Mau Mau and witchcraft became intertwined, both in the understandings of colonial authorities and of ordinary Kamba. And these overlapping terms highlight some of the ways in which both Mau Mau and *uoi* derived their power – in official colonial narratives and in the recollections of ordinary Kamba – from their ambiguity.

First, the use of the terms *kithitu cha Mau Mau* and *ng'ondu* to talk about Mau Mau oathing, Mau Mau de-oathing, and oaths to cleanse *uoi* suggests commonalities in the ways in which Mau Mau and *uoi* were conceived. Violence and separation are central, common threads underlying the narratives of both Mau Mau and witchcraft. Certainly in the minds of colonial authorities and also in stories of many Kamba people both Mau Mau and witchcraft, or *uoi*, were treated as bearers of violence. Both the violence of Mau Mau and the violence of witchcraft, in addition to doing material and spiritual harm, also caused significant divisions within communities and rendered those involved in Mau Mau

---

[58] The Machakos "witch-cleansing" campaigns are discussed in detail in the next chapter.

and/or *uoi* activities literal and figurative outsiders whose membership in recognized communities, be it the local community of the village or the colonial community of "loyal" subjects, needed to be restored through cleansing. Because Mau Mau and witchcraft wrought violence and separation and could be employed to reinforce each other, they could be dealt with through overlapping oathing practices.

In a related vein, terminological overlap suggests that Kamba people accorded a killing capacity to the Mau Mau oath, to oaths used to cleanse Mau Mau, and to oaths used cleanse *uoi*. A key element of any oath that falls under the rubric *kithitu* is its ability to instantly kill an adherent who later violates the oath. References to Mau Mau oaths, oaths to cleanse Mau Mau, and oaths to cleanse *uoi* as *kithitu* and/or *ng'ondu* suggest that Kamba people took seriously the bonds of all of these oaths even though the movements precipitating their employ originated outside Kamba communities.

Second, the use of *kithitu cha Mau Mau* and *ng'ondu* to discuss Mau Mau oaths, oaths to cleanse Mau Mau, and oaths to cleanse *uoi* points to additional shared characteristics of Mau Mau and *uoi*. Like violence and separation, secrecy and ambiguity were also common themes in stories of Mau Mau and *uoi*. Despite years of anthro-administrative inquiry, Kamba witchcraft was still in many ways obscure to British colonial authorities during the 1950s, due in large part to Kamba people's attitudes towards *uoi* as a power and a substance necessarily shot through with secrecy.

Further, as colonial discourse about Mau Mau among the Kikuyu drew strong connections among Mau Mau, the subversion of Kikuyu "traditional" religion, and Kikuyu black magic or witchcraft, it also concentrated on the killing capacity of Kikuyu Mau Mau oaths. It is not surprising then that with the persistent obscurity of Kamba *uoi* and the consistency of colonial attitudes about the ambiguous divide between "black magic" and "white magic," British colonial authorities perceived relations between Kamba Mau Mau and Kamba witchcraft, read Kamba Mau Mau oaths as a corrupted *kithitu*, and agreed to the use of *kithitu* and/or *ng'ondu* to deal with the intertwined problems of Mau Mau and *uoi* in Machakos.

While the oral encyclopedia of Kamba *uoi* is common knowledge to nearly every adult Kamba, the particulars of Mau Mau among the Kamba were and remain ambiguous in large part because the pledge to secrecy and the killing capacity of Mau Mau *kithitu* rendered their details unspeakable. Like British colonial authorities, Kamba people often read *uoi* and Mau Mau as constituent elements of the same situation of disorder. It is logical then that they viewed Mau Mau and *uoi* as rectifiable through the same or similar varieties of *kithitu*.

The overlaps between Mau Mau oaths, oaths to cleanse Mau Mau, and oaths to cleanse *uoi* were not simply semantic and conceptual, however. They were procedural as well. First, known or suspected Mau Mau and known or suspected witches were collected by the same sorts of authorities and in similar manners during the mid-1950s. Once brought to administrative centers, alleged Mau Mau and alleged witches were interviewed by colonial authorities in an effort to determine the scope of their activities. And similar procedures to cleanse Mau Mau and witchcraft, or *uoi*, were carried out by specially appointed "experts" in oath administration recognized as such both by colonial authorities and by ordinary Kamba.

Overall, the killing power accorded *kithitu* made it usable as a way of oathing Kamba *to* the Mau Mau movement. But at the same time, the same power rendered varieties of *kithitu* rehabilitative tools for de-oathing the Mau Mau adherent and for cleansing a *mu'unde m'uoi*. During Mau Mau, *kithitu cha Mau Mau* first created a separate community of Mau Mau adherents (willing or otherwise). But in the same context, the *kithitu* was also returned to its preexisting function, reforming broken communities and serving as "a remedy against any threat of disunity or conflict that can hit the community."[59]

THE COLONIAL STATE, OATHING, AND WITCHCRAFT

The Mau Mau-era cleansing ceremonies entailing *kithitu* and *ng'ondu* were not the first instances in which colonial officials had considered or used supernatural methods and means to deal with challenges to state authority related to supernatural beliefs and practices. Rather, the state's use of Kamba cleansing ceremonies and recognized Kamba ritual experts constituted another chapter in a broader, long-standing series of debates about the roles of local cosmologies and cultures, and how their concomitant supernatural practices and beliefs could, or should, play out in colonial governmentality. Prior to Mau Mau, colonial officials had considered whether legislation should distinguish between practitioners of black magic and white magic, if the administration should sanction the importation of witchdoctors when the presence of such practitioners was requested by local people, and if colonial law permitted the application of local cleansing oaths in addition to or in substitution for colonial legal sanctions against witches convicted under the Witchcraft Ordinance. The primary themes of these discussions reemerged in varying degrees in Mau

---

[59] Grignon, "The *Kithitu*," 5.

The World of Oathing and Witchcraft

Mau-era policies concerned with cleansing Mau Mau and witchcraft in Ukambani.

Interwar-era debates over the development and revision of the Kenya Witchcraft Ordinances included important discussions over whether the legislation should draw a distinction between white and black magic. The chief justice of the Supreme Court of Kenya voiced his opinion that the 1909 anti-witchcraft legislation was too broad and created "the possibility of bringing within the purview of the Ordinance healing or beneficent 'white' magic, or proceedings by priests of recognised religions which, though partaking of the supernatural are otherwise harmless."[60] In dealing with this issue, subsequent legislation constructed the creation of fear through witchcraft activities, in addition to witchcraft activities *writ large*, as a crime to be prevented and disciplined by the legislation. The legislation effectively set up a protection for witchdoctors practicing white magic, while outlawing the practice of black magic.

Distinctions between black magic and white magic are also present in correspondence transmitted among district officers and district commissioners in Kamba areas of Kenya and dating from the fifteen years before Mau Mau. Discussions concerned whether it would be efficacious and appropriate to "import" *waganga* from the coast to perform cleansings at the request of local Kamba populations. These discussions touched on issues such as the "reputation" of the *waganga*, on the sorts of services they would perform, on Kamba people's requests that such services be obtained, and how regularly Kamba people had employed *waganga* in the past. These strands are apparent in the 1940 letter from the district commissioner, Machakos, addressed to his counterpart in the coastal province of Kwale. The District Commissioner's office wrote,

> The people of Kikumbuliu Location North of Kibwezi have asked that Mwaka Tengu, a well known general practitioner of Mariakani should pay them a visit for the purpose of exorcising certain of their number – mainly women – who have recently become adepts in witchcraft.
>
> I would be most grateful if you would find out whether Mwaka Tengu is willing to undertake this task and what his charges would be.[61]

This letter touches on Mwaka Tengu's reputation, on the Kikumbuli Kamba's desire to employ him, and the purposes for which they wished

---

[60] KNA AP/1/1009, letter from R. W. Hamilton, Chief Justice, to the Chief Secretary, 22 August 1917.
[61] KNA CC/13/39, letter from the Office of the District Commissioner, Machakos, to the District Commissioner, Kwale, 21 November 1940.

to "import" the "witchdoctor." An earlier letter from the district commissioner, Kwale, to the district officer, Kitui, also attends to these issues. The district commissioner wrote,

> With reference to your note on the subject of Mwakatengu, an mganga of this district, I have made enquiries and have found Mwakatengu is a well known and respected mganga, whose principal function among Duruma (the tribe to which he belongs) is the administration of native oaths. If the necessary traveling expenses are forthcoming, I will endeavour to persuade him to visit Kitui.[62]

These letters foreground another element of relations between the state and the supernatural – the bureaucratization of the witchdoctor and of magical activities. With the sort of spectacular matter-of-factness characterizing much colonial discourse about African witchcraft, the letters evidence classically bureaucratic concerns with efficiency and finances, and cast Mwakatengu as in the employ of the state. Thus, the cleansings of Mau Mau and of witches in 1950s Machakos were not the initial instances in which discussions of cleansing, oathing, and witchdoctors were woven into the fabric of colonial governmentality.

The five years immediately preceding Mau Mau also witnessed a heated debate about oathing that formed part of broader exchanges among members of the colonial administration about the inefficacy of the Witchcraft Ordinance and the extent to which "Native Law and Custom" could be legally employed to deal with witchcraft and related crimes. The discussion is captured in an exchange of letters between district and provincial authorities in Kikuyuland and the Nairobi administration. It came about in part through a case put forward by a district commissioner in Central Province in response to an earlier, but oft-ignored, request from Nairobi that district officers and commissioners forward the particulars of witchcraft cases to Nairobi.

In the district commissioner's jurisdiction, a Kikuyu man had been tried and convicted under the Witchcraft Ordinance. However, while this might seem an acceptable result to members of the colonial administration, the district commissioner explained that a conviction under the colonial law was essentially meaningless to Kikuyu people because it offered no way of cleansing the convicted witch so he could be reintegrated

---

[62] KNA CC/13/39, letter from the District Commissioner, Kwale, to the District Officer, Kitui, 12 November 1936.

The World of Oathing and Witchcraft   179

into the local community. As the district commissioner explained to his provincial higher-ups,

> Unfortunately the Witchcraft Ordinance does not allow a settlement of this case which is acceptable in Kikuyu law. The Native Tribunals of this District feel strongly that when a man has been convicted of witchcraft and sentenced to imprisonment, on his release his clan are entitled to order him to cleanse himself by taking the "Muma" oath.[63]

The district commissioner thus acknowledged the parallel Kikuyu system of law existing alongside the colonial one and recognized the authority that "Native Law and Custom" retained in the eyes of black Kenyans in his district.

Raising the issue to the next level of the administration and articulating its terms more sharply, the provincial commissioner of Central Province explained more fully the district commissioner's dilemma in a letter to the judicial adviser in Nairobi. He explained,

> The District Commissioner, Fort Hall considers that if a man is convicted under the witchcraft ordinance only imprisonment can be given, and that the cleansing ceremony would be illegal. As the cleansing ceremony is in Native eyes the essential part, he desires to uphold the authority of the elders in insisting on such ceremony.[64]

This extract points not only to the co-existence of colonial and local codes and authorities but also to how they typically came into conflict and contradiction. The provincial commissioner queried the legal adviser whether

> it would be legal and desirable in witchcraft cases, if instead of trying them under the Ordinance (the intention of which is entirely obscure to the Native mind) I would be proper to charge the accused with witchcraft contrary to Native law and custom, and if after evidence is led he is convicted, for the Tribunal to give the correct sentence in Native law i.e. "to take the Muma oath and pay two rams for cleansing purposes."[65]

The provincial commissioner's query thus reiterated long-standing colonial debates over the efficacy of the Witchcraft Ordinance vis-à-vis native

---

[63] KNA MAA 7/835, letter from District Commissioner, Fort Hall, to the Hon. Provincial Commissioner, Nyeri, 29 November 1946.
[64] KNA MAA 7/835, letter from the Provincial Commissioner, Central Province, to the Judicial Adviser, Nairobi, with copies to the District Commissioners, Fort Hall, Nyeri, and Kiambu, 4 November 1946.
[65] Ibid.

mentalities and suggested substituting "Native law and custom" in the *criminal* arena. Asserting the primacy of colonial law over Kikuyu codes, the judicial adviser replied,

> In view of the existence of a comprehensive statutory enactment, expressly designed to apply to cases of native witchcraft, it would not be legitimate, in my opinion, to invoke native law and custom, either in substitution for, or even in addition to, the law contained in the Ordinance. This is clearly a matter in which we are obliged to apply the maxim that statute ousts common law. If the Witchcraft Ordinance is unsatisfactory the proper remedy is to get it amended.[66]

These discussions of what role "Native law and custom" related to witchcraft should be allowed to play in the colonial administration of justice indicate that while in some instances local supernatural practices and authorities could be incorporated into colonial governance, they could not be permitted to supplant colonial codes. In certain circumstances, oathing and cleansing were regarded as bulwarks to law and order, but in other instances they could be read as a potential challenge to the primacy of the state legal system.

By the eve of Mau Mau, colonial debates about the utility and legality of oathing practices included a new element and resulted in increased legal strictures on oathing. With the beginnings of anti-colonial unrest in the late 1940s, colonial officials began to attribute a political character to oathing and then later to regard oathing as a political tool. In his legal history of politicized oathing in Kenya, Philip Durand argues that Mau Mau oathing had a different aim and nature from earlier oathing practices. He writes,

> when oathing began to be used to further political aims, the oath assumed a different character than when used in traditional form and for traditional purposes. The object of the oath, rather than to settle disputes, was to foster unity.[67]

While raising important issues about politicized oathing in Kenya, Durand is mistaken in regarding the settlement of disputes and the fostering of unity as separate issues and goals. Rather, the reintegration of disputants and malefactors and the concomitant restoration of community cohesion

---

[66] KNA MAA 7/835, letter from the Judicial Adviser to the Hon. Provincial Commissioner, Central Province, Nyeri, 15 April 1947.
[67] Philip P. Durand, "Customary Oathing and the Legal Process in Kenya," *Journal of African Law* 14 (1970), 19.

were and remain a key end of oathing. In the period before Mau Mau, colonial proponents of the use of local oathing practices in the resolution of conflicts – over land, family, witchcraft, and other matters – read oathing as a means to foster the sort of unity or community that would support the state's goals of the maintenance of law and order. During Mau Mau, many colonial officials regarded oathing as creating a new sort of unity or community centered on its direct, active opposition to the colonial state. In turn, by establishing programs that incorporated oathing to cleanse Mau Mau and witchcraft, members of the colonial administration drew upon oathing as a means by which to reformulate a "loyal" community and to foster unity against Mau Mau.

Concerns about political oathing contributed to revisions of the sections of the Kenya Penal Code related to oathing in 1950 and again in 1955. Sections on oathing in earlier additions of the code had focused primarily on disciplining oaths to commit "capital" or other "unlawful offences."[68] Reflecting colonial concerns and black Kenyans' assertions that people were being forced to take political oaths, the 1950 revisions introduced a new emphasis on the role of "compulsion" in oath taking. The code's stand on what constituted "compulsion" in the context of politicized oathing can be succinctly summed up as follows:

> Compulsion is a defence to a charge of taking an unlawful oath providing that the person oathed, within five days of its administration (or within five days after the termination of any physical force or sickness which prevents the person from acting), reports to the stipulated authorities (the police or a commanding officer if within the services) everything he knows about the matter, including person or persons by whom and in whose presence, and the place where and the time when the oath or engagement was administered or taken.[69]

The "compulsion" defense thus summarized also set up the bureaucratic procedure through which the state aimed to curb and combat anti-colonial oathing. Indeed, the paragraph echoes informant testimony describing the "interviews" which preceded cleansings of Mau Mau and *uoi*. The introduction of "compulsion" as a defense in cases of anti-colonial, political oathing thus served to give people who had participated – willingly or otherwise – in Mau Mau oathing a means by which to reestablish their loyalty to the state and to reintegrate themselves into the larger "loyal" community.

---

[68] *The Kenya Penal Code (1948).*
[69] Durand, "Customary," 21.

Another revision to the code, the 1955 Penal Code Amendment Ordinance, rendered administering "unlawful" oaths a separate, capital offense.[70] The penal code and related case law served to link political oathing with the broadly defined offense of sedition. The 1950 and 1955 changes to the Kenya Penal Code thus spoke to the context of Mau Mau oathing.

Overall, colonial concerns about Mau Mau oathing certainly took in political issues – such as challenges to the state's ability to maintain law and order and the constitution of anti-colonial communities – and the state drew upon law in efforts to deal with these issues. But many colonial officials also read Mau Mau as a supernatural situation that could be dealt with through methods and means like cleansing. The colonial state's practices of Mau Mau de-oathing were in various ways outgrowths of long-standing debates over what role local supernatural beliefs and practices should play in colonial governmentality. They were also part of far-reaching discussions over how the state should legally define and discipline local beliefs and practices.

In addition, the compulsion defense to charges of illegal oathing also suggests that many members of the colonial administration regarded Mau Mau oathing as motivated not simply by politics but also by people's fears of material and supernatural Mau Mau retribution. Since many colonial authorities in Ukambani saw witchcraft practices as contributing to the environment of fear and the fracturing of the "loyal" community in Kamba districts in much the same way that Mau Mau activities did, the witch-cleansings instituted in 1950s Machakos strongly resembled the bureaucratic model for de-oathing Mau Mau. The following chapter describes and analyzes the Machakos witch-cleansings querying their short- and long-term efficacy and asking to what extent they were a part of the larger imperial "fantasy" of the "civilizing mission" and to what degree they were an outgrowth of the particular socio-historical context of mid-1950s Machakos.

---

[70] See *The Laws of Kenya*, Ordinance No. 52 of 1955. The Ministry of African Affairs index of capital cases contains numerous cases of Mau Mau oathing. See Anderson, *Histories of the Hanged*.

8

Cleansing Ukambani Witches

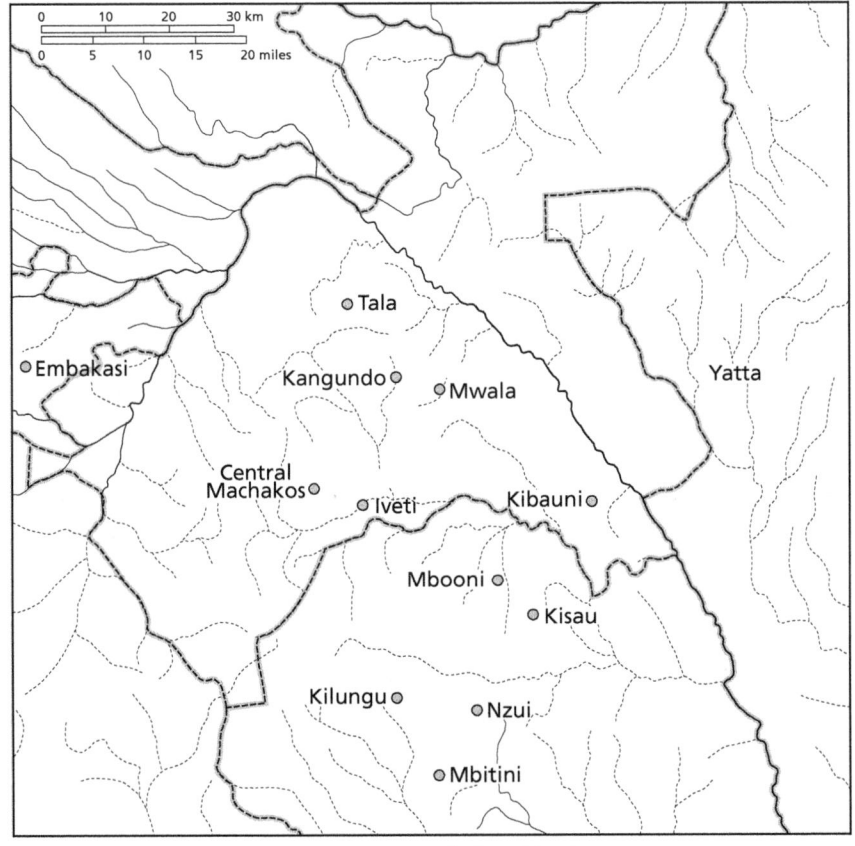

Locations in Machakos District

In the mid-1950s in Machakos, close to one thousand Kamba witches and witchdoctors responded to state officials' requests that they surrender their paraphernalia for public burning and publicly renounce witchcraft – a pair of practices that colonial authorities imagined would cleanse these practitioners of prior bad acts. In return, witches and witchdoctors could expect amnesty from the government and a clean slate from their neighbors. This campaign, referred to as the Machakos witch-cleansings, comprised the final set of "critical events" through which colonial authorities linked a breakdown in law and order to Kamba witchcraft beliefs and practices. While preceding colonial anti-witchcraft policies had sought to discipline witchcraft by denying its existence, or at least its efficacy, the Machakos witch-cleansings, in contrast, aimed instead to discipline witchcraft beliefs and practices by acknowledging and mobilizing their power.

Drawing on archival sources, this chapter examines in depth how and why the colonial administration in Machakos came to believe that Mau Mau and witchcraft were entangled in Ukambani. It addresses where the Machakos witch-cleansings fit in a history of state-sanctioned witchcraft activity and situates them within larger colonial debates over whether the state should endorse or forbid the use of supernatural methods and means to manage supernatural problems. By tracing how the production of anthropological knowledge about witchcraft in mid-century Machakos contributed to administrative policy and practice, this chapter demonstrates why the witch-cleansings took the particular forms that they did.

Accounts of the Machakos witch-cleansings exist outside the colonial archive as well, occupying significant *lieux de mémoire* in Kamba histories of Mau Mau and of the state's entanglement with *uoi* more broadly.[1] Accordingly, this chapter analyzes oral data and engages the central question left wanting by archival sources: *Why* did Kamba people submit themselves to a colonial campaign to cleanse *uoi*? In answering this question, it demonstrates how oral histories trouble the state's easy narrative of volition. It reveals the coercion underpinning the campaign, illustrating how the witch-cleansings were yet another permutation of the "routine violence" seeping through state-society relations during Mau Mau.[2]

This chapter also shows how oral histories disrupt state chronologies that situate the witch-cleansings in Machakos solely within the context of Mau Mau and/or exclusively under state actors' purview. Narratives of earlier witch-cleansing campaigns conducted by an evangelical church

---

[1] Nora, "Memory and History."
[2] Pandey, *Routine Violence*.

in Machakos and of anti-*uoi* activities undertaken in the district by non-Kamba cleansers from the coast during the rebellion each complicate the sociology of power in Ukambani.

ENTANGLING THE STATE AND THE SUPERNATURAL

The impetus for the Machakos witch-cleansings ultimately originated with the concerns of ordinary Kamba across the district that brought knowledge about the flourishing of *uoi* in the context of Mau Mau to the attention of chiefs and headmen in the district. For example, as an elderly Kamba woman explained, "This movement against all the witchcraft came from the people in the villages who went and complained to the sub-chiefs about it," while an ex-chief recollected similarly that reports of *uoi* and Mau Mau "came from the people themselves."[3] Another elderly Kamba man stated succinctly, "There was a lot of witchcraft during Mau Mau. There was an outcry from the people, so the Government had to take action."[4]

Kamba functionaries, in turn, broached the florescence of *uoi* to British administrators in their areas, suggesting that as the state had engaged in de-oathing Mau Mau, it should develop a campaign to cleanse the related threat of witchcraft. For example, during an August 1954 meeting of the Eastern Area Chiefs, Chief Muthoka introduced the possibility of state intervention in witchcraft, and in November the group agreed to set up protocols for dealing with witchcraft in Ukambani.[5]

Colonial records also indicate that the chief of Mbitini, Simeon Musyoki, was particularly influential in the organization of the Machakos witch-cleansings. As the 1954 Machakos District Annual Report explained, "it was thought gently but firmly to tackle the *uoi* problem. Chief Simeon Musyoki, the new Chief of Mbitini, gave the lead, which was followed in Nzaui and Kikumbulyu," after the problem of two thousand Kamba across two locations having taken the Mau Mau oath had been "cleaned up."[6]

In attending to the roles of chiefs like Musyoki, oral evidence also addresses some of the ways in which *uoi* and Mau Mau operated in

---

[3] Jeremy Newman, *Machakos Interviews*. Unpublished interview transcripts, 1974. Personal collection of François Grignon. Hereafter, *Machakos Interviews*. Mary Muendi, Ukia Mkt., 5 March 1974, and John Mutua, Kiteta Location, 3 November 1974.
[4] S. M., Mbooni, September 2004.
[5] KNA BB/PC/EST/12/15, Eastern Area Handing Over Report, 21 November 1955, "Witchcraft Appendix," 2.
[6] KNA DC/MKS 1/1/32, Machakos District Annual Report 1954, 9.

tandem across mid-century Machakos. For example, one informant explained,

> Chief Simeon (Musyoki) was brought to Mbitini to finish Mau Mau and *uoi*. The chief who was previously in Mbitini failed to do so.... *Uoi* practitioners were killing people the same way Mau Mau killed. The previous chief resigned because of threats from the Mau Mau.... The previous chief had a letter threatening him and asking him to step down. That's why they wanted to finish *uoi* at this time. People were killing using *uoi*.[7]

Lethal violence threatened and wrought by Mau Mau and *uoi* thus targeted administrative actors and harmed ordinary people.

Oral histories further emphasize direct connections between political and supernatural unrest, indicating that Mau Mau insurgents allied with *uoi* practitioners to employ power and paraphernalia against the state. Elderly interviewees from Nzawi and neighboring market areas explained that *muti* (a mélange of harmful *uoi* substances) and *nzevu* (*uoi* used to "confuse" its object) were used by Mau Mau adherents against administrative authorities – *muti* being applied more often to chiefs and headmen and *nzevu* to British officials.[8] Typical assertions were "People who were involved with Mau Mau got some *muthea* (the same thing as *muti* or *nzevu*) and then used it to fight the Europeans. They got this *muthea* from the witchdoctors" or "this *nzevu* was used by Mau Mau members to fight the European colonialists."[9] While much colonial propaganda turned on how the Emergency was evidence that black Kenyans had lost their senses, Kamba narratives address how Mau Mau used *nzevu* against members of the colonial administration in an effort to make them lose theirs.

But while Mau Mau may have deployed *nzevu* against British officers, various administrative documents indicate that colonial officials were *not* confused about the long history of witchcraft beliefs and practices challenging colonial order in Ukambani. J. C. Nottingham, who as a young district officer was the British authority most engaged in the planning and implementation of the witch-cleansings, concluded in the "Witchcraft Appendix" to the 1955 Eastern Area Handing Over Report, "I am convinced now that witchcraft, which was until recently the real government of Eastern Area, is the biggest single barrier to progress in Ukambani

---

[7] P. K. M., Welfare, September 2004.
[8] See Chapter 3 for explanations of *muti* and *nzevu*. Nzawi has a reputation as the most *uoi*-saturated location in Machakos. See Chapter 5.
[9] M. M., Machakos, September 2004; K. N., Nzawi, September 2004; M. M., Nzawi, September 2004.

today."[10] Persuaded of the degree to which witchcraft permeated Kamba communities and cognizant of widespread discussions of Kikuyu witchcraft being tied up in Mau Mau, British administrators were willing to take seriously the arguments of chiefs and headmen that Mau Mau in Ukambani "crept in not along modern politico-nationalistic channels, but through the dark sewers of sorcery and magic in the south" and was being supported by Kamba witches and witchdoctors.[11]

The enhanced emphasis on "closer administration," which the Machakos district commissioner cited as the "biggest weapon on the side of the Government" in fighting Mau Mau, further disposed British officials to follow the lead of Kamba authorities in simultaneously combating Mau Mau and cleansing *uoi*.[12] Discussing the witch-cleansings, Nottingham stipulated in the "Witchcraft Appendix," "I want to emphasise here that I was pushed into this by the Chiefs, who were in turn pushed into it by public opinion."[13] And fifty years later he reiterated, "The witch-cleansings were only possible because of the Emergency and the closer administration of the period."[14] The next section examines how though they were brought to bear by the concerns of ordinary Kamba and channeled through Kamba functionaries, the witch-cleansings were imagined and implemented through formal anthro-administrative inquiries undertaken by British officials.

THE ANTHROPOLOGY OF *UOI* ERADICATION

In writing that "on witchcraft all movements such as Mau Mau must be built," Nottingham voiced the perceptions of the colonial administration in Ukambani more generally.[15] This mind-set, in turn, precipitated the anthro-administrative inquiry through which the Machakos witch-cleansings were conceptualized and executed. In an article for the *Journal of African Administration*, Nottingham recalled that

> as clear indications came in that the Kikuyu and Kamba Mau Mau were using and adapting Kamba "witchcraft" in their campaign of subversion,

[10] KNA BB/PC/EST/12/15, "Witchcraft Appendix," 11.
[11] KNA DC/MKS 1/1/32, Machakos District Annual Report 1954, 9.
[12] CO 822/780, "Kenya Newsletter, No. 44," 19 May 1954. Nottingham recalled that during Mau Mau, "chiefs were functioning almost as junior D.O.s." J. C. Nottingham, Nairobi, January 2004. Hereafter, Nottingham Interview I.
[13] KNA BB/PC/EST/12/15, "Witchcraft Appendix," 2.
[14] Nottingham Interview I.
[15] KNA BB/PC/EST/12/15, "Witchcraft Appendix," 11.

the District Commissioner of Machakos felt that the opportunity which a properly controlled inquiry might give to learn something of its techniques and their alleged effects should not be missed and so he gave advice and instructions for carrying out an investigation.[16]

The formalized anthro-administrative inquiries into *uoi* carried out by Nottingham and by Government Sociologist Godfrey Wilson aimed to establish witchcraft as a "knowable" and, hence, "governable" category of administration bounded by colonial expertise and productive of fresh policies for combating sociopolitical unrest in Mau Mau-era Machakos.[17] The 1955 Machakos District Annual Report portrayed the campaign as growing out of Nottingham's and Wilson's inquiries and described the participants, the scope, and the procedures of the witch-cleansings. It explained,

> Mr. John Nottingham was District Officer, Eastern Area, and delved considerably into the problems of witchcraft.... [H]e amassed much useful knowledge, which has since been considered by the Government Anthropologist, Dr. Wilson. Further, lines of approach are being explored on the recommendations of Dr. Wilson. Of interest is the ceremony at Mumbumbuni in Kisau Location in October, 1955, when 700 witches, 50 warlock and 20 witchdoctors burnt their paraphernalia. In Western area there was an extra small experimental campaign into the realms of sorcery, and in December, 204 witches and 50 witchdoctors in the Wautu section Kilumbu openly admitted their arts and crafts and gave up a formidable number of implements.
>
> Nzawi in the Southern Area had previously conducted a big ceremonial burning of witches' paraphernalia in May and a large cleansing ceremony held at Makueni was attended by every woman in the settlement.[18]

Most generally, the annual report points to the depth and breadth of colonial concerns about "the extent to which both black 'Uoi' and white 'Uwe' witchcraft ha[d] a grip on the lives of the people" in Ukambani.[19] But on a deeper level, it indicates how in imagining and implementing the witch-cleansings, the colonial state aimed to discipline inherently secret witchcraft beliefs and practices through public performances of colonial governmentality.

---

[16] J. C. Nottingham, "Sorcery Among the Akamba," 2.

[17] In addition to reporting his own findings which did not vary significantly from Nottingham's, Wilson was tasked with critiquing Nottingham's work for officials in Nairobi. See BB/PC/EST/12/15, memo from Government Sociologist Godfrey Wilson to the provincial commissioner, Southern Province, 26 January 1956. [Enclosure]: Godfrey Wilson, "Witchcraft and Medicine in Machakos, 1955," 1–15.

[18] KNA PC/SP1/3/2, Machakos District Annual Report 1955, 6.

[19] Ibid.

PHOTOGRAPH 3. British and Kamba authorities at a Machakos witch-cleansing, circa 1955. J. C. Nottingham, second from right. (Photograph courtesy of J. C. Nottingham.)

Published four years after the conclusion of Machakos witch-cleansings, Nottingham's *Journal of African Administration* article depicts the campaign as a solidly non-magical administrative exercise. In the following paragraphs, the article elaborates the chronology, constitution, and carrying-out of the witch-cleansings, expanding and in some instances diverging from balder administrative narratives. It reads,

> As a result of the revelations of the inquiry, a considerable public demand arose for an effective, once for all, cleansing of the witches. The usual Kamba method of cleansing a self-confessed witch, of any category, is to recircumcise her, however advanced her age in the presence of her family. Apart from the Government and the Church, many of the more advanced Kamba were extremely angry when unconfirmed rumors came in that such ceremonies were in fact taking place, organized by families tired of waiting for the Government to decide what they were going to do. Needless to say such remedies were wholly unacceptable to Government. Another way employed with a witch who is wholly suspect but is not judged bad enough for *king'ole*, is to give her an *ndundu* oath within the family circle. This oath, which involves the slaughter by her relatives of a valuable bull, would never be idly given. In Kamba tradition, the witch who has been given such an oath, takes

her paraphernalia and hides it away very secretly, and from that day forth never touches it again. Were this custom still binding, it might have been a relatively unobjectionable means of cleansing witches who did not shelter beneath the Christian umbrella, but it no longer retains any force.

But all the methods contained seeds of their own inevitable failure in that magical elements were intrinsic in the ceremonies attached to them; nor were they universal in that they ignored the large numbers of at least nominal Christians concerned. A small African committee which had been trying to find a solution, eventually recommended a wholly unmagical approach which was finally adopted. At Mbumbuni in Kisau on 14th October 1955, all the witch-doctors and witches assembled together to a full-locational *baraza* of several thousand people; one by one they filed past a large pit and threw their trash on to the expectant furnace blazing beneath. They were then lectured by their Chief. Several of the more prominent ex-(we hope) witchdoctors gave demonstrations of the conjuring trickery by which they had duped their clients for many years. Government's ace of trumps, the Witchcraft Ordinance, was read and handed out, and three heavy sentences recently imposed under it were announced. This ceremony had a deep immediate effect: how long it will last is impossible to assess.[20]

Though vivid and detailed, the article's descriptions of the Machakos campaign are at odds with other archival and ethnographic accounts of cleansing *uoi*. First, the emphases on the destruction of witchcraft paraphernalia and on the debunking of practices of witchdoctors suggest that witch-cleansings were targeted primarily toward bought *uoi* rather than toward inherited *uoi*, which Kamba (and oftentimes colonial authorities) have typically perceived as the more virulent and pervasive form. Second, the descriptions of the witch-cleansings seem to reflect a very European perspective, one in which fire would be sufficient to destroy witchcraft without the addition of any supernatural mechanism.[21] But the destruction of paraphernalia alone is insufficient to cleanse a *mu'unde m'uoi* completely, and an oath is also required to complete the process. Third, in discounting the *ndundu* cleansing oath, the article underestimates the persistent power of oathing practices among Kamba people and the regularity of Kamba Christians' participation in oathing. Fourth, stripping Kamba magic from the witch-cleansings, the article instead privileges the

---

[20] Nottingham, "Sorcery," 11–12.
[21] Nottingham sprinkles his writings with Shakespearian quotes concerning the Macbeth "witches." In conversations with the author he offered the caveat that he knew nothing of African "witchcraft" before commencing the Machakos inquiry. Nottingham Interview I; J. C. Nottingham, Nairobi, June 2004. Hereafter, Nottingham Interview II.

"magic of the state" – bureaucracy and lawfare – as the primary power at work in the campaign.[22]

These discrepancies can be plausibly attributed both to the genre in which Nottingham was writing and to the limits of colonial knowledge production. From a discursive standpoint, they likely reflect simplifications of a complex cosmology and colonial situation made for the benefit of an audience without nuanced knowledge of Kenya who anticipated widely applicable narratives of colonial knowledge production and governmentality.[23] In narrating the witch-cleansings for a publication aimed to instruct in and celebrate British colonial bureaucracy, it would have been important to emphasize that imperial practice, not local "superstitions," held ultimate sway. Yet, at the same moment, such discrepancies could also indicate that colonial efforts to anthropologize witchcraft merely scratched the surface of *uoi*.

Finally, anthro-administrative accounts of the witch-cleansings all raise the following question: "*Why* did Kamba men and women agree to bring their paraphernalia to be burned and to subject themselves to this spectacular exercise in disciplinary colonial bureaucracy?" Drawing upon Euro-American images of witchcraft, Nottingham's article suggests that there is no concrete answer. He wrote, "the real motive behind their mass surrender of these objects is not easy to assess, though there have been similar episodes in the historical past; nor can one even now be absolutely sure that they were not deluded as those involved in the Salem tragedy in America."[24] When more than five decades later I posed the "why" question to Nottingham, he paused thoughtfully and said, "I don't really know. I suppose you would have to ask the people who brought it."[25] Following his suggestion, my research assistant and I asked elderly Kamba people to share their memories of the Machakos witch-cleansings, memories which wove together stories of the campaign that were in many ways different from those found documentary sources.

---

[22] Taussig, *The Magic*, 5; Comaroff and Comaroff, "Law and Disorder in the Postcolony," 30.
[23] Referencing Nottingham's article, editorial notes in the *Journal of African Administration* explained: "Some of the most difficult and delicate problems which confront administrative officers in Africa arise from widespread belief in witchcraft and the practice of sorcery. Witchcraft ... is still a most powerful influence in Africa today but it is not easy to obtain articles which describe its administrative and legal repercussions in a practical and dispassionate manner." See PRO CO 955/21, Editorial Policy and Editors' Notes, January 1959.
[24] Nottingham, "Sorcery," 2.
[25] Nottingham Interview II.

ROUNDING UP WITCHES AND BUREAUCRATS

Oral histories of elderly Kamba enliven bureaucratically oriented narratives, depicting "what it was like" to be cleansed of *uoi* in the fraught context of Mau Mau-era Machakos. They introduce new actors and attitudes into the supernatural state of Ukambani and shed light on precisely how witches came to be cleansed. They offer accounts of violent coercion that crucially contest colonial claims about the volitional nature of the witch-cleansings. In doing so, recollections of the witch-cleansings exhibit dissonances not simply with the documentary record but also among themselves.

At first glance, it might seem that such dissonances would preclude using oral histories to tease out more meaningful stories of the Machakos witch-cleansings. But, as Justin Willis explains, dissonances themselves offer historical information. He writes,

> Dissonances can tell us very much both about the ways in which people structure and understand the past – that is, about ways in which they turn disparate fragments of knowledge into history....
>
> Dissonances often show that people are aware of conflicting interpretations of the past and that they have a considerable and diverse range of historical knowledge.[26]

As in Willis's work on rural Tanzania, the dissonances in stories of the Machakos witch-cleansings reveal ways of being and knowing, both past and present. In much the same way that documentary sources like Nottingham's article and official reports have been shaped by attention to audience, aims, and protocols of production, so too have oral histories been actively considered rather than simply recounted.

While the oral histories of elderly Kamba who had been employed by the colonial administration during the 1950s concur in many respects with explanations of the witch-cleansings found in colonial documents, they include important dissonances with the archival record, attending strongly to coercion and complicating notions of colonial authority. For example, the recollections of an informant who served as an assistant chief in Mbitini from the Mau Mau period into the 1980s concentrate on the bureaucratization of witch-cleansing and concomitant coercion.

---

[26] Justin Willis, "Two Lives of Mpamizo: Dissonance in Oral History," *History in Africa* 23 (1996): 321–322.

Describing himself as having been "in charge" of the witch-cleansings in his area, the former functionary noted,

> I had people in every village who were working for the government to find out who had *uoi* and a manager whose work it was to know all the practitioners in a village, and then to take those people to their chiefs. The managers brought all the practitioners in the village to their sub-chiefs.... They [practitioners] used to leave their paraphernalia at the chief's office. It was burned.... There was not one big *baraza*. *Uoi* was burned Monday–Friday from 10 A.M. to 4 P.M. The *uoi* was brought and burned continuously.[27]

This account sets up a hierarchy of witch-finding and a new category of expert, the "witchcraft manager," tying each to the state's bureaucratization of activities that were once the sole, impermeable purview of Kamba diviners and elders. Though he acknowledged the role of Kamba elders in selecting witchcraft managers, explaining that "the *atumia* chose people," the ex-assistant chief privileged his own authority over the selection process noting, "those people were approved by the assistant chief."[28] Rather than situating the primary, active responsibility for the witch-cleansings in British officials, his account instead establishes a more localized pyramid of administrative power.

The ex-assistant chief explained further that British officials' participation in the witch-cleansings was largely confined to offering formal permission for their Kamba subordinates to undertake the campaign. He noted,

> We got permits from the D.O. so that if a *uoi* victim went to report the *uoi* there would be no consequences. The practitioners were beaten hard if they refused to surrender their paraphernalia and they could not report this to the D.O. and D.C. because there was good cooperation with the chief and the assistant chief. The D.C. and D.O.s were aware of the cleansings.[29]

Echoing this account, an ex-headman explained how the witch-cleansings were similarly authorized in his location. He noted, "First the headman met with the chief, the chief informed the D.O. in Makueni, and he gave the authority to look for *uoi* practitioners."[30]

---

[27] P. K. M., Welfare, September 2004. The phrase "Monday-Friday from 10 A.M. to 4 P.M." is likely this informant's backward projection. The phrasing suggests that the "witchcraft" burnings were all-day affairs.
[28] Ibid.
[29] P. K. M., Welfare, September 2004.
[30] M. M., Nzawi, September 2004.

PHOTOGRAPH 4. Burning witchcraft in Mau Mau–era Machakos. (Photograph courtesy of J. C. Nottingham.)

Oral histories of "ordinary" Kamba outside the administration's employ bear out these ex-officials' contentions. For example, one informant indicated that

> Assistant chiefs organized it [cleansing] with the *atumia*. They sent the youth to bring the *uoi* practitioners.... Because they were known, they were all gathered up and taken to the chief's office at Nziu for cleansing. The *atumia* knew who the witches were.... The D.C. would give the chief a permit.[31]

A contemporary similarly noted, "He [the district commissioner] gave a '*barua*' – a permit, a letter, at a public meeting announcing the day on which the *uoi* practitioners would be taken."[32]

Responding to a question about the rationale behind such formal state sanction, the ex-assistant chief noted that it was intended to protect Kamba functionaries. He elaborated,

> We feared being reported by the suspects of practicing *uoi* ourselves. If we had consent from the D.O./D.C., then we wouldn't have *uoi*. There

---

[31] K. N., Nzawi, September 2004.
[32] J. M. N., Nzawi, September 2004.

was a woman at the chief's place called Kathembe Mauguu ... an expert *mu'unde m'uwe* retained by the Government to identify *uoi*.[33]

Here the tension between knowledge of *uoi* and the practice of *uoi* again emerges, indicating that having too much knowledge could have disciplinary, or in the case of the witchdoctor Kathembe (who was later killed), even deadly consequences.

State sanction served also to protect Kamba functionaries from *colonial* law pertaining to *uoi*. Because the 1925 Witchcraft Ordinance rendered witchcraft *accusations* a crime, Kamba chiefs and headmen were restricted from identifying witches (even in the course of a governmental campaign) without the express permission of British officials, lest the alleged witches turn accusations back at them in the courts.

The oral histories of ordinary Kamba concentrate even more strongly on the violence – epistemological and practical, threatened and carried out – underpinning the witch-cleansings.[34] Coercive models of collection and cleansing described in these histories can be loosely grouped according to the methods they employed and the reactions they engendered or were intended to engender.

Numerous informants explained that people were driven to submit to the witch-cleansings through threats of arrest and of subsequent violence. As one elderly Kamba recalled, "The chief told the headmen that they should threaten the people involved with arrest and severe punishment."[35] A contemporary explained simply that practitioners had agreed to burn their paraphernalia because "they were threatened with beatings" while another elderly Kamba noted simply that refusal to surrender oneself for cleansing was "not an option."[36]

Elderly Kamba also noted that women were coerced with sexual torture into producing *uoi* paraphernalia. Recounting her experience, one woman explained, "It was all done at the chief's office. Sometimes soda bottles were inserted in women's private parts to make them bring their *uoi*."[37] Her account is supported by that of a contemporary who elucidated,

> Some people denied having *uoi* and refused to surrender their *uoi* paraphernalia voluntarily. They were forced through beatings and torture. In

---

[33] Ibid.
[34] Maurice Bloch, *How We Think They Think: Anthropological Approaches to Cognition, Memory and Literacy* (Boulder: Westview Press, 1998).
[35] M. M., Nzawi, September 2004.
[36] M. N., Machakos, September 2004; K. N., Nzawi, September 2004.
[37] M. W., Machakos, September 2004.

some instances, objects like bottles would be inserted in women's private parts to force them to reveal their *uoi* after they experienced pain.[38]

Though always horrific, accounts of sexualized violence against alleged female *uoi* practitioners are perhaps less jarring if one recalls the regularity with which female *uoi* practitioners were subjected to punitive bodily harm via *king'ole* or vigilantism.[39] Given that the most powerful form of Kamba *uoi* resides squarely in women's bodies and is linked to their reproductive capacities, it is unsurprising that oral histories introduced tortuous methods of cleansing centered on women's reproductive regions.

Oral histories also present more mild varieties of coercion that referenced earlier models through which the state had dealt with dangerous, disorderly persons and through which the Kamba had managed *uoi*. For instance, addressing how alleged witches did *not* cheerfully volunteer to be cleansed, an informant noted, "They were coerced. The D.C., the chiefs, and the villagers coerced them. A date was set by which the witches had to be cleansed or leave the area." If they did not agree, he added, they were "chased away."[40]

This statement reflects both Kamba and colonial precedents for disciplining witches and the spatially fraught context of Mau Mau. While banishing an unrepentant *mu'unde m'uoi* from her (or his) village was an alternative to *king'ole* killing, colonial legislation offered the option of dealing with recidivist "witches" and other intractable supernatural practitioners by "shifting" them from their home locations to opposite ends of the colony or at least to the administrative *boma*. Further, to many people in Ukambani threats of expulsion likely conjured up images of the forced relocation of Kikuyu into "safe villages" and of the internment of known/suspected/potential Mau Mau in concentration camps far from home.[41]

Finally, an elderly Machakos man attributed a mercenary quality to the witch-cleansings, depicting them as a money-making enterprise on the part of local members of the administration. He explained,

> This was also the time of the movement against witchcraft. It didn't mean that witchcraft had increased. Those people just wanted money and this was one way of getting it. People were threatened and told to pay Shs.30/- [shillings, or *shilingi* in Kiswahili]. They were taken into the Chief's

---

[38] W. N., Machakos, September 2004.
[39] See also, the discussion in Chapter 4 about a female *mu'unde m'uoi* subjected to sexualized torture.
[40] J. N. K., Kilungu, September 2004.
[41] See Elkins, *Imperial Reckoning*, 233–236.

centers and questioned about the *kithitu* and other charms. Shs.30/- had to be paid before release and for being treated as a normal person. Those who did not pay were taken away to camps as at Kibaoni with an askari and the next day they would come back hungry and most of them then agreed to pay and were then released. Some suspected of taking the oath were arrested and treated in the same way. It was mostly old men and women who were the victims and after the money was collected it was taken to the DO's office. There was a time also when the askaris were taking young girls and one was engaged and her man came to try to get her released and he was shot. The askari said the DO had told them to shoot when guarding. The DO then stopped that regulation.[42]

The threat and actuality of physical displacement stand out clearly in this narrative alongside less typical notions about Mau Mau, witchcraft, and money. Though uncharacteristic of oral histories of the era, statements attributing a mercenary quality to the witch-cleansings nonetheless reflect important attitudes about the colonial state as a primarily economic enterprise and hint at the ways in which Kamba people might have read the state's avowed concerns with local problems as excuses for intervention and extraction.

Yet although strands of violence, displacement, and discord shoot through oral histories of the witch-cleansings, many elderly Kamba cited the celebrations that accompanied the conclusions of the campaign and retain the opinion that the witch-cleansings were useful. Typical statements are that the campaign "was a good idea because it 'finished' *uoi*" or that the witch-cleansings were "thought to be a good idea because *uoi* is not a good practice... [T]he Government had the authority and ability to enforce measures."[43] Descriptions of the public, locational celebrations that put an official, participatory stamp on the conclusion of the campaign are also common. For example, one elderly Kamba explained,

> *Uoi* was bad. The policy was to finish *uoi* and Mau Mau. The final day was at Malala. There was a gathering to celebrate ... with meat, etc. People were told to love each other.... Each sub-location had to produce a bull. This meant that everyone contributed and went to witness the end of the Mau Mau and the witch-cleansings.[44]

Oral histories suggest that despite their coercive and oft-times violent character, colonial efforts to cleanse *uoi* in the context of Mau Mau were taken seriously by ordinary Kamba people and that many read the Machakos

---

[42] *Machakos Interviews*, Zachayo Mulandi Ngao, Kiteta Location, 2 November 1974.
[43] L. N. N., Kangundo, August 2004; E. M. M., Tawa, September 2004.
[44] P. K. M., Welfare, September 2004.

witch-cleansings as authentic and efficacious. However, not everyone in Machakos regarded the witch-cleansings favorably. The next section addresses how the campaign raised the ire of members of the district's evangelical churches by shining a spotlight on the persistence of *uoi*, a paganism of which they thought their adherents had already been cleansed.

CHURCH CHALLENGES AND PRE-MAU MAU CLEANSINGS

With varying degrees of specificity, documentary and oral sources demonstrate how state actors and fundamentalist Christians clashed over cleansing witches. The recollections of elderly Kamba men and women, many of them Africa Inland Mission (AIM) members from central Machakos, complicate narratives of this conflict even further by introducing new chronologies and conceptions into the history of cleansing *uoi* in Ukambani. Some informants indicated that the Mau Mau-era campaign was not the first instance of witch-cleansings being undertaken by white authorities and their Kamba collaborators in Machakos. In turn, AIM adherents from in and around Mbooni and Kilungu in particular offered accounts that denied not simply the efficacy of *uoi* – and to a lesser extent of Mau Mau – but the presence of *uoi* and Mau Mau in the district at all.

The AIM's history in Machakos, together with its overall "faith and prayer" character, contoured adherents' speech and silence regarding cleansing.[45] Although missionary efforts overall were considerably less successful in Ukambani than they were in nearby Kikuyu areas, Machakos had been the "bailiwick" of the AIM since the opening of the colonial era.[46] The first AIM missionaries arrived at Nzawi in 1895 where they encountered the fearsome Kamba prophetess, Syombesa, who is widely reputed to have used her supernatural powers to "chase away" the pioneer missionaries and to kill their leader.[47] Once a foothold was established in Machakos, AIM missionaries treated conversion not as a straightforward issue of rejecting paganism in favor of Christianity, but as a totalizing substitution of a primitive lifeway for a "modern" lifestyle and "rational" mentality in which witchcraft could play no part.[48]

[45] Tignor, "Kamba Political Protest," 244.
[46] Ibid.; The Africa Inland *Mission* later became the Africa Inland *Church*, and as such many Kamba refer to it by that name even when speaking of the colonial era.
[47] Bob Odalo, "Syombesa Immortalized," *Daily Nation (DN)* 26 June 2006. And M. M., Nzawi, 2004.
[48] See also, David Sandgren, "Kamba Christianity." For a strongly mission-centered view, see James Muli Mbuva, "Witchcraft among the Akamba and AIM" (M. A., Fuller Theological Center, School of World Missions, 1992).

On the first level, these histories of Christianity and cleansing illustrate the charged character of conversion. In doing so, they point to the conflictual nature of relations between British colonial officials and church authorities, emphasizing the intrusion of religious adherence on administrative practice. More deeply, however, these sources show how claims of *forgetting* and/or *not knowing* themselves form a kind of knowledge.

In discussing cleansing *uoi* in the 1950s, some elderly Kamba brought up a series of earlier campaigns sponsored by the Mukaa branch of the AIM during the mid-1920s. As one Kamba woman pointed out, "People used to gather their *uoi* and burn it in the church compound."[49] Explaining how Christianity had led to a "deterioration of the strength of local *uoi*" and an increase in the purchase of *uoi* from Kitui and Tanzania, another elderly Kamba described the scope and aims of the Mukaa cleansings, noting,

> In 1924 I saw people burning *uoi* at the Mukaa AIC church. They used to burn it using open fire and I saw some of the paraphernalia "jump" from the fire. The same people who burnt their *uoi* later started going out [to Kitui and Tanzania] to purchase witchcraft.... They could not get it locally.... In 1926, most of the *uoi* in this area was burned.... The *kanisa* (church) ... organized it.... It was done after church services, not once, but several times.... Between 400 and 600 [people].... It was done occasionally for those who were accepted as Christians, new members of the church. It was done when they joined the church. After the generation that burned the witchcraft in 1926, there came another generation in the 1940s which started going back to *uoi*.[50]

Despite organizational similarities, the goals of Mukaa cleansings and those of the Mau Mau era were different. While the state-sponsored cleansings had the practical goal of reducing intertwined witchcraft and Mau Mau-related disorder, the Mukaa campaign was as much about ensuring a complete conversion by cleansing the spiritual stain of "pagan" *uoi* as it was about purging paraphernalia. And while oral recollections of the Mau Mau-era cleansings attended to coercion, many discussions of the Christian cleansings sought to emphasize the volitional nature of the burnings, and by extension, the voluntary nature of conversion. For example, the previous informant added, "People were told and advised that *uoi* was bad. The burning was not a 'must'. It was for those who accepted Christianity after the preaching against *uoi*. It was voluntary."[51]

---

[49] M. N., Kilungu, August 2004.
[50] P. M., Kilungu, August 2004.
[51] Ibid.

The Mukaa campaign relied on Kamba people who had been incorporated into the institutional hierarchy of the church and who worked with white church leaders. Christian *atumia* did a substantial part of the outreach work of convincing current and potential Kamba Christians to burn their *uoi* during the Mukaa cleansings. Describing the protocols of the Mukaa ceremonies the elderly man cited earlier noted,

> They [church leaders] went to every family. There were no headmen like there are now, and the chiefs and sub-chiefs were not Christians. There was no government policy on the matter, but the church representatives preached against *uoi*.... The church representatives were Africans. The Europeans used to live at the church station. There were also white ladies.... They used to take old Kamba men, the *atumia*. They were accompanied by white ladies.[52]

Responding to a question about who had *envisaged* the Mukaa cleansings, a contemporary replied that "people who became Christians" were burning *uoi* and that while "it was not a church policy," the churches "proposed that *uoi* should be burnt. They supported them because *uoi* brings loss."[53] Such accounts suggest that though Kamba people recognized white missionaries' engagement with the issue of *uoi*, they located ultimate responsibility for the Mukaa cleansings in Kamba Christians on the ground rather than in their institutional higher-ups in much the same way that they would situate primary authority and responsibility for the state-sponsored cleansings of the Mau Mau era in Kamba chiefs and headmen.[54]

While informant testimony indicates that Christians – both Kamba converts and AIM missionaries – engineered and executed the Mukaa campaign, both oral and written sources indicate that AIM authorities and adherents raised strenuous objections to the state-sponsored cleansings of the 1950s and denied the existence of *uoi* in their locations. For example, many elderly Kamba from in and around AIM bastions like Mbooni explained that they did not witness the cleanings of the 1950s because the church, which also precluded them from acknowledging the existence of *uoi*, discouraged attendance. In an explanation typical of that offered by many AIM adherents, an informant recalled that he did not

---

[52] Ibid.
[53] M. M., Tawa, September 2004.
[54] A complete survey of relevant district and provincial reports found no mention of the Mukaa campaign, suggesting that the "cleansings" were carried out without the state's participation, or perhaps even without its knowledge.

attend the cleansings because "Church people did not go.... Christians did not go because they did not believe in *uoi*." When asked if Christians thought the cleansings were pointless, he noted, "According to the Bible, Christians are not supposed to cooperate with non-Christians." Another elderly Kamba man reiterated the AIM's opposition, noting, "Some Christians did not go to the burnings because of their faith. The churches said that *uoi* was not 'true' and so the cleansings were 'false.'"[55]

Other AIM adherents typically asserted one of four lines: (1) neither *uoi* nor Mau Mau was present in their communities, (2) no relationship between Mau Mau and *uoi* existed in their locations, (3) they had no knowledge whatsoever of high-profile, well-publicized cleansings, or (4) witches and Mau Mau were cleansed on a wholly voluntary (and sometimes jolly) basis. For example, the following exchange with an elderly AIM informant incorporated three of these strands.

> Q: Was it difficult to get people to admit to having taken the Mau Mau oath?
> EKM: No, they admitted freely.
> Q: Did you hear stories or rumors about Mau Mau mixing with *uoi*?
> EKM: No. Here there was nothing like that.
> Q: Why might the Government have gotten that idea?
> EKM: No idea.
> Q: Were there *uoi* cleansings in other parts of Ukambani?
> EKM: Yes, in Kibauni, but I don't know anything.[56]

Overall, Kamba Christians' claims about the supernatural state of mid-century Machakos are as interesting for what they leave out as for what they include, suggesting not simply what many elderly AIM adherents thought should be left unsaid, but what sorts of knowledge they deemed unspeakable.[57]

Additional oral recollections demonstrated that religious belief intruded on administrative practice. A number of elderly Kamba recalled that chiefs and headmen who belonged to the AIM refused to participate in the cleansings, or to even admit that witchcraft existed in their locations. Explaining the perspective of a chief who belonged to the AIM and who had declined to have anything to do with the

---

[55] S. M., Mbooni, September 2004; J. K. K., Tawa, September 2004.
[56] E. K. M., Machakos, September 2004. For various perspectives on the importance of rumor, gossip, and sentiment in understanding occult issues, see Pamela J. Stewart and Andrew Strathern, eds., *Witchcraft, Sorcery, Rumors and Gossip* (Cambridge: Cambridge University Press, 2004).
[57] Rolph-Trouillot, *Silencing the Past*.

cleansings, an informant noted, "The Kiteta Chief refused because he said *uoi* didn't exist.... He said *uoi* didn't exist because he was a Christian.... There was only one denomination, the AIC, and its members did not involve themselves in the *uoi* cleansings."[58] Elaborating the relationship between AIM authority and administrative practice, a contemporary explained, "In our area people were not arrested because the chief refused to have people arrested. He said in his area there was no *uoi*. There was some influence from the AIC church because the village headmen were sometimes heading up the church as well."[59] Overall, the AIM stance on witchcraft resulted in Kamba who were both AIM congregants and colonial functionaries denying *uoi* and subsequently refusing to discipline it.

Nottingham's frustrated writings and his recollections fifty years after the cleansings also indicate that AIM ideology and efforts undermined administrative practice. Expressing frustration with the philosophical and practical intractability of the "evangelising bodies," he noted his "regret" that they "all combined to resist the Government's campaign by every means in their power."[60] Nottingham attributed objections of the AIM et al. to what he called "the split-second, blinding flash, conversion nature of their Christianity," writing, "they cannot believe that anyone who has come to know Jesus in their Church, and who has once been saved, could possibly still hide their witchcraft materials from them and come to Church."[61] The degree of the church's disillusioned anger in the face of the state-sponsored campaign was still so present in Nottingham's mind six decades later that he recounted readily how a pastor affiliated with the AIM's Mbooni branch had confronted him on the street shortly after the state-sponsored cleansings, calling Nottingham a "devil" for instituting them and claiming that he was appalled at having witches in his congregation so publicly exposed.[62]

It would seem that during the decades between the Mukaa and Mau Mau cleansings, the AIM operated under the misapprehensions that Kamba adherents had undergone a totalizing conversion and that witchcraft was thus a non-issue among them. The state-sponsored campaign

---

[58] E. M. M., Tawa, September 2004.
[59] W. N., Machakos, September 2004.
[60] In addition to the AIM, Nottingham cited the Gospel Furthering Fellowship which he termed a "militant splinter group" of the AIM, the Salvation Army, and the Seventh Day Adventists.
[61] KNA BB/PC/EST/12/15, "Witchcraft Appendix," 5.
[62] Nottingham Interview I.

shattered these notions, exposing the weakness of the church, revealing conversion as a veneer, and juxtaposing these failures with the relative success of the state. The AIM, however, was not the sole corpus of cosmological actors with roots outside Ukambani to become tightly wrapped up in cleansing *uoi* nor was the Mukaa campaign the only incidence of cleansing Kamba witches to occur outside the campaign organized by Nottingham. The following section explores how practitioners from the Swahili Coast came to cleanse *uoi* and provide Kamba people with protective magic during Mau Mau.

COASTAL CLEANSERS AND KAMBA CHIEFS

Oral histories offered by elderly Kamba from Nzawi and its environs introduce new cleansing agents into the history of combating *uoi* in Mau Mau-era Ukambani.[63] As one informant succinctly summarized,

> The chief took the *atumia* to the D.C. They wanted permission to "finish" *uoi*. They organized someone from Mombasa, an Mdigo.... Before no one had been brought from Mombasa.... He was famous.... There was no one equally effective in this area.... The *atumia* gathered witches and asked for their paraphernalia. It was collected, and the witches were given something to make them act possessed and fall down.[64]

Further complicating the sociology of power, recollections like that above reinforce the extent to which the state accorded active authority in managing *uoi* to Kamba functionaries and indicate the significant roles played by the *atumia* and ordinary Kamba in bringing about the cleansings. Casting cleansing as a forced exercise, these histories illustrate how coercion was not necessarily confined to blunt instruments, but entailed the violence of supernatural compulsion as well. They introduce important elements of Kamba cosmology – possession and protective magic – otherwise absent from accounts of Mau Mau,

---

[63] Among many communities in Kenya, cleansers or witchdoctors who are recruited from outside the community are believed to be more efficacious than "local" practitioners. Kamba people often cite practitioners from the Kenya coast like Kabwere as being particularly effective. See the discussion surrounding Mwaka Tengu in the previous chapter. In his well-regarded treatise on Kamba customary law in Machakos District, Penwill explained, "The Kamba themselves consider that the most potent wizards come from Tharaka, and speak highly of the work of the Nyamwezi (whom they regard as peculiarly allied to them and with whom they stand in a special relationship), the Giriama and the Duruma. The island of Pemba is recommended for advanced study." Penwill, *Kamba Customary*, 93.

[64] M. N., Kilungu, August 2004.

and broaden supernatural geographies, indicating that Kamba witches were both cleansed away from Machakos and cleansed by non-Kamba practitioners who were invited to the Nzawi area and who deployed their own protocols to counter Kamba *uoi*.

Oral histories indicate that cleansing was rooted in Kamba dissatisfaction with the supernatural state of Mau Mau-era Machakos. For example, one elderly informant from Nzawi underscored how the cleansings relied on the initiatives of ordinary Kamba, noting

> Local people were fed up with *uoi* practitioners and sent for him [Kabwere].... They didn't know anyone else who could cleanse perfectly. They didn't know any powerful witchdoctors around. They [the colonial government] gave him [Kabwere] permission to operate.[65]

A contemporary from nearby Mbooni offered a subtly different account, focusing on the action and activities of *nzama*, which were reminiscent of those of a precolonial *king'ole* confronting *uoi*. He explained,

> SM: *Nzama* were responsible for the "cleansings." They met secretly without women and identified all the *uoi* practitioners. They arrested them with *askaris*. They asked them questions about *uoi*, and those who refused to answer were given the substance.
> Q: Who else was involved?
> SM: The chiefs, the assistant chiefs, the elders and the APs.
> Q: Were the D.O. and D.C. involved?
> SM: They gave instructions to the chiefs to do the cleansings. Sometimes they were present.
> Q: Were they responsible for sending to Mombasa for help?
> SM: The chiefs and the *nzama* did it for the location.
> Q: Did they get a permit or permission?
> SM: No.[66]

Comments like these further shed light on how ordinary people have perceived what constituted authority, by whom it was exercised, and how this was indicated. They point to how in the fraught, dangerous context of the mid-1950s, the Kamba located power in discernible on-the-ground action rather in the apex of the administrative pyramid.

Oral histories from around Nzawi also show how outsider involvement changed cleansing protocols and procedures, illustrating that the type of ceremony performed by Kabwere, Kibauni, and their coastal counterparts was different from the *kithitu*-based protocols described in

[65] J. M. N., Nzawi, September 2004.
[66] S. M., Mbooni, September 2004.

documentary records and hinted at by other oral sources. The cleansing activities of coastal witchdoctors instead used "magical water" as a central element. For example, one elderly Kamba explained simply that "the witches were given something to make them act possessed and fall down."[67] His contemporary elaborated,

> Kabwere came to the market and people fell down because of his magic... He gave special water to those who refused to surrender their *uoi* and water to others to neutralize them. The people drank it and fell down. Normal people took it as protection. The witches were forced from their homes.[68]

Accounts further pointed to the multi-functionality of this magical water, which one elderly Kamba pointedly described as a "truth serum," explaining how upon its administration, witches "fell down and confessed" and were then "sent to produce their paraphernalia."[69] Cleansings that induced a possession-like state in *uoi* practitioners causing them to confess their malevolent activities, driving them to produce their paraphernalia, and ultimately neutralizing their *uoi*, would have been easily assimilable to Kamba people given the shape and centrality of possession in Kamba cosmology.[70] Overall, such cleansings demonstrated how coercion was not confined to the epistemological violence delivered through threats or to the physical violence wrought by bottles and beatings but was carried out through supernatural compulsion as well.

Recollections further insist that the magic water was only punitive when administered to *uoi* practitioners and instead offered supernatural protection against *uoi* when taken by ordinary Kamba. For example, an elderly Kamba asserted, "The water had protective qualities against witches."[71] His contemporary explained, "Normal people took it [the water] as protection."[72] Given the prevalence of protective magic in Kamba cosmology, it is surprising such mentions of its use in the danger-laden context of Mau Mau-era Machakos are so rare.

Scant documentary evidence speaks directly to the involvement of coastal cleansers. In the "Witchcraft Appendix," Nottingham noted, "It

---

[67] M. N., Kilungu, August 2004.
[68] S. M., Mbooni, September 2004.
[69] W. N., Machakos, September 2004.
[70] See, Mahone, "Psychology," and Katherine Luongo, "Prophecy, Possession, and Politics: Negotiating the 'Supernatural' in Twentieth Century Machakos, Kenya" *International Journal of African Historical Studies* (Forthcoming, 2012).
[71] J. M. N., Nzawi, September 2004
[72] S. M., Mbooni, September 2004.

was also suggested we should bring up the famous Ghiriama Wizard from Kilifi; in this game reputations grow with distance, and the further you live away the more mysterious, and hence the more terrifying your medicine is."⁷³ According to files on the witch-cleansings, this suggestion went nowhere officially, likely in part because of the British squeamishness with importing witchdoctors across tribal and administrative lines for official administrative purposes, a reservation which persisted despite the Machakos administration's employ of Kamba ritual specialists.

As Mariano Pavanello notes, in "doing" history professionally, an ambiguity exists between investigation and narration while in "doing" history locally, an ambiguity persists between narration and event.⁷⁴ Accordingly the dissonances in archival and oral renderings of cleansing *uoi* in Machakos do not demonstrate one set of narratives to be necessarily "true" and the other to be equally "false." Rather, they suggest practical, historical gaps between colonial discourse and practice, between nominal and practical authority, and between exercised and perceived responsibility.

All accounts of cleansing *uoi* share themes of coercion and of reintegration. Kamba methods of cleansing social malefactors had never been purely voluntary, and indeed, British administrators came to understand this well. For example, Nottingham explained that the "original method" the state had envisioned "assumed" that a "general wish" among "witches" would motivate them to "bring all their stuff and burn it." He added that given the knowledge about the "workings" of *uoi* and "its hold on the Akamba" gleaned through anthro-administrative inquiry, the initial program seemed "incredibly naïve" and had obviously failed.⁷⁵

Nevertheless, what witch-cleansings achieved throughout the twentieth century in Machakos was to publicly accomplish and recognize the transformation of witches into "good" people who could be reincorporated into their respective communities. However, despite the avowed success of the state-sponsored campaign, *uoi* threats in Ukambani did not end with the Mau Mau era. The conclusion traces the proliferation of witchcraft and other aspects of supernatural insecurity in Kenya and beyond.

---

[73] KNA BB/PC/EST/12/15, "Witchcraft Appendix," 4.
[74] Mariano Pavanello, "L'Evénement et la Parole, la Conception de l'histoire et du Temps Historique dans les Traditions Orales Africaines: Le Cas des Nzema," *Cahiers d'études africaines* 171 (2003): 471.
[75] "Witchcraft Appendix," 3. November 1955.

9

Epilogue

Does the belief in witchcraft avail to an accused person the defence of provocation, and if so, under what circumstances? There is a long line of authorities ... to illustrate the vexing nature of the issue both pre- and post the colonial era.[1]

WITCHCRAFT AND (POSTCOLONIAL) PROVOCATION

On a summer night in Malindi District, Patrick Tuva Mwanengu crept into the home of his kinsmen and hacked to death his uncle, Gona Mwanengu Gona, as Gona slept among members of the family. In the murder trial that followed, the question of witchcraft initially arose on cross-examination as prosecution witnesses testified that they were familiar with allegations that the deceased had practiced witchcraft. The defense counsel subsequently argued that accused's belief in the witchcraft of the deceased constituted legally mitigating provocation.

In taking up witchcraft and provocation, the trial judge's directions to the assessors offered startlingly contradictory advice. The judge first offered a straightforward explanation of provocation, emphasizing the elements of proximity and immediacy necessary to establish the legally mitigating condition. In contrast, his directions concerning witchcraft broke with convention. The judge wrote,

> Belief in witchcraft is widespread among many communities in Africa. The belief can be deeply entrenched in the believer, who, convinced that

[1] Patrick Tuva Mwanengu and Republic. Criminal Appeal 2727 of 2006. In the Court of Appeal of Kenya at Mombasa. http:///www.kenyalaw.org Hereafter, *Patrick Tuva Mwanengu*.

the woes in his family are caused by the wizard or witch, will strike the latter without reflection. So that in considering the defence of provocation you must see the wide picture surrounding the claim. The cumulative effect of events culminating with the final blow.[2]

This direction proffered an avenue to treat the (alleged) witchcraft of the deceased as legally mitigating provocation without the necessary conditions of immediacy and proximity being attached.

Yet despite the contradictory character of his directions to the assessors, the judge relied on the standard definition of provocation and precedent in two earlier witch-murder cases, *Eria Galikuwa* and *Fabiano Kinene*, which emphasized proximity and immediacy, in rendering his judgment.[3] Finding Patrick Tuva Mwanengu guilty of premeditated murder, he wrote, "The deceased did nothing to the accused or any person under his care to have provoked him."[4]

As with so many cases of witch-murder, *Patrick Tuva Mwanengu* was heard on appeal. Echoing the trial judge's directions to the assessors, the appellant's counsel argued that the circumstances of the case added up to a sort of "'slow punctured' provocation." The counsel for the state, mobilizing language reminiscent of the judgment in *Kumwaka*, "pleaded passionately" with the appeals court justices "not to sanction the opening of a window for believers in witchcraft to unleash death and mayhem."[5]

The appellate court found that the original judgment had neglected to attend to two witch-murder cases, *Chivatsi* and *Yovan*, which superseded those cited in the original judgment.[6] These later cases established that a threat to kill made by the deceased, together with other circumstances that would stimulate in the accused a genuine belief in the witchcraft of the deceased, amounted to provocation. Accordingly, the justices substituted a conviction of manslaughter for that of murder, arguing that given the totality of the circumstances of the case, Patrick Tuva Mwanengu "was entitled to the benefit of the doubt."[7] The decision of the appellate court attracted the interest of both the public and the legal establishment.[8]

---

[2] Ibid.
[3] Ibid. *Fabiano* is discussed in Chapter 6.
[4] Ibid.
[5] Ibid.
[6] Ibid.
[7] Ibid.
[8] Esther Onchana, "Law Report: Instance Where Witchcraft Is Regarded as Legal Provocation," *DN*, 15 September 2008. Online.

By now the circumstances of the case and the attendant legal wrangling should seem familiar to the reader. What might be surprising initially is that Patrick Tuva Mwanengu killed his uncle in 2002, and that the case was heard in Kenya's courts between 2005 and 2007. The case is simply the most recent addition to a long legal genealogy stretching from the early 1900s to the present day in which witchcraft-driven violence has challenged the state's ability to maintain law and order. *Patrick Tuva Mwanengu* (and similar cases) point not only to a remarkable historical consistency in the motives and means surrounding witchcraft-driven violence in Kenya but also to notable continuities in how the legal system has approached such violence.

A primary aim of this book has been to provide a history to the cases of witchcraft-driven violence and to related law and policy approaches that have persisted into the postcolonial era. The Kenyan judicial system continues to rely on the Witchcraft Ordinance, virtually unchanged in language and implementation since the colonial era, as the primary deterrent to and instrument for prosecuting witchcraft accusations *and* activities. Kenyan jurisprudence dealing with witch-killings, in turn, continues to focus on "the same fears expressed more than 70 years ago in the *Kumwaka case* (supra)."[9] The postcolonial continuities in Kenya's rationales and rules regarding witchcraft contrast strongly with the approaches of African nations which have gone so far as to integrate occult practitioners into the legal system.[10]

WITCHCRAFT AND (UNDER)DEVELOPMENT

> Kenya Power & Lighting came to give us electricity ... but the witches chased them away.
> – Kiosk proprietor, outside Kangundo, 2004

In his excellent study of contemporary Taita, Kenya, Smith traces how witchcraft and development are popularly perceived to share an invisible ability to get things done in a globalized environment that discourages gain and reinforces lack. But, he notes, at the same moment, witchcraft also offers a language of power through which both ordinary people and authorities articulate why the predicted and promised fruits of development often fail to be born. Smith locates the deep history of official, administrative

---

[9] *Patrick Tuva Mwanengu*.
[10] Geschiere, *The Modernity of Witchcraft*. See also, Tebbe, "Witchcraft and Statecraft."

perspectives on the interpenetration of witchcraft and development in the development schemas of the post–World War II era. He writes,

> Colonial administrations regarded popular resistance to these schemas as antimodern, irrational, and even occult and thus, ironically, set the precedent for associating witchcraft with everything that was outside the control of the state, a discourse that postcolonial leaders would develop further.[11]

This book has shown how official administrative discourse from Ukambani supports this view. Yet, it has analyzed administrative attitudes toward witchcraft and development even more deeply and broadly, demonstrating how from the opening years of the colonial era state authorities regarded witchcraft as an impediment not simply to particular development schemas but to the administrative project of development writ large.

This official attitude has been consistently rearticulated from the early twentieth century onward. Indeed, a June 2009 article entitled "Witch's Hand Seen in Coast Poverty," that ran in Kenya's major daily, addressed the provincial commissioner's (typical) remarks attributing the Coast Province's lack of educational and economic development to "backward practices like witchcraft."[12] Ordinary Kenyans' assertions that witchcraft is the primary reason that they have been unwilling or unable to comply with development dictates has also reinforced state discourse. For example, as I waited for the country bus in yet another unelectrified location in Machakos, the proprietor of the local kiosk apologized for having no chilled beverages as he handed me a warm Stoney Tangawizi (a Coca-Cola brand beverage), noting that "Kenya Power & Lighting came to give us electricity ... but the witches chased them away," as other patrons muttered in assent.[13] The body of statements like these underscores the ways witchcraft continues to work as a convenient category not simply for assimilating personal distress but also for explaining away all sorts of what could be termed "official misfortune" – the inability to establish order and implement policy.

WITCHCRAFT AND POLITICS

> More than 300 parents are up in arms after the local administration barred them from holding a protest march to demand that he [a witch-doctor] exorcise demons that he allegedly "planted" at Ithani Primary

---

[11] Smith, *Bewitching Development*, 28–29.
[12] Mazera Nduyra, "Witch's Hand Seen in Coast Poverty," *DN*, 17 June 2009. Online.
[13] Outside Kangundo. September, 2004.

school.... [T]he protesting parents are strongly supported by [the] Kitui Central MP.[14]

– *Daily Nation*, 2002

Throughout the first half of the twentieth century colonial authorities imagined and implemented the epistemological "work" of witchcraft, attending to the strong association between witchcraft and lack – of law, of development, and of overall order.

This book has demonstrated that colonial authorities overwhelmingly discounted the ability of witches to actually do magic. Yet it has also shown the ways in which state officials readily engaged with the power of *beliefs* in the efficacy of supernatural practitioners like witches and the concomitant power of such persons to challenge the authority of the state.

In the postcolonial period, state actors (and aspirants) have conceived of and worked with witchcraft in ways significantly different from those of their predecessors. Rather than being considered simply as a potentially political challenge to the state, witchcraft has been mobilized discursively *and* practically in struggles over access to and maintenance of state power. Witchcraft has been used by officials of the postcolonial Kenyan state and by those aspiring to political power to explain why they have been unable to adequately access and/or retain power or why their opponents have been able to do so.

Unsurprisingly, discussions of the interpenetration of witchcraft and politics in Ukambani abound. Most notably, in 2003, gossip about malevolent witchcraft swirled around the election eve death by drowning of a prominent Kamba MP, and six weeks later newspapers carried reports of the arrest of a "suspected witchdoctor" interfering in the campaign of another Kamba politician. As the *Daily Nation* reported, "The man was handed over to the police by agents of Mr. Charles Kilonzo, who accused him of having ill motives against their candidate. The suspect told his interrogators that that he was sent by one of the aspirants to work against Mr. Kilonzo."[15]

But the postcolonial intertwining of witchcraft and politics is not always necessarily negative. While witchcraft can explain away political misfortunes and missteps, claims-making about witchcraft has also operated as way of developing political power within or in opposition to

[14] "Respect Cultural Beliefs," *DN*, 15 February 2002. Online.
[15] Katherine Luongo, "A Self-Evident Death? Reading Water and Witchcraft in the News of a Kenya MP's Death," *Journal of the University of Michigan International Institute* (March 2005):15. Also Bob Odalo and Victor Nzuma, "Man Held over Witchcraft Claim in Yatta," *DN*, 27 June 2003.

the state. For example, in 2000 a pair of opposition leaders took a public stand against witchcraft in Ukambani. As press reports summarize,

> A Cabinet minister and an opposition party leader led a Kitui mob in a raid on the clinic of Tanzanian herbalist-cum-magician on Monday and threw him out. Minister Francis Nyenze and Social Democratic Party leader Charity Ngilu accused Dr. Juma Ibrahim of unleashing evil spirits on residents and vowed to use all means to protect the people.... [T]hey took an assortment of funny paraphernalia.[16]

In this instance, taking a stand against witchcraft enabled the two politicians to highlight their concern for and active attention to the welfare of their constituents endangered by supernatural activities. At the same moment, such an engagement with witchcraft enabled the opposition politicians to foreground the lack of state presence in and the absence of state concern with the supernaturally-fraught space of Ukambani.

Witchcraft also surfaced in wide-ranging analyses of Kenya's hotly contested and violent 2007 elections. For instance, the Kenyan press carried reports of a defeated MP who attributed his loss to voters having been bewitched by his rival who had ordered spells cast upon them and live goats buried at polling places across the MP's stronghold.[17] More subtly, the Waki Commission, which conducted an official inquiry into the election violence, classed "witchcraft" as a form of "hate speech." Its report noted, for instance, that leaflets circulating widely in a district heavily populated by supporters of the Kibaki regime had accused the opposition candidate, Raila Odinga, of being "a terrorist, devil worshipper, communist, expert in overthrowing governments, tribalist, and deceptive, dishonest, *practising witchcraft to win the presidency*."[18]

MU'UNDE M'UOI AND MAJINI

> Kambas are natural office clerks, soldiers, and domestic servants; but watch out for potions, freak accidents and charms under the bed – these are the spell-casters of Kenya.[19]
>
> – Wrong, *It's Our Turn to Eat*, 2009

---

[16] "Ngilu and Nyenze Lead Raid," *DN*, August, n.d., 2000.
[17] Phionah Mwadilo, "Kenya Minister Blames Loss on Witchcraft," *EAS*, 31 December 2007; http://www.allafrica.com.
[18] The Waki Report: Findings of the Commission of Inquiry into the Post-Election Violence in Kenya. October 2008. 216. My emphasis. http://www.eastandard.net/downloads/Waki_Report.pdf.
[19] Noted journalist Michaela Wrong trenchantly summarizes persistent ethnic stereotypes in contemporary Kenya. Michaela Wrong, *It's Our Turn to Eat* (New York: HarperCollins, 2009), 43.

The shape of beliefs and practices related to *uoi* has remained remarkably consistent from the colonial era into the present day, but whether the level of witchcraft practices overall has increased or decreased since independence in the early 1960s is a point of contention among Kamba people. In response to the broad question, "Has the level of *uoi* activity increased, decreased, or remained the same over your lifetime?" most elderly Kamba interviewees responded that malevolent supernatural activity had both increased *and* decreased in their lifetimes.[20]

These men and women explained that while varieties of "traditional" *uoi*, had decreased over their lifetimes, they had also witnessed an upsurge in new or revitalized forms of malevolent "supernatural" activities which they maintained could be equally categorized under the broad rubric of "*uoi*." Christianity, and to a significantly lesser extent "government law," elderly Kamba argue, are each responsible for the decline in traditional *uoi*. Responses such as "Witchcraft has gone down ... more people have become Christians" and "witchcraft has gone down due to Christianity" are typical.[21]

Indeed, domestic and foreign mainline, evangelical, and Pentecostal churches operating in Kenya have focused a harsh lens on witchcraft in recent years. In a shift away from earlier dicta proposing Christianity and witchcraft only as ineluctably incompatible, recent Christian discourses have argued instead that Christian beliefs and practices from the mundane to the metaphysical can and should be mobilized to combat broad-spectrum witchcraft. For example, in the well-stocked bookstore of Nairobi's august Catholic Cathedral, numerous texts dealing with Catholicism's role in countering African witchcraft are available for purchase, while a few streets over vendors hawk "gutter press" pamphlets with such dramaturgic titles as "The Dangers of Witchcraft Covenant Practices!" and "How to Identify and Break Curses" produced by the plethora of millenarian-oriented storefront churches that has exploded around Nairobi's east.[22]

---

[20] For example, B. M., Nairobi (Pipeline), August 2004; K. K., Kangundo, August 2004; R. K., Kilungu, September 2004; J. M. N., Nzawi, September 2004.

[21] M. M., Tawa, September 2004; S. M., Mbooni, September 2004.

[22] See for example, Aylward Shorter and Joseph N. Njiru, *New Religious Movements in Africa* (Nairobi: Paulines Publications of Africa, 2001). Also, *AFER African Ecclesial Review* 45.3 (September 2003), a special volume on "Evil Practices in Africa, Obstacles to Authentic Christianity." Both works were purchased at the Catholic Cathedral shop. The two pamphlets cited above were produced in mid-2004 by Steven Gichuhi Ministries International in Nairobi. I am grateful to Matthew and Jolene Carotenuto for obtaining these pamphlets for me.

These discourses penetrated American presidential politics during the country's "Kenyan" elections of 2008[23] when video surfaced of Kenyan pastor, Thomas Muthee, publicly "treating" then vice-presidential candidate Sarah Palin against witchcraft some years earlier.[24] Muthee, a frequent visitor to Wasilla's Pentecostal church, performed a laying-on-of-hands ceremony as a witchcraft prophylaxis. The pastor had built his large ministry and his reputation as a "witch-finder" by "chasing away" an elderly woman who was alleged to run a "divination clinic" and who lived near the site of numerous traffic accidents in Kiambu. Muthee claimed that he had successfully banished a "witch" in the course of "spiritual warfare."[25] Palin attributed her successful gubernatorial bid in part to Muthee's intervention.[26]

Informants' testimony that traditional *uoi* is on the downturn could indicate a shift in discursive practices related to *uoi* rather than in *uoi* practices themselves. As one elderly Kamba man noted with subtlety, "People don't talk much [about witchcraft] because of Christianity. It has driven people underground."[27] The inherently invisible and largely secretive character of *uoi* renders a quantifiable assessment of traditional *uoi*'s upsurge or diminishment virtually impossible.

The discussions of elderly men and women also introduced additional categories of harmful supernatural actors and actions. Many interviewees assert that there has been an increase in the presence and activities of *majini* in Ukambani, particularly in recent years.[28] *Majini*, evil spirits, which are believed to be mobilized by humans to help people achieve material success, are typically thought to emanate from outside the afflicted community, in recent years coming increasingly from the Persian Gulf. Assessing the supernatural state of contemporary Ukambani, informants regularly stated simply that "*Majini* have gone up." Others assert that *majini* activity had supplanted traditional *uoi* because of the efficacy of *majini* mobilization for achieving worldly wealth and power. As one

---

[23] Matthew Carotenuto and Katherine Luongo, "*Dala* or Diaspora? Obama and the Luo Community of Kenya," *African Affairs* 103.481 (2009): 197–219.

[24] Max Blumenthal, "The Witch Hunter Anoints Sara Palin," *Huffington Post*, 28 September 2008. Online.

[25] See the Web site of Muthee's World of Faith Ministries; http://www.wofchurchke.org.

[26] Hannah Strange, "Palin Linked Electoral Success to Prayer of Kenyan Witch-Hunter," *Times Online*, 16 September 2008.

[27] J. K. K., Tawa, September 2004.

[28] M. N., Kilungu, August 2004; B. M., Kilungu, August 2004; J. K., Kilungu, August 2004. *Jini* (plural *majini*), in Kiswahili or "jinn(s)" in English, are evil spirits originating from the Swahili Coast and more broadly from the Indian Ocean World. In 2004, informants in Kilungu told my research assistant and me about a recent spate of *majini* activity brought about by outsiders posing as thermos salespeople.

elderly Kamba man suggested, "Traditional witchcraft has gone down, but *majini* have gone up because they can be used for gain."[29] *Majini* then are key constituents of a larger coterie of malevolent supernatural actors mobilized in the service of material gain in contemporary Kenya.[30] The swell in moneymaking, black magic actors and activities is an ironic turn in light of the colonial-era decision to strike the phrase "for the purposes of gain" in revising the Witchcraft Ordinance of 1909.[31]

WITCHCRAFT AND THE WORLD

> In many countries in the world there is a strong belief in the power of witches. There are also a great many reports of individuals being killed after being accused of practicing witchcraft. The Council should acknowledge that it is entirely unacceptable for individuals accused of witchcraft to be killed including through extrajudicial processes. It should call upon Governments to ensure that all such killings are treated as murder and investigated, and prosecuted and punished accordingly.[32]
> – Statement of the U.N. Special Rapporteur on extrajudicial, summary or arbitrary executions, 2009

In recent years, witchcraft has gone global, but not merely through the increasing prominence of transnational supernatural actors like *majini*. This book has illustrated the global reach of witchcraft (and concomitant violence) in the first half of the twentieth century, tracing how witchcraft mattered far beyond the bounds of community and colony, becoming an object of empire-wide concern and stimulating the development of an anthro-administrative complex of knowledge and practice. In the intervening fifty years since the end of colonialism in Africa, the worldwide

---

[29] M. M., Nzawi, September 2004.
[30] For analysis of the currency of discourses of "devil worship" and politics among Kikuyu and Kalenjin communities, see Yvon Droz, "Si Dieu veut ... ou suppôts de Satan. Inceritudes, Millérnarisme et Sorcellerie chez les Migrants Kikuyu," *Cahiers d' Etudes africaines* 37.1 (1997): 85–117. Droz's analysis is one of the most comprehensive on devil worship in Kenya. See also, Hervé Maupeu, "Les Élections"; and Stephen Ellis and Gerrie Ter Haar, *Worlds of Power: Religious Thought and Political Practice in Africa* (New York: Oxford University Press, 2004). The Kikamba-language audio cassette, "Frederick Muule," offers a narrative of "devil worship" in Kamba communities. I am grateful to Hervé Maupeu for purchasing this cassette for me on River Road in Nairobi in July 2004.
[31] See Chapter 2.
[32] Philip Alston, "Statement by Professor Philip Alston, Special Rapporteur on Extrajudicial, Summary or Arbitrary Executions" (paper presented at the United Nations Human Rights Council, Geneva, Switzerland, 3 June 2009); http://www.refworld.org.

reach of witchcraft has become even more pronounced as concerns about witchcraft and related violence have entered the global legal arena through the avenue of asylum.

As the Special Rapporteur's statement indicates, witch-murder has captured the attention of international organizations like the United Nations. In autumn of 2008, a rapid assessment conducted by the United Nations High Commissioner for Refugees (UNHCR) revealed that Africans have recently sought protection at UNHCR offices on the continent and in Kuala Lumpur, claiming fear of persecution for their (alleged) witchcraft activities and the absence of state protection from violence prompted by witchcraft accusations as grounds for asylum.[33] Such claims are not without historical antecedents. As this book has shown, colonial records contain reports of Africans accused of witchcraft seeking sanctuary at the administrative *boma*, of administrative officers deporting accused witches to other parts of the colony in order to preempt witch-murders, and other, similar occurrences. Clear precedent for such claims does not exist, however, in international refugee law and praxis.

Recent sources also show that the UNHCR has had to cope with the problem of witchcraft accusations and witchcraft-driven violence in its refugee camps in Africa. The agency has established "customary courts" to deal with a variety of disputes among camp residents, including witchcraft accusations.[34] It has also implemented various educational programs in the camps, a significant aim of which is combating witchcraft beliefs and practices.[35] This book has underscored the historical precursors of these interventions. Customary law was a key element of administration in British colonial Africa, and the notion that witchcraft could be "educated out of existence" was a prominent trope in colonial anthro-administrative discourse. Nonetheless, the problem of witchcraft-driven violence has yet to be definitively solved – inside or outside the camps. And history suggests that a colonial report's assertion leveled in 1927, "Eventually the power of the witch doctor will vanish before the spread of education but this process will inevitably be a long one," might have been unduly optimistic.[36]

[33] Jill Schnobelen, "Witchcraft Allegations, Refugee Protection and Human Rights: A Review of the Evidence. Research Paper No. 169," United Nations High Commissioner for Refugees, 2009; http://www.refworld.org.

[34] Rosemary da Costa, "The Administration of Justice in Refugee Camps, a Study of Practice," United Nations High Commissioner for Refugees, 2006; http://www.refworld.org.

[35] For example, Bryn Boyce, "Witchcraft Allegations Plague Southern Chad's Camps," 25 October 2008, United Nations High Commissioner for Refugees; http://www.refworld.org.

[36] PRO CO 533/382/13, Native Affairs Department Annual Report 1927, n.p.

Immigration authorities in the global North have also been grappling with witchcraft claims similar to those made before the UNHCR. For example, in 2005, a Canadian lawyer secured a stay of deportation for a Nigerian client, arguing that witchcraft accusations leveled against his client together with the prevalence of witch-murder in Nigeria would endanger the client's life were he returned to Nigeria.[37]

Unsurprisingly, assessing witchcraft allegations in asylum cases has been challenging for immigration courts. Like courts of the colonial era, contemporary immigration courts operate largely within a dual framework of institutional incredulity and ignorance vis-à-vis witchcraft. In much the same way that colonial justices relied upon native assessors to evaluate claims about witchcraft, contemporary immigration officials have drawn upon the expertise of anthropologists to assess the validity, and thus the legal usability, of asylum seekers' claims about witchcraft in their countries of origin.

Overall, this book has demonstrated the ever-present potential for violence wrought by "living in a world with witches."[38] It has shown that although colonial authorities did not believe in witchcraft per se, they did comprehend how witchcraft beliefs and practices did a range of work – social and political, epistemological and material – in communities across the African continent. As today's bureaucrats grapple anew with the various challenges produced by inhabiting a world in which witches still reside, witchcraft remains a crucial concern of the twenty-first century.[39]

---

[37] Schnobelen, "Witchcraft Allegations," 38.
[38] Ashforth, "On Living," 206.
[39] Ibid.

Glossary

askari (Kiswahili) – Soldier; guard
boma (Kiswahili) – The colonial administrative center in a given location
jini (Kiswahili) – A spirit, often malevolent, often hailing from the Swahili Coast or Saudi Peninsula
king'ole – A law; an act; an institution. A *king'ole* council was composed of select *atumia* and was responsible for sanctioning serial malefactors like witches or thieves in the precolonial era.
kivala (Kikamba) – A substance used to elicit a confession from a *mu'unde m'uoi*; "truth serum"
kithitu (Kikamba) – The most deadly Kamba oath
konzesya (Kikamba) – A variety of *uoi* causing prolonged, wasting illness in its target
malu (Kigiriama) – Compensation; a fine, especially for the commission of adultery
mchawi (Kiswahili) – Witch; witch doctor; sorcerer
mganga (Kiswahili) – Witch doctor; healer
mu'unde m'uoi – Literally, "witch person"; witch; witch doctor; sorcerer
mu'unde m'uwe – Literally, "healing person"; witch doctor; healer
mutumia (Kiswahili) – Kamba male elder
ndia (Kikamba) – A variety of *uoi* causing deafness in its target
ndundu (Kikamba) – A variety of *kithitu* used to cleanse *uoi*
ng'ondu (Kikamba) – A variety of *kithitu* used to counter *uoi*; also used to cleanse the Mau Mau oath
nzevu (Kikamba) – A variety of *uoi* causing confusion in its target

nzama (Kikamba) – Councils of *atumia* similar to the *king'ole* but having broader functions in deciding conflicts between individuals and/or parties; co-opted into the colonial administration under the Native Tribunals Act (1911)

uchawi (Kiswahili) – Witchcraft; black magic; "magical harm"; sorcery

uoi (Kikamba) – Witchcraft; black magic; "magical harm"; sorcery

uwavi (Shimakonde) – Witchcraft; sorcery

uwe (Kikamba) – Witchcraft; white magic, "healing"

Bibliography

Archival Sources and Interviews

Kenya National Archives, Nairobi (KNA)

African Affairs (MAA)
Attorney General (AG)
District Commissioner, Kiambu (DC/KBU)
District Commissioner, Kitui (DC/KTI)
District Commissioner, Machakos (DC/MKS)
Judicial Department (AP)
Legal Affairs (MLA)
Native Medicine and Witchcraft, Kwale (CC)
Provincial Commissioner, Central Province (PC/CP, VQ)
Provincial Commissioner, Eastern Province (BB/PC/EST)
Provincial Commissioner, Nyanza (PC/NZA)
Provincial Commissioner, Southern Province (PC/SP)
Rehabilitation Advisory Committee (VP)

Public Records Office, Kew Gardens, Great Britain (PRO)

Africa, original correspondence (CO 847)
African Studies Branch, original correspondence (CO 955)
Colonial Social Science Research Council (CO 901)
East Africa, original correspondence (CO 822)
Gambia, original correspondence (CO 87)
Kenya, government gazettes (CO 542)
Kenya, original correspondence (CO 533)
Kenya, sessional papers (CO 544)
Political and Other Departments, general correspondence before 1906, Africa (FO 2)
Research Department, original correspondence (CO 927)

Bibliography

London School of Economics Library Archives, London (LSE)

IAI/2/1, International Institute of African Languages and Cultures Bureau Minutes (1931–1950)
LSE, MALINOWSKI/10/10 African Papers (1934)
LSE, MALINOWSKI/9/2 Loose Notes (1926)

Rhodes House, Oxford (RH)

Papers of the Anti-Slavery Society (Mss Brit Emp s 19)
Papers of the London Group on African Affairs (Mss Afr s 1427)

School of Oriental and African Studies (SOAS)

Ueda, Hitoshi. "Witchcraft and Sorcery in Kitui of Kamba Tribe." Presented to Institute of African Studies, University of Nairobi, Research Seminar No 25. 22 June 1971. SOAS PP MS 42 Whiteley Collection File SL/14: Kitui Witchcraft.

Kenya National Archives Murembi Library Collection

Hobley, Charles William. Mss. 27 Ethnology of Akamba Manuscript. Mss. 97/2.
Ueda, Hitoshi. "Kithitu among the Kamba of Kenya – the Case Study of Kilonzo's Kithitu." Kenya National Archives Mss. 83–821 390 EUD. N.D

Government Documents

Great Britain. Parliamentary Debates, Commons, 5th ser., vol. 249 (1932), cols. 857–858.
Law Reports Containing Cases Determined by the High Court of East Africa, and by the Court of Appeal for Eastern Africa, and by the Judicial Committee of the Privy Council on Appeal from that Court. Nairobi: Government Printer.
Law Reports Containing Decisions of the Court of Appeal for Eastern Africa. Nairobi: Government Printer.
Law Reports of Kenya: Containing Cases Determined by the Supreme Court, Kenya Colony and Protectorate and by the Court of Appeal for Eastern Africa and by the Judicial Committee of the Privy Council on Appeal from that Court. Nairobi: Government Printer.
Law Reports of Kenya. http://www.kenyalaw.org,
The Commission of Inquiry into the Administration of Justice in Kenya, Uganda and the Tanganyika Territory in Criminal Matters Affecting Natives (Bushe Commission). Cmd. 4623. London: His Majesty's Stationery Office, 1934.
The Commission of Inquiry into Post-Election Violence (Waki Commission), *The Waki Report: Findings of the Commission of Inquiry into the Post-Election Violence in Kenya*. October 2008. http://www.eastandard.net/downloads/Waki_Report.pdf.

Bibliography

Jomo Kenyatta University Library, University of Nairobi

Penal Code of Kenya (1930): Division IV – Offences against the Person, Chapter XIX Murder and Manslaughter. Afr. Docs. J 750.155.P4 1930.

Newspapers and Periodicals

Daily Nation (DN), 1985–2009.
East Africa, 1931–1932.
East African Standard (EAS), 1931–2009.
The Times of London (ToL), 1931–1932.

Pamphlets

"The Dangers of Witchcraft Covenant Practices!" *Steven Gichuhi Ministries International*. Nairobi. June 2004.
"How to Identify and Break Curses." *Steven Gichuhi Ministries International*. Nairobi. June 2004.

Web Site

World of Faith Ministries. http://www.wofchurchke.org.

Audiocassette

"Frederick Muule." Kikamba. Nairobi. July 2004.

Interview Transcripts

Newman, Jeremy. *Machakos Interviews.* Unpublished interview transcripts, 1974. Personal collection of François Grignon.
Sungi, William Mutemi and Raphael Nguli, eds. *Akamba Oral Historical Texts.* Unpublished interview transcripts, 1977. Nairobi: Kenya National Archives, Murembi Library Collection.

Interviews

In the following list, Kamba informants' names are coded by initials, and place-names in Machakos District refer to the closest location or market-center while those in Nairobi to the particular Nairobi neighborhood. Kamba people are cited in the text by their initials.

Nairobi

J. C. Nottingham. Interviewed by the author. Nairobi. City Center. January 2004. June 2004. July 2004.
M. K. Birth date unknown. Interviewed by J. Mbithi wa Mutunga and the author. Notes. Nairobi. Kibera. July 2004.

B. W. Born circa 1930. Interviewed by J. Mbithi wa Mutunga and the author. Notes. Nairobi. Pipeline. July 2004.

D. K. Born circa 1970. Interviewed by J. Mbithi wa Mutunga and the author. Notes. Nairobi. Industrial Area. July 2004.

Machakos District

K. K. Born circa 1918. Interviewed by J. Mbithi wa Mutunga and the author. Tape recording and notes. Kangundo. August 2004.

K. M. Born circa 1910. Interviewed by J. Mbithi wa Mutunga and the author. Tape recording and notes. Kangundo. August 2004.

M. N. Born circa 1910. Interviewed by J. Mbithi wa Mutunga and the author. Tape recording and notes. Kangundo. August 2004.

L. N. N. Birth date unknown. Interviewed by J. Mbithi wa Mutunga and the author. Tape recording and notes. Kilungu. August 2004.

M. M. N. Birthdate unknown. Interviewed by J. Mbithi wa Mutunga and the author. Tape recording and notes. Kilungu. August 2004.

P. M. Born circa 1912. Interviewed by J. Mbithi wa Mutunga and the author. Tape recording and notes. Kilungu. August 2004.

J. M. Born circa 1918–1919. Interviewed by J. Mbithi wa Mutunga and the author. Tape recording and notes. Kilungu. August 2004.

M. N. Born circa 1920. Interviewed by J. Mbithi wa Mutunga and the author. Tape recording and notes. Kilungu. August 2004.

B. M. Born circa 1925. Interviewed by J. Mbithi wa Mutunga and the author. Tape recording and notes. Kilungu. August 2004.

R. K. Born circa 1925. Interviewed by J. Mbithi wa Mutunga and the author. Tape recording and notes. Kilungu. August 2004.

J. N. K. Born circa 1922. Interviewed by J. Mbithi wa Mutunga and the author. Tape recording and notes. Kilungu. September 2004.

J. K. S. Born circa 1927. Interviewed by J. Mbithi wa Mutunga and the author. Tape recording and notes. Kilungu. September 2004.

M. W. Birth date unknown. Interviewed by J. Mbithi wa Mutunga and the author. Tape recording and notes. Imani. September 2004.

P. K. M. Birth date unknown. Interviewed by J. Mbithi wa Mutunga and the author. Tape recording and notes. Welfare. September 2004.

R. S. K. Birth date unknown. Interviewed by J. Mbithi wa Mutunga and the author. Tape recording and notes. Welfare. September 2004.

K. N. Born circa 1921. Interviewed by J. Mbithi wa Mutunga and the author. Tape recording and notes. Nzawi. September 2004.

M. M. Born circa 1898. Interviewed by J. Mbithi wa Mutunga and the author. Tape recording and notes. Nzawi. September 2004.

J. M. N. Born circa 1939. Interviewed by J. Mbithi wa Mutunga and the author. Tape recording and notes. Nzawi. September 2004.

J. K. Born circa 1916. Interviewed by J. Mbithi wa Mutunga and the author. Tape recording and notes. Tawa. September 2004.

J. K. K. Born circa 1922. Interviewed by J. Mbithi wa Mutunga and the author. Tape recording and notes. Tawa. September 2004.

E.M.M. Born circa 1902. Interviewed by J. Mbithi wa Mutunga and the author. Tape recording and notes. Tawa. September 2004.

N. D. M. Born circa 1904. Interviewed by J. Mbithi wa Mutunga and the author. Tape recording and notes. Tawa. September 2004.

M. M. Born circa 1930s. Interviewed by J. Mbithi wa Mutunga and the author. Tape recording and notes. Tawa. September 2004.

M. K. Born circa 1927. Interviewed by J. Mbithi wa Mutunga and the author. Tape recording and notes. Tawa. September 2004.

S. K. Born circa 1934. Interviewed by J. Mbithi wa Mutunga and the author. Tape recording and notes. Tawa. September 2004.

S. M. Born circa 1913. Interviewed by J. Mbithi wa Mutunga and the author. Tape recording and notes. Mbooni. September 2004.

W. N. Born circa 1919. Interviewed by J. Mbithi wa Mutunga and the author. Tape recording and notes. Machakos. September 2004.

E. K. M. Born circa 1914. Interviewed by J. Mbithi wa Mutunga and the author. Tape recording and notes. Machakos. September 2004.

M.M. Born circa 1935. Interviewed by J. Mbithi wa Mutunga and the author. Tape recording and notes. Machakos. September 2004.

M. W. Born circa 1930. Interviewed by J. Mbithi wa Mutunga and the author. Tape recording and notes. Machakos. September 2004.

M. N. Born circa 1922. Interviewed by J. Mbithi wa Mutunga and the author. Tape recording and notes. Machakos. September 2004.

M. M. Born circa 1935. Interviewed by J. Mbithi wa Mutunga and the author. Tape recording and notes. Machakos. September 2004.

Other Works

Ainsworth, John. "On a Journey from Machakos to Kitwyi." *Geographical Journal* 7.4 (April 1896): 406–412.

——— "A Description of the Ukamba Province, East Africa Protectorate, and Its Progress under British Administration." *Journal of the Manchester Geographic Society* 16 (1900): 178–196.

Alston, Philip. "Statement by Professor Philip Alston, Special Rapporteur on Extrajudicial, Summary or Arbitrary Executions." Paper presented at the United Nations Human Rights Council, Geneva, Switzerland, 3 June 2009.

Ambler, Charles. *Kenyan Communities in the Age of Imperialism: The Central Region in the Late Nineteenth Century*. New Haven: Yale University Press, 1988.

——— "What Is the World Going to Come To? Prophecy and Colonization in Colonial Kenya." In *Revealing Prophets: Prophecy in Eastern African History*, edited by David M. Anderson and Douglas H. Johnson, 221–239. Athens: University of Ohio Press, 1999.

Amin, Shahid. *Event, Metaphor, Memory: Chauri Chaura 1922–1992*. Berkeley: University of California Press, 1995.

Anderson, David M. "Black Mischief: Crime, Protest, and Resistance in Colonial Kenya." *Historical Journal* 36 (1993): 851–877.

Histories of the Hanged: The Dirty War in Kenya and the End of Empire. New York: W.W. Norton, 2005.

Ashforth, Adam. *Madumo: A Man Bewitched*. Chicago: University of Chicago Press, 2000.

"On Living in a World with Witches: Everyday Epistemology and Spiritual Insecurity in a Modern African City (Soweto)." In *Magical Interpretations, Material Realities: Modernity, Witchcraft, and the Occult in Postcolonial Africa*, edited by Henrietta L. Moore and Todd Sanders, 206–225. London: Routledge, 2001.

Witchcraft, Violence and Democracy in South Africa. Chicago: University of Chicago Press, 2005.

Bailey, Michael D. "The Disenchantment of Magic: Spells, Charms, and Superstition in Early European Witchcraft Literature." *American Historical Review* 111.2 (April 2006): 383–404.

Balandier, M. Georges. "The Colonial Situation: A Theoretical Approach." In *Africa: Social Problems of Change and Conflict*, edited by Pierre L. Van den Berghe, 34–61. San Francisco: Chandler, 1965.

Benton, Lauren. *Law and Colonial Cultures: Legal Regimes in World History, 1400–1900*. Cambridge: Cambridge University Press, 2002.

Beresford-Stooke, G. "An Akamba Ceremony Used in Times of Drought." *Man* 28 (August 1928): 139–140.

Berman, Bruce. *Control and Crisis in Colonial Kenya: The Dialectic of Domination*. Nairobi: East Africa Educational Publishers, 1990.

Berman, Bruce and John Lonsdale. "Coping with the Contradictions: The Development of the Colonial State in Kenya, 1895–1914." *Journal of African History* 20 (1979): 487–505.

"Louis Leakey's Mau Mau: A Study in the Politics of Knowledge." *History and Anthropology* 5 (1991): 143–204.

Unhappy Valley, Conflict in Kenya and Africa, Book One: State and Class. Nairobi: East African Educational Publishers, 1992.

Unhappy Valley, Conflict in Kenya and Africa, Book Two: Violence and Ethnicity. Nairobi: East African Educational Publishers, 1992.

Berry, Sara. "Hegemony on a Shoestring: Indirect Rule and Access to Agricultural Land." *Africa* 62.3 (1992): 327–355.

Bissell, William Cunningham. "Colonial Constructions: Historicizing Debates on Civil Society in Africa." In *Civil Society and the Political Imagination in Africa: Critical Perspectives*, edited by John and Jean Comaroff, 124–159. Chicago: University of Chicago Press, 1999.

Urban Design, Chaos, and Colonial Power in Zanzibar. Bloomington: Indiana University Press, 2011.

Bloch, Maurice. *How We Think They Think: Anthropological Approaches to Cognition, Memory and Literacy*. Boulder: Westview Press, 1998.

Bond, George Clement and Diane Ciekawy. "Introduction: Contested Domains in the Dialogues of 'Witchcraft'." In *Witchcraft Dialogues: Anthropological and Philosophical Exchanges* edited by George Clement Bond and Diane Ciekawy, 1–38. Athens: Ohio University, Center for International Studies, 2003.

Bornstein, George. "How to Read a Page: Modernism and Material Textuality." *Studies in the Literary Imagination* 32.1 (1999): 29–58.
Branch, Daniel. "On Her Majesty's Supernatural Service: Ethnography, Magic and the War against Mau Mau." Unpublished paper. November 2004.
  Defeating Mau Mau, Creating Kenya. Cambridge: Cambridge University Press, 2009.
Brown, G. Gordon and Bruce Hutt. *Anthropology in Action: An Experiment in the Iringa Province of the Tanganyika Territory*. London: Humphrey Milton, 1935.
Buell, Raymond Leslie. *The Native Problem in Africa*. New York: Macmillan, 1928.
Canguillhem, Georges. *The Normal and the Pathological*. New York: Zone Books, 1991.
Carothers, J. C. *The Psychology of Mau Mau*. Nairobi: Government Printer, 1954.
Corfield, F. D. *Historical Survey of the Origins and Growth of Mau Mau*. London: H.M.S.O., 1960.
Chanock, Martin. *Law, Custom and Social Order: The Colonial Experience in Malawi and Zimbabwe*. Portsmouth, NH: Heinemann, 1985.
Chevenix Trench, Charles. *The Men Who Ruled Kenya: The Kenya Administration 1892–1963*. London: Radcliffe Press, 1993.
Ciekawy, Diane. "Witchcraft and Statecraft: Five Technologies of Power in Coastal Kenya." *African Studies Review* 41.3 (1998): 119–143.
Cohen, David William and E. S. Atieno Odhiambo. *Burying SM: The Politics of Knowledge and the Sociology of Power in Africa*. Portsmouth, NH: Heinemann, 1992.
  The Risks of Knowledge: Investigations into the Death of the Hon. Minister John Robert Ouko in Kenya, 1990. Athens: Ohio University Press, 2004.
Cohn, Bernard. *Colonialism and Its Forms of Knowledge: The British in India*. Chicago: University of Chicago Press, 1996.
Cohn, Bernard and Nicholas B. Dirks. "Beyond the Fringe: The Nation State, Colonialism and Technologies of Power." *Journal of Historical Sociology* 1.2 (1988): 224–229.
Cooper, Frederick. *Decolonization and African Society: The Labor Question in French and British Africa*. Cambridge: Cambridge University Press, 1996.
Comaroff, John L. and Jean Comaroff. "Law and Disorder in the Postcolony: An Introduction." In *Law and Disorder in the Postcolony*, edited by John L. and Jean Comaroff, 1–56. Chicago: University of Chicago Press, 2006.
Crais, Clifton, ed. *The Culture of Power in Southern Africa: Essays on State Formation and Political Imagination*. Portsmouth, NH: Heinemann, 2003.
Cummings, Robert J. "Aspects of Human Porterage with Special Reference to the Akamba of Kenya: Towards an Economic History, 1820–1920." Ph.D. diss., University of California, Los Angeles, 1975.
  "The Early Development of Akamba Local Trade History, c.1780–1820." *Kenya Historical Review* 4.1 (1976): 85–110.

da Costa, Rosemary. "The Administration of Justice in Refugee Camps, a Study of Practice." United Nations High Commissioner for Refugees, 2006. http://www.refworld.org.

Das, Veena. *Critical Events: An Anthropological Perspective on Contemporary India*. Delhi: Oxford University Press, 1995.

Davis, Natalie Zemon. *Fiction in the Archives: Pardon Tales and Their Tellers in Sixteenth Century France*. Stanford: Stanford University Press, 1987.

De Hart, Jane Sherron. "Oral Sources and Contemporary History: Dispelling Old Assumptions." *Journal of American History* 80.2 (September 1993): 582–595.

De Rosny, Eric. "Justice and Sorcellerie." Unpublished paper. November 2005.

Deutsch, Jan-Georg. "Celebrating Power in Everyday Life: The Administration of the Law and the Public Sphere in Colonial Tanzania, 1890–1914." *Journal of African Cultural Studies* 21 (2002): 95–100.

Dirks, Nicholas. "Colonial Histories and Native Informants: Biography of an Archive." In *Orientalism and the Postcolonial Predicament: Perspectives on South Asia*, edited by Carol Breckenridge and Peter van der Veer, 279–313. Philadelphia: University of Pennsylvania Press, 1993.

——— "The Policing of Tradition: Colonialism and Anthropology in History." *Comparative Studies in Society and History* (1997): 182–212.

Dressman, Mark. "Theory *into* Practice? Reading against the Grain of Good Practice Narratives." *Language Arts* 78.1 (2002): 50–58.

Droz, Yvon. "Si Dieu veut ... ou suppôts de Satan. Inceritudes, Millérnarisme et Sorcellerie chez les Migrants Kikuyu." *Cahiers d'études africaines* 37.145 (1997): 85–117.

Dundas, Charles. "History of Kitui." *Journal of the Royal Anthropological Institute of Great Britain and Ireland* 43 (July–December 1913): 480–549.

——— "Native Laws of the Bantu Tribes of East Africa." *Journal of the Royal Anthropological Institute of Great Britain and Ireland* (January–June, 1921): 217–278.

Durand, Philip P. "Customary Oathing and the Legal Process in Kenya." *Journal of African Law* 14 (1970): 17–33.

Elkins, Caroline. *Imperial Reckoning: The Untold Story of Britain's Gulag in Kenya*. New York: Henry Holt, 2005.

Ellis, Stephen and Gerrie Ter Haar. *Worlds of Power: Religious Thought and Political Practice in Africa*. New York: Oxford University Press, 2004.

Evans-Pritchard, E. E. *Witchcraft, Oracles, and Magic among the Azande*. Oxford: Clarendon Press, 1937.

Fadiman, Jeffrey. *When We Began There Were Witchmen: An Oral History from Mount Kenya*. Berkeley: University of California Press, 1993.

Feierman, Steven. "Colonizers, Scholars, and the Creation of Invisible Histories." In *Beyond the Cultural Turn*, edited by Victoria E. Bonnell and Lynn Hunt, 182–216. Berkeley: University of California Press, 1999.

Fields, Karen E. *Revival and Rebellion in Colonial Central Africa*. Princeton: Princeton University Press, 1985.

Foucault, Michel. *The Archaeology of Knowledge*. New York: Pantheon, 1982.

Gadsen, Fay. "Further Notes on the Kamba Destocking Controversy." *International Journal of African Historical Studies* 7.4 (1974): 681–687.

Geschiere, Peter. *The Modernity of Witchcraft: Politics and the Occult in Postcolonial Africa*. Charlottesville: University of Virginia Press, 1995.
Ghai, Y. P. and J. P. W. B. McAuslan. *Public Law and Political Change in Kenya: A Study of Legal Framework of Government from Colonial Times to the Present*. Nairobi: Oxford University Press, 1970.
Giblin, James and Jamie Monson, eds. *Lifting the Fog of War*. Boston: Brill, 2010.
Ginio, Ruth. "Negotiating Legal Authority in French West Africa: The Colonial Administration and African Assessors, 1903–1918." In *Intermediaries, Interpreters, and Clerks: African Employees in the Making of Colonial Africa*, edited by Benjamin N. Lawrence, Emily Osborne, and Richard L. Roberts, 115–138. Madison: University of Wisconsin Press, 2006.
Ginzburg, Carlo. *The Cheese and the Worms: The Cosmos of a Sixteenth Century Miller*, trans. John Tedeschi and Anne C. Tedeschi. Baltimore: Johns Hopkins University Press, 1980.
    Clues, Myth and the Historical Method, trans. John Tedeschi and Anne C. Tedeschi. Baltimore: Johns Hopkins University Press, 1989.
Gordon, H. L. "The Mental Capacity of the African." *Journal of the African Society* 33.132 (July 1934): 226–243.
Gray, John. "Opinions of Assessors in Criminal Trials in East Africa as to Native Custom." *Journal of African Law* 2.1 (Spring 1958): 5–18.
Gregory, Robert G., Robert M. Maxon, and Leon P. Spencer, eds. *A Guide to the Kenya National Archives*. Syracuse: Program of Eastern African Studies, 1968.
Grignon, François. "Le Politicien Entrepreneur en Son Terroir: Paul Ngei à Kangundo (Kenya), 1945–1900." Ph.D. diss., Université de Montesquieu, 1997.
    "The *Kithitu* Oath in Ukambani Politics: A Moral Contract in Kenyan Politics." Paper presented at the ASA-UK Bi-annual Meeting, London, Great Britain, 1998.
Guha, Ranajit. "Chandra's Death." In *A Subaltern Studies Reader, 1986–1995*, edited by Ranajit Guha, 34–62. Minneapolis: University of Minnesota Press, 1997.
Hailey, William Malcolm. *An African Survey*. London: Oxford University Press, 1938.
Harris, Joseph B. *Recollections of James Joseph Mbotela*. Nairobi: East Africa Publishing House, 1977.
Heald, Suzette. *Controlling Anger: The Anthropology of Gisu Violence*. Oxford: James Currey, 1998.
Hobley, C. W. *An Ethnology of the A-kamba and Other East African Tribes*. Cambridge: Cambridge University Press, 1910.
    Bantu Beliefs and Magic. London: Frank Cass, 1922.
    "Some Reflections on Native Magic in Relation to Witchcraft." *Journal of the African Society* 33.132 (July 1934): 243–249.
Hunt, Nancy Rose. *A Colonial Lexicon of Birth Ritual, Medicalization, and Mobility in the Congo*. Durham: Duke University Press, 1999.
Huxley, Elspeth. *Murder at Government House*. 1937. Reprint, London: J. M. Dent and Sons, 1987.

Hynd, Stacey. "Imperial Gallows: Capital Punishment, Violence and Colonial Rule in Britain's African Territories, c.1908–68." Ph.D., diss., Oxford University, 2007.
"Killing the Condemned: The Practice and Process of Capital Punishment in British Africa, 1900–1950s." *Journal of African History* 49.3 (2008): 403–418.
Jackson, Kennell. "Gerhard Lindblom and the First Treatment of the Akamba Clans." In *Hadith 2: Proceedings of the 1968 Conference for the Historical Association of Kenya*, edited by Bethwell A. Ogot and Andrew Brockett, 42–59. Nairobi: East African Publishing House, 1970.
"An Ethnohistorical Study of the Oral Traditions of the Kamba." Ph.D. diss., University of California, Los Angeles, 1972.
"The Family Entity and Famine among the Nineteenth-Century Akamba of Kenya: Social Responses to Environmental Stress." *Journal of Family History* 1.2 (1976): 193–216.
Kanogo, Tabitha. *Squatters and the Roots of Mau Mau, 1905–63*. Nairobi: East African Educational Publishers, 1987.
Kavyu, Paul. "Rain Making and Prophecy in Kamba People" (Seminar Paper No. 54). Paper presented at the Institute of African Studies, University of Nairobi, December 1973.
Kenyatta, Jomo. *Facing Mount Kenya: The Tribal Life of the Gikuyu*. Introduction by Bronislaw Malinowski. London: Secker and Warburton, 1938.
Kershaw, Greet. *Mau Mau from Below*. Nairobi: East African Educational Publishers, 1997.
Killingray, David. "The Maintenance of Law and Order in British Colonial Africa." *Africa* 340 (1985): 411–437.
Kimambo, Isaria N. "The Economic History of the Kamba." In *Hadith 2: Proceedings of the 1968 Conference for the Historical Association of Kenya*, edited by Bethwell A. Ogot and Andrew Brockett, 79–103. Nairobi: East African Publishing House, 1970.
Kimilu, David N. *Mukamba wa Wo*. Kampala: East Africa Literature Bureau, 1962.
Krapf, J. L. *Travels, Researches, and Missionary Labors during an Eighteen Years Residence in East Africa*. Boston: Ticknor and Fields, 1860.
Lalu, Premesh. "The Grammar of Domination and the Subjection of Agency: Colonial Texts and Modes of Evidence." *History and Theory, Theme Issue* 39 (December 2002): 45–68.
Lambert, H. E. "Land Tenure among the Kamba." *African Studies* 6.3 (September 1947): 131 147.
Lawrence, Benjamin N., Emily Osborne, and Richard L. Roberts. "Introduction: African Intermediaries and the 'Bargain' of Collaboration." In *Intermediaries, Interpreters, and Clerks: African Employees in the Making of Colonial Africa*, edited by Benjamin N. Lawrence, Emily Osborne, and Richard L. Roberts, 3–34. Madison: University of Wisconsin Press, 2006.
Leakey, L. S. B. *Mau Mau and the Kikuyu*. London: Metheun, 1954.
Defeating Mau Mau. 1954. Reprint, 1977. London: Metheun.
Lewis, Joanna. *Empire and State-Building: War and Welfare in Kenya 1925–1952*. Oxford: James Currey Press, 2000.

Lindblom, Gerhard. *The Akamba in British East Africa: An Ethnological Monograph*. Uppsala: Appelbergs Boktryckeri Aktiebolag, 1920.
Lonsdale, John. "When Did the Gusii (or Any Other Group) Become a Tribe?" *Kenya Historical Review* 5.1 (1997): 122–133.
"Mau Maus of the Mind: Making Mau Mau and Remaking Kenya." *Journal of African History* 31.3 (1990): 393–421.
Low, D. A. and John Lonsdale. "Introduction: Towards the New Order, 1945–1963." In *History of East Africa, Volume III*, edited by D. A. Low and A. Smith, 1–63. Oxford: Clarendon Press, 1976.
Lugard, Frederick. *The Dual Mandate in British Tropical Africa*. London: W. Blackwood and Sons, 1922.
Luongo, Katherine. "A Self-Evident Death? Reading Water and Witchcraft in the News of a Kenya MP's Death." *Journal of the University of Michigan International Institute* (March 2005): 15.
"If You Can't Beat Them, Join Them: Government Cleansings of Witches and Mau Mau in 1950s Kenya." *History in Africa* 33.1 (2006): 451–471.
"Motive Rather than Means: Legal Genealogies of Witch-Killing Cases." *Cahiers d' études africaines* 189–190 (2008): 35–57.
"Domestic Dramas and Occult Acts: Witchcraft and Violence in the Arena of the Intimate." In *Domestic Violence and the Law in Colonial and Postcolonial Africa*, edited by Emily S. Burrill, Richard L. Roberts, and Elizabeth Thornberry, 179–200. Athens: Ohio University Press, 2010.
"Polling Places and 'Slow-Punctured' Provocation: Occult-Driven Cases in Postcolonial Kenya's High Courts." *Journal of Eastern African Studies* 4.3 (2010): 577–591.
Lynch, Michael. "Archives in Formation: Privileged Spaces, Popular Archives, and Paper Trails." *History of the Human Sciences* 12.2 (1999): 65–87.
Mackenzie, Fiona D. *Land, Ecology, and Resistance in Kenya, 180–1952*. Portsmouth, NH: Heinemann, 1998.
Mahone, Sloan. "The Psychology of Rebellion: Colonial Medical Responses to Dissent in British East Africa." *Journal of African History* 47 (2006): 241–258.
Mamdani, Mahmood. *Citizen and Subject: Contemporary Africa and the Legacy of Late Colonialism*. Princeton: Princeton University Press, 1996.
Mann, Kristin and Richard Roberts. "Law in Colonial Africa." In *Law in Colonial Africa*, edited by Kristin Mann and Richard Roberts, 3–60. Portsmouth, NH: Heinemann, 1991.
Matson, A.T. and Thomas P. Ofcansky. "A Bio-Bibliography of C. W. Hobley." *History in Africa* 8 (1981): 253–260.
Maupeu, Hervé. "Les Élections Comme Moment Prophétique. Narrations Kikuyu Des Elections Générales de 2002 (Kenya)." *Politique Africaine* 90 (Juin 2003): 56–77.
Mbuva, James Mbuli. "Witchcraft among the Akamba and the Africa Inland Church, Kenya." M.A. thesis, Fuller Theological Seminary, 1992.
McCollough, Jock. *Colonial Psychiatry and "the African Mind."* Cambridge: Cambridge University Press, 1995.
McDonald, James Ronald Leslie. *Soldiering and Surveying in British East Africa, 1891–1894*. London: Edward Arnold, 1897.

Middleton, John. "Kenya: Administration and Changes in African Life, 1912–1945." In *History of East Africa*, edited by Vincent Harlow and E. M. Chilver, 333–392. Oxford: Clarendon Press, 1965.

Middleton, John and E. H. Winter. *Witchcraft and Sorcery in East Africa*. London: Routledge and Kegan Paul, 1963.

Mitchell, Timothy. "The Limits of the State: Beyond Statist Approaches and Their Critics." *American Political Science Review* 85.1 (March 1991): 77–96.

Moffett, J. P. "Government Sociologists in Tanganyika. A Government View." *Journal of African Administration* 4.3 (July 1952): 100–103.

Moore, Sally Falk. "Treating Law as Knowledge: Telling Colonial Officers What to Say to Africans about Running 'Their Own' Native Courts." *Journal of History and Society* 26.2 (1992): 11–46.

Morris, H. F. and James S. Read. *Indirect Rule and the Search for Justice*. Oxford: Clarendon Press, 1972.

Munro, J. Forbes. *Colonial Rule and the Kamba: Social Change in the Kenya Highlands, 1889–1939*. London: Oxford University Press, 1975.

Mutongi, Kenda. *Worries of the Heart: Widows, Family, and Community in Kenya*. Chicago: University of Chicago Press, 2007.

Mutungi, Onesmus K. *The Legal Aspects of Witchcraft in East Africa*. Nairobi: East African Literature Bureau, 1977.

Myrick, Bismarck. "Colonial Initiatives and Kamba Reaction in Machakos District: The Destocking Issue, 1930–1938." In *Three Aspects of Crisis in Colonial Kenya*, edited by Bismarck Myrick, David L. Easterbrook, and Jack R. Roelker, 1–26. Syracuse: Maxwell School of Citizenship and Public Affairs, 1975.

"Native Research Work." *Habari: A Newspaper for the Nations of the Kenya Colony* 6.2 (May 1927): 3–5.

Nora, Pierre. "Between Memory and History: *Les Lieux de Mémoire*." *Representations* 26 (Spring 1989): 7–24.

Nottingham, J. C. "Sorcery among the Akamba of Kenya." *Journal of African Administration*. 11.1 (January 1959): 2–14.

Ogembo, Justus M. *Contemporary Witch-Hunting in Gusii, Southwestern Kenya*. Lewiston, NY: Edwin Mellen Press, 2006.

Ojwang, J. B. "Kenya: Preventative Detention in Context." In *Preventative Detention and Security Law: A Comparative Study*, edited by Andrew Harding and John Hatchard, 105–122. Norwell, MA: Kluwer Academic, 1993.

Orde Browne, G. St. J. "Mount Kenya and Its People: Some Notes on the Chuka Tribe." *Journal of the Royal African Society* 15.59 (April 1916): 225–233.

"Witchcraft and British Colonial Law." *Africa: Journal of the International Institute of African Languages and Cultures* 8.4 (1935): 481–487.

Osborne, Myles. "Changing Kamba, Making Kenya, 1880–1964." Ph.D. diss., Harvard University, 2008.

"The Kamba and Mau Mau: Ethnicity, Development, and Chieftainship, 1952–1960." *International Journal of African Historical Studies* 43.1 (2010): 63–87.

Osborne, Thomas. "The Ordinariness of the Archive." *History of the Human Sciences* 12.2 (1999): 51–64.

Pandey, Gyanendra. "Voices from the Edge: The Struggle to Write Subaltern Histories." In *Mapping Subaltern Studies and the Postcolonial*, edited by Vinayak Chaturvedi, 281– 299. London: Verso Press, 2000.
Routine Violence: Nations, Fragments, Histories. Stanford: Stanford University Press, 2006.
Parsons, Timothy. "'Wakamba Warriors Are Soldiers of the Queen': The Evolution of the Kamba as a Martial Race, 1890–1970." *Ethnohistory* 46.4 (Fall 1999): 671–701.
Pavanello, Mariano. "L' Evénement et la Parole, la Conception de l'histoire et du Temps Historique Dans les Traditions Orales Africaines: Le Cas des Nzema." *Cahiers d'études africaines* 171 (2003): 461–481.
Peacock, F. "Witchcraft and Its Effect on Crime in East Africa." *Police Journal and Quarterly Review for Police Forces in the Empire* (1929): 121–131.
Pedersen, Susan. "National Bodies and Unspeakable Acts: The Sexual Politics of Colonial Policy Making." *Journal of Modern History* 63 (1991): 647–680.
Pels, Peter. "The Anthropology of Colonialism: Culture, History, and the Emergence of Western Governmentality." *Annual Review of Anthropology* 26 (1997): 168–183.
Penwill, D. J. *Kamba Customary Law*. London: McMillan, 1951.
Perham, Margery. "Some Problems of Indirect Rule in Africa: A Paper Read at a Joint Meeting of the African Society and the Royal Society of Arts." Reprinted from the *Journal of the Royal Society of Arts* as an appendix for the *Journal of the African Society* 34 (1935): 1–23.
Peterson, Derek. *Creative Writing: Tradition, Book-keeping and the Work of the Imagination in Colonial Kenya*. Portsmouth, NH: Heinemann, 2004.
Pratten, David. *The Man-Leopard Murders: History and Society in Colonial Nigeria*. Bloomington: Indiana University Press, 2007.
Rathbone, Richard. *Murder and Politics in Colonial Ghana*. New Haven: Yale University Press, 1993.
Roberts, C. Clifton. "African Natives under the English System of Penal Law." *Journal of Comparative Legislation and International Law*, Third Series 15.4 (1933): 169–175.
"Witchcraft and Colonial Legislation." *Africa: Journal of the International Institute of African Languages and Cultures* 8.4. (1935): 488–503.
Rosberg, Carl G. and J. C. Nottingham. *The Myth of "Mau Mau": Nationalism in Kenya*. New York: Praeger, 1966.
Ross, W. McGregor. *Kenya from Within: A Short Political History*. London: George Allen and Unwin, 1927.
Sadowsky, Jonathan. *Imperial Bedlam: Institutions of Madness in Colonial Southwest Nigeria*. Berkeley: University of California Press, 1999.
Sandgren, David. "Kamba Christianity: From Africa Inland Church to African Brotherhood Church." In *East African Expressions of Christianity*, edited by Thomas Spear and Isaria Kimambo, 169–195. Oxford: James Currey, 1999.
Schapera, Isaac. *Some Problems of Anthropological Research in the Kenya Colony*. London: Oxford University Press, 1949.
"Anthropology and the Administrator." *Journal of African Administration* 3.3 (July 1951): 128–135.

Schumaker, Lyn. *Africanizing Anthropology: Fieldwork, Networks, and the Making of Cultural Knowledge in Central Africa.* Durham: Duke University Press, 2001.

Schnobelen, Jill. "Witchcraft Allegations, Refugee Protection and Human Rights: A Review of the Evidence." Research Paper No. 169. United Nations High Commissioner for Refugees, 2009. http://www.refworld.org.

Scott, David. "Colonial Governmentality." *Social Text* 43 (1995): 191–219.

Seidman, Robert B. "Witch Murder and Mens Rea: A Problem of Society under Radical Social Change." *Modern Law Review* 28 (1965): 46–61.

Smith, James Howard. *Bewitching Development: Witchcraft and the Reinvention of Development in Neoliberal Kenya.* Chicago: University of Chicago Press, 2008.

Shadle, Brett. "'Changing Traditions to Meet Current Altering Conditions': Customary Law, African Courts and the Rejection of Codification in Kenya, 1930–60." *Journal of African History* 40.3 (1999): 389–411.

——— *"Girl Cases": Marriage and Colonialism in Gusiiland, Kenya, 1890–1970.* Portsmouth, NH: Heinemann, 2006.

Shetty, Sandhya and Elizabeth J. Bellamy. "Postcolonialism's Archive Fever." *Diacritics* 30.1 (2002): 28–45.

Shorter, Aylward and Joseph N. Njiru. *New Religious Movements in Africa.* Nairobi: Paulines Publications of Africa, 2001.

Shumaker, Lyn. *Africanizing Anthropology: Fieldwork, Networks, and the Making of Cultural Knowledge in Central Africa.* Durham: Duke University Press, 2001.

Somba, John Ndeti. *Akamba Mirror: Some Notable Events in the Machakos District of Kenya, 1889–1929 A.D.* Nairobi: Kesho Publishing, 1979

Sorrenson, M. P. K. *Origins of European Settlement in Kenya.* Nairobi: Oxford University Press, 1968.

Spivak, Gayatri Chakravorty. "The Rani of Sirmur: An Essay in Reading in the Archives." *History and Theory* 24.3 (1985): 247–272.

Starn, Randolph. "Truths in the Archives." *Common Knowledge* 8.2 (2002): 307–401.

Stewart, Pamela J. and Andrew Strathern, eds. *Witchcraft, Sorcery, Rumors and Gossip.* Cambridge: Cambridge University Press, 2004.

Stoler, Ann Laura. "'In Cold Blood': Hierarchies of Credibility and the Politics of Colonial Narratives." *Representations* 37 (1992): 151–189.

——— *Race and the Education of Desire: Foucault's History of Sexuality and the Colonial Order of Things.* Durham, NC: Duke University Press, 1995.

——— *Carnal Knowledge and Imperial Power: Race and the Intimate in Colonial Rule.* Berkeley: University of California Press, 2002.

——— "Colonial Archives and the Arts of Governance, on Content in the Form." In *Refiguring the Archive*, edited by Carolyn Hamilton Verne Harris, Jane Taylor, Michele Pickover, Graeme Reid, and Rezia Shah, 83–128. Capetown: David Philip, 2002.

——— *Along the Archival Grain: Epistemic Anxieties and Colonial Common Sense.* Princeton: Princeton University Press, 2009.

Stoler, Ann Laura and Frederick Cooper. "Beyond Metropole and Colony: Rethinking a Research Agenda." In *Tensions of Empire: Colonial Cultures in a Bourgeois World*, edited by Ann Laura Stoler and Frederick Cooper, 1–57. Berkeley: University of California Press, 1997.

Tate, H. R. "Notes on the Kikuyu and Kamba Tribes of British East Africa." *Journal of the Royal Geographic Society of Great Britain and Ireland* 34 (January–June 1904): 130–148.

Taussig, Michael. *The Magic of the State*. New York: Routledge, 1997.

Tebbe, Nelson. "Witchcraft and Statecraft: Liberal Democracy in Africa." *Georgetown Law Journal* 96 (2007): 185–236.

Thomas, Lynn M. *Politics of the Womb: Women, Reproduction and the State in Kenya*. Berkeley: University of California Press, 2003.

Thomas, Nicholas. *Colonialism's Culture: Anthropology, Travel, and Government*. Princeton: Princeton University Press, 1994.

Tignor, Robert. "Kamba Political Protest: The Destocking Controversy of 1938." *African Historical Studies* 4.2 (1971): 235–251.

The Colonial Transformation of Kenya: The Kamba, Kikuyu, and Masai from 1900–1939. Princeton: Princeton University Press, 1976.

Thompson, Joseph. *Through Masai Land, a Journey of Exploration among the Snowclad Volcanic Mountains and Strange Tribes of Eastern Equatorial Africa*. London: Sampson, Low, Marston, Searle, and Rivington, 1885.

Thomas, Anthony E. "Oaths, Ordeals, and the Kenyan Courts: A Policy Analysis." *Human Organization* 33.1 (1974): 59–70.

Throup, David. *Economic and Social Origins of Mau Mau, 1945–1953*. Athens: Ohio University Press, 1988.

Trouillot, Michel-Rolph. *Silencing the Past: Power and the Production of History*. Boston: Beacon Press, 1995.

Waller, Richard. "Witchcraft and the Law in Colonial Kenya." *Past and Present Society* 180.1 (October 2003): 241–275.

West, Harry G. *Kupilikula: Governance and the Invisible Realm in Mozambique*. Chicago: University of Chicago Press, 2005.

Ethnographic Sorcery. Chicago: University of Chicago Press, 2007.

White, Hayden. *The Content in the Form: Narrative Discourse and Historical Representation*. Baltimore: Johns Hopkins University Press, 1987.

White, Luise. "True Stories: Narrative, Event, History, and Blood in the Lake Victoria Basin." In *African Words, African Voices: Critical Practices in Oral History*, edited by Luise White, Stephan Miescher, and David William Cohen, 281–304. Bloomington: Indiana University Press, 2002.

Willis, Justin. "Two Lives of Mpamizo: Dissonance in Oral History." *History in Africa* 23 (1996): 319–332.

Wrong, Michela. *It's Our Turn to Eat*. New York: HarperCollins, 2009.

Index

affective states 19, 23, 51, 52–53, 57–58, 92, 129, 130, 140–141, 153–154, 171, 210
    anger 58, 137–138, 202
    envy or jealousy 7, 57
    fear 52–53, 62, 68, 88, 97, 116, 118, 120, 127, 137–138, 142–143, 145, 166, 171, 177, 182, 209
    pleasure 51
Africa Inland Mission (AIM) 42–43, 56, 184, 198–199, 202–203
    Mukaa Cleansings 199–203
    See also missionaries
Ainsworth, John, 38–41, 43
anthro-administration 6
    anthro-administrators 11, 30, 79, 85, 122, 187
    government anthropologist and government sociologist 11, 46, 85–86, 123, 188
    "men-on-the-spot" 72–74, 83, 85, 110–123, 132
    professionalization 23, 84–85
    See also Malinowski, Bronislaw; Schapera, Isaac
    synergy 11–12, 27, 82, 87, 132
anthropology 4, 10–12, 17, 19–21, 24, 26–27, 74, 79, 83–85, 87–89, 96, 123, 132, 160, 187–191, 217
Anti-Slavery and Aborigines Protection Society 23, 116
    See also Rex versus Kumwaka s/o Mulumbi and 69 Others; Wakamba Witch Trials

archives 19, 46, 74, 99, 101, 105, 111, 122, 130, 132, 138, 160, 167, 170–171, 184, 190, 198, 200, 205–206
Ashforth, Adam 8, 18
assessors 79–82, 102, 108, 110, 131, 136, 145–147, 150–151, 207–208, 217
asylum 27, 216–217
atavism 9, 45, 105, 108, 120, 159, 169–170, 187, 198–199
    See also Inquiry into the Administration of Justice in Criminal Matters Affecting Natives in Kenya, Tanganyika, and Uganda/Bushe Commission; *Rex versus Kumwaka s/o Mulumbi and 69 others*

Barrett-Lennard, Fiennes 119–121
Barth, Jacob 101, 128
beliefs
    "real but mistaken belief" 136, 138, 147, 149, 151, 155, 208
    witchcraft 3–4, 7–8, 9, 45, 51, 76, 86, 88–89, 105, 113, 120, 123, 127, 130–133, 137–138, 144, 147–148, 154, 184, 186, 188, 207–208, 211–212, 216
Benton, Lauren 121
Berman, Bruce 10, 11, 13, 38–39, 72–73, 77, 159
Berry, Sara 10
best practice, 23, 70, 85, 96, 131, 146, 155, 160, 166, 187, 191

Branch, Daniel 169
British justice 2, 4, 13, 22, 80, 86, 98, 102, 109, 113–122, 126–128, 130–133, 140, 157
bureaucratization 11, 42, 72, 178, 190–194

capital cases 21, 27, 76, 81, 97, 100, 105–106, 124, 129–131, 140, 147, 181–182
  Rex versus Charo Hinzano 139–141, 145, 149–156
  Rex versus Fabiano Kinene s/o Mukye, Seperiano Kiwanuka s/o Kintu, Albert Iseja s/o Kintu 135, 136, 137–138, 208
  Rex versus Karoga wa Katheni 107, 109
  Rex versus Kimutai arap Mursoi 135, 136, 137, 146, 148
  Rex versus Maganyo s/o Ochiel 139–142, 144–145, 149–150, 151–156
  Rex versus Petero Wabwire s/o Malemo 138
  Rex versus Weyulo binti Kakonzi 139–141, 142–144, 146–149, 151–156
  See also precedent
caravans 26, 33, 37–40
  See also IBEAC
"categories of dangerous persons" 62–63, 70, 89, 196
  See also mu'unde m'uoi; recidivism
Chanock, Martin 13
chiefs 18, 41, 77–78, 91, 107, 163, 165, 172–173, 185, 192–193, 195, 200–202, 204
  See also functionaries; Indirect Rule; Machakos Witch–Cleansings; Simeon Musyoki 185–186
Christianity
  Christian Kamba 189–190, 198–203, 213–214
  idiom of cleansing 171–172
  See also Africa Inland Mission (AIM); missionaries
Ciekawy, Diane 19
circumcision 35–36, 55, 189
  See also uoi
clans or mbai 26, 34–35, 44, 64, 67
  witchcraft 35, 54
    Amutei 35

Atanga 35
cleansing 13, 18, 25, 27, 61–63, 67, 69, 107, 112, 160–161, 167–168, 171–174, 178–180, 184, 186–187, 190, 197, 199, 203
  Coast cleansers 37, 185, 203, 205
    See also magic, protective, "magical water"; witchdoctor
  kivala 63, 205
  ndundu, 66, 69–70, 189, 190
  ng'ondu 174–176
coercion 11, 72, 166–167, 168, 173, 181, 184, 192, 195, 199, 203, 205–206
  See also Mau Mau; violence
"colonial lexicon" 5–6, 8, 70, 91
Colonial Office 20, 23, 124–125, 128, 130–134
  See also Inquiry into the Administration of Justice in Criminal Matters Affecting Natives in Kenya, Tanganyika, and Uganda/Bushe Commission; networks
Cooper, Frederick 11
cosmology
  colonial 18, 45
  Kamba 18, 26, 35, 45, 47, 71, 82, 95, 159, 176, 191, 203, 205
Court of Appeal for Eastern Africa 4, 22, 97, 98, 102, 104, 109–111, 112, 114–116, 121, 129, 135–136, 152
criminalization 5, 15, 76, 91–94, 96, 99, 104, 124, 157
  See also capital cases; Kenya Penal Code; law, criminal; Witchcraft Ordinances
"critical events" 25–26, 45, 47, 51, 70, 72, 159, 184
custom 75, 80–81, 99, 104, 115, 119, 132–133, 140, 167, 178–180
  See also law, customary

de-oathing, 27, 160–161, 167–169, 171–173, 185
  See also cleansing; Mau Mau
Destocking Controversy of 1938 16, 164
  Ukamba Members Association 164
development and underdevelopment 11–12, 70, 82–83, 85–87, 89, 209, 211
discipline 98, 128, 140, 167, 182, 184, 188, 191

Index

discourse 6–7, 9, 19, 71, 99, 130–131, 141, 153, 162, 165, 170, 178, 206, 209–210, 211, 216
diviner 39, 59–61, 63, 93, 214
See also uoi
Dundas, Charles 33, 36, 54, 62
Durand, Philip 180–181

elders or *atumia* 36–37, 40–41, 48, 61, 63, 65, 67, 77, 88–89, 100, 107–109, 112, 163, 192–194, 200, 203
See also king'ole; nzama
embodiment 51, 52, 54, 56–57, 58, 59, 66, 68, 88–89, 104, 106, 123, 153–154
See also uoi
ethnography 99, 104, 110, 130, 167–168, 172, 175, 184, 190
Evans–Pritchard, E.E. 24, 49–50
Expertise 12, 23, 86, 99, 108–109, 131, 133–134, 140, 152, 168, 176, 188, 216
"experts–of–the–local" 77, 79, 81–82, 146–147, 157
See also assessors; translation

famine or *mayua* 25, 32–33, 34, 37, 43
See also rainmakers
Feierman, Steven 45–46
functionaries 44, 79, 81, 88–89, 91–93, 95, 165, 167, 172, 185–186, 192, 194–195, 203
See also chiefs; headmen; Indirect Rule; nzama

Geschiere, Peter 18, 50
Ginio, Ruth 80
governmentality 10, 11, 71–72, 105, 130, 166, 176, 178, 188, 191, 200
Governor–in–Council 4, 102, 110–111, 114, 116, 121, 132–134, 139, 147, 149, 152, 155
"grave and sudden provocation" 15, 18, 27, 111, 130, 135, 136–137, 139, 141–142, 149, 207–209
Grignon, François 68
Guha, Ranajit 102

Hailey, William 74, 85–86
headmen 15, 41, 77–78, 88–89, 91–93, 97, 100, 165, 170, 185, 193, 201

Hobley, C.W. 11, 30, 36, 64–65, 74–75, 85, 110
Hunt, Nancy Rose 5
Huxley, Elspeth 1, 3
Hynd, Stacey 75, 112, 140, 156

Imperial British East Africa Company (IBEAC) 30, 38–41
See also caravans
Indirect Rule 10, 41, 74–75, 80, 82–83, 107, 109, 111, 199
closer administration 159, 163, 165, 187
See also chiefs; functionaries; Mau Mau; "middle figures"; nzama
Inquiry into the Administration of Justice in Criminal Matters Affecting Natives in Kenya, Tanganyika, and Uganda/Bushe Commission 102, 124–128, 130
International Institute of African Languages and Culture, 132

Jackson, Kennell 31, 33, 35
Journal of African Administration 23, 25, 187, 189–191
judicial settings 2, 104, 106, 110–112, 151–152
jurisprudence 4, 15, 22, 107, 128, 129–130, 209

Kavyu, Paul 32
Kenya Penal Code 3, 76, 97, 104–10, 147, 151, 181–182
See also criminalization; murder; oathing
Kenyatta, Jomo 34, 164
Kikuyu 4, 16–17, 43
Kikuyu Central Association, 164
Mau Mau 159–161, 168, 170–172, 175, 187, 196, 198
See also screening
relationship to Kamba 33–34, 43
witchcraft 107, 168, 175, 179–180, 187
king'ole 3, 15, 37, 41–42, 61–70, 71–72, 76–77, 95–97, 99, 106–10, 112, 189, 196, 204
council 15, 37, 61–62, 112
discipline 61–65
family involvement 63–65, 106, 189
law 61–62
parallel institution of justice 3, 42, 66, 95, 97, 110, 112

kithutu 26, 45–48, 66–71, 76, 166, 172–175, 197, 204
  See also affective states; Mau Mau
Kitui 16, 20, 32–33, 35, 42, 139, 178, 199, 211
knowledge 7–9, 13, 73, 83, 99, 109, 125, 134, 140, 145, 160, 184–185
  anthro–administrative 5, 10–13, 26, 30, 71–2, 74, 89, 104, 133, 161, 174–175, 178, 182, 187–188, 191, 206, 215
    See also Machakos Witch–Cleansings; networks
Krapf, J.L. 37

lack 50, 58, 200, 209, 211
law
  and order 3–4, 10, 45, 48–49, 80, 86, 98, 122, 131, 140, 146, 157, 159, 161, 165, 180, 184, 209, 211
  civil 15, 76, 113
  criminal 14, 15, 21–22, 90–94, 125–126, 213
  customary 13–14, 46, 75–76, 78, 80–82, 104, 107–109, 125, 216
  lawfare 15, 191
Lawrance, Benjamin 77
Leakey, Louis 168–169
Lindblom, Gerhard 34, 51, 52, 58, 63, 106, 109
lineage 34, 44, 51, 54
  mbaa 35
  utoi 35
"living in a world with witches" 6, 7, 9, 18, 217
London Group on African Affairs 116, 117–118
  See also Rex versus Kumwaka s/o Mulumbi and 69 Others; Wakamba Witch Trials
Lonsdale, John 10, 38–39, 77, 168
loyalty 162–165, 175, 181
  Kamba Association 163–164, 165
  Akamba Union 87, 164
    See also Destocking Controversy, Ukamba Members Association
Lugard, Frederick 75, 122, 123
  See also Indirect Rule; Melland, Frank

Machakos 16, 20, 24, 32, 35, 40–41, 47, 94, 99–100, 160, 164, 172–175, 178, 184, 186, 188, 192, 198, 210

Machakos Witch–Cleansings 13, 18, 25, 27, 47, 69, 174, 182, 184, 186–191, 196–199
  See also anthro–administration; Indirect rule, closer administration; *Journal of African Administration*; Mau Mau; Nottingham, J.C.; orality; *uoi*
magic 6, 8, 49–50, 53, 59, 168–169, 177–178, 190, 209
  "black" 89–90, 159, 175, 176, 188, 215
  protective 48, 58, 66, 203, 205
  "magical water" 205
    See also cleansing
  state 160, 191
  "white" 89–90, 175, 176, 188
"magical harm" 8, 19, 49, 58, 90–91, 93, 154
  See also uoi
"malice aforethought" 105, 126, 136, 146
Malinowski, Bronislaw 11, 23, 85–86
Mamdani, Mahmood 14
Mann, Kristin 22
manslaughter 105, 135, 137, 145–146, 148, 208
martial race 16, 162–163, 212
Mau Mau 13, 17, 25, 27, 69, 157, 159–160, 164–168, 173, 197
  adherents 27, 159, 167, 170, 176, 185
  cleansing 160, 167–168, 171–176, 178, 181
  contamination 160–163, 165, 173
  guerrillas or insurgents 17, 159, 167, 173, 185
  in Nairobi 17, 160–165, 172–173
  oath 27, 159–160, 162, 164, 165, 166–171, 173–175, 180–182, 185
  witchcraft's relation to Mau Mau 18, 27, 169, 184–187
    See also Indirect Rule, closer administration
McDonald, James 39
medical examiner's form 152–153
Melland, Frank 122–123
  Mwanalesa, 122
    See also anthro–administration; Lugard, Frederick; *Rex versus Kumwaka s/o Mulumbi and 69 others*
memory 26, 191, 199, 205
  "*lieux de mémoire*" 24, 47, 121, 174, 184
    See also orality

mentalities
  colonial 11, 43, 83, 104, 120, 187
  local 8, 15, 105, 113, 117–121, 123, 125–127, 131, 136–137, 147, 169–170, 180, 198
"middle figures" 10, 38, 54, 77, 145–146
  See also "experts-of-the-local"; functionaries; witchdoctor
missionaries 16, 30, 42–43, 184, 198, 200, 213
  See also Africa Inland Mission (AIM)
mitigation 18, 22, 107, 118, 127–128, 129–130, 132, 133, 134, 135, 147, 207–208
modernity 9, 18, 71, 99, 113, 116, 198, 209–210
Munro, J. Forbes 30, 35, 41, 78
murder 3–5, 14, 27, 65, 79, 97, 100, 103–107, 110, 122–123, 127, 129, 132, 135, 137, 139, 143–145, 149–152, 208, 215, 217
  See also "grave and sudden provocation"; Kenya Penal Code; "malice aforethought"; mitigation
muthani/athani 31–32, 38
Muthee, Thomas 214
Mutungi, Onesmus 68
mu'unde m'uoi 36–37, 49–51, 55–56, 61–66, 105–107, 112–113, 174, 176, 190, 194, 196
  See also *uoi*; witchcraft; witchdoctor
mu'unde m'uwe 36–37, 40, 50, 90, 195
  See also healing; white; witchdoctor

narrative 21, 103, 121, 140–144, 174, 184, 186, 189, 198
  testimony 141, 143–144
networks 13, 22, 23, 74, 86, 90–91, 97–98, 109, 125, 130–131, 164, 167, 178–180, 215
Nottingham, J.C. 25, 47, 186–191, 202–203, 206
  See also anthro-administration; *Journal of African Administration*; Machakos Witch-Cleansings
nzama 37, 66–67, 77–79, 109, 204
  See also Indirect Rule
Nzaui/Nzawi 30, 94, 198, 203–204
Newman, Jeremy 31

official misfortune 9, 210

oaths 35, 45–46, 66–70, 71, 107, 159–160, 162, 164, 165, 166, 167, 174–175, 178–181, 190
  See also affective states, fear; cleansing, *ndundu*; *kithitu*; Mau Mau
orality 24, 30, 34, 46, 99, 103, 185, 198, 200–201
oral history 18, 27, 30, 32–33, 192, 194–196, 199, 203–206
  dissonance 192, 206
oral tradition, 30, 32–33
Osborne, Emily 77

Palin, Sarah 214
paraphernalia 7, 56, 59, 60, 138, 139, 142, 144, 173, 185–186, 190, 195, 199, 202–203, 205
  See also Machakos Witch-Cleansings; *uoi*; witchdoctor
Pavanello, Mario 206
Penwill, D.J. 46, 50, 52, 105
Pratten, David 130
poison 52–53
precedent 104, 106–107, 115, 135–136, 138, 146–148, 182, 216
prophets
  Masuku wa Musya 32, 37
  Syokimau 31–32, 37, 41–42
  See also *muthani/athani*; rainmakers
Syombesa 198
  See also Africa Inland Mission (AIM)
publics 2, 3, 23, 45, 110–112, 121

rainmakers, 31–32, 34, 35, 93
  See also famine/*mayua*
reasonableness 135, 138–139, 145, 147
  See also belief, "real but mistaken"; mentalities, local
recidivism 3, 62–63, 65–66, 76, 95, 106–107, 110, 143–144, 196
  See also "categories of dangerous persons"; *mu'unde m'uoi*; witch
Rex v. Kumwaka s/o Mulumbi and 69 Others 98–100, 102–104, 106–107, 110–111, 113, 115, 121–123, 127, 129, 130–132, 133, 135, 137, 138, 148, 208, 209
  See also *king'ole*; *uoi*; Wakamba Witch Trials
Roberts, Richard 22, 77

Schapera, Isaac 23, 86–87
  See also anthro–administration
screening 166, 170–172, 173, 176
  Rehabilitation Advisory Committee 168–169
    "myth of Mau Mau" 169
    "Report on the Sociological Causes Underlying Mau Mau with Some Proposals on the Means of Ending It" 169–172
  See also coercion; Mau Mau
Shadle, Brett 14, 73
Simeon Musyoki 185–186
Smith, James Howard 21, 57, 209–210
sorcery 2, 49–50
spirits 60–61, 212
  aimu 37, 48
  possession 20, 42–44, 203, 205
  majini 214–215
  shrines/*ithembo* 37, 39, 55
Stoler, Ann Laura 19, 166
supernatural 4, 6, 8, 17–19, 25, 31, 34–35, 40, 43–44, 49, 68, 71, 73, 88, 91–92, 97, 98, 128, 157, 159–160, 171, 176, 178, 182, 184, 186, 189–190, 192, 201, 211–213
Supreme Court of Kenya 3, 22, 94, 98, 100, 107, 109, 111, 113–114, 119, 135, 139, 144, 151, 177
  contemporary cases 27

Tate, H.R. 33–34
Thomas, Lynn 14, 25
Thompson, Joseph 33
Tebbe, Nelson 49
Tignor, Robert 30, 42
translation, 25, 79–82, 95, 108–109

uchawi 49, 50, 88, 90
Ueda, Hitoshi 31, 51, 57, 68
uganga 50, 90, 177–178
Ukambani 16, 20–21, 24, 26, 30, 32, 38, 41, 46–47, 52, 54, 66, 71, 73, 77, 88, 96, 99, 121, 160–161, 167, 172–173, 184–187, 192, 210, 212, 214
uoi 5–6, 17–18, 24–27, 36–37, 42, 44–58, 63–65, 71–72, 76, 88–91, 104, 106, 110, 112, 121, 173–175, 181, 184–185, 187–190, 193, 195–198, 200–206, 213–214
  bought 6–7, 49, 53–54, 190

  See also paraphernalia; witchdoctor
  embodied 6, 8, 36, 49, 51, 54, 88–89, 106
    See also circumcision; *mu'unde m'uoi*
  inherited 36, 53, 54–56, 88–90, 95, 190
  typologies 7, 53
    konzeysa 54
    muthea/muti 53–54, 186
    ndia 7, 54, 104
    nzevu, 186
    See also cleansing, *ndundu*; magic, "black"; "magical harm"; witchcraft
United Nations High Commissioner for Refugees (UNHCR) 27, 216
uwe 5–7, 8, 17, 26–27, 37, 42, 44–50, 58, 89, 121, 188
  healing 6–7, 8, 50, 59, 91, 93
    See also magic, "white"; witchdoctor

victim 52, 99, 104–16
vigilantism 66, 76, 105, 196
violence 5–6, 9, 15, 22, 27, 39–40, 44, 96–97, 101, 174, 184–186, 195, 197, 203, 205, 209, 216
  discursive 6
  juridical 6, 15, 42, 71, 76, 78, 95, 106, 122
  sexual 106, 195–196
volition 171, 184, 192, 199, 201, 206

Wakamba Witch Trials 3–4, 7, 9, 15, 23, 25–26, 42, 97, 98, 121, 127, 132
Waller, Richard 19, 22, 91–92
"ways–of–being–in–the–world" 26, 30, 51, 52, 67, 70, 71, 88–89
  Kamba-ness 48, 51, 53, 67, 70
West, Harry G. 7, 18, 47, 50, 52
White, Luise 46
Willis, Justin 192
Wilson, Godfrey 46, 188
  See also anthro–administration; Machakos Witch–Cleansings
witch 3, 13, 17, 27, 36–37, 42, 49, 54–56, 76, 90, 93–94, 96–97, 100–101, 103–128, 129, 137–138, 142–143, 148–150, 173–174, 184, 187, 189–190, 195–196, 206, 207–208, 210–211, 214, 217
  See also "categories of dangerous persons"; *mu'unde m'uoi*; *mu'unde m'uwe*; recidivism

witchcraft 3–4, 8, 11–12, 17, 20–21,
    23–28, 45, 47–49, 71, 88–95,
    98, 100, 103–128, 129, 157,
    160, 173–174, 177–180, 184,
    198–203, 207–217
  accusations 6, 15, 92–93, 195, 209,
    216–217
  See also mu'unde m'uoi; mu'unde m'uwe
Witchcraft Ordinances 5, 26, 71, 91–94,
    96, 104, 128, 137–138, 176–177,
    178, 190, 209
  1909 Ordinance 91, 177, 215
  1918 Ordinance 92
  1925 Ordinance 93, 195
  Legislative Council debates 91–93
  See also criminalization; law, criminal;
    affective states, fear
witchdoctor 15, 37, 44, 50, 54, 58–59,
    67, 90, 93–94, 106–107, 127,
    135, 147, 155, 173–174,
    176–178, 184–187, 190, 205,
    210–211, 216
  debates over state employ 178–180, 182
  See also cleansing

BOOKS IN THIS SERIES

1 *City Politics: A Study of Léopoldville, 1962–63*, J. S. LaFontaine
2 *Studies in Rural Capitalism in West Africa*, Polly Hill
3 *Land Policy in Buganda*, Henry W. West
4 *The Nigerian Military: A Sociological Analysis of Authority and Revolt, 1960–67*, Robin Luckham
5 *The Ghanaian Factory Worker: Industrial Man in Africa*, Margaret Peil
6 *Labour in the South African Gold Mines*, Francis Wilson
7 *The Price of Liberty: Personality and Politics in Colonial Nigeria*, Kenneth W. J. Post and George D. Jenkins
8 *Subsistence to Commercial Farming in Present Day Buganda: An Economic and Anthropological Survey*, Audrey I. Richards, Fort Sturrock, and Jean M. Fortt (eds.)
9 *Dependence and Opportunity: Political Change in Ahafo*, John Dunn and A. F. Robertson
10 *African Railwaymen: Solidarity and Opposition in an East African Labour Force*, R. D. Grillo
11 *Islam and Tribal Art in West Africa*, René A. Bravmann
12 *Modern and Traditional Elites in the Politics of Lagos*, P. D. Cole
13 *Asante in the Nineteenth Century: The Structure and Evolution of a Political Order*, Ivor Wilks
14 *Culture, Tradition and Society in the West African Novel*, Emmanuel Obiechina
15 *Saints and Politicians*, Donald B. Cruise O'Brien
16 *The Lions of Dagbon: Political Change in Northern Ghana*, Martin Staniland
17 *Politics of Decolonization: Kenya Europeans and the Land Issue 1960–1965*, Gary B. Wasserman
18 *Muslim Brotherhoods in Nineteenth-Century Africa*, B. G. Martin
19 *Warfare in the Sokoto Caliphate: Historical and Sociological Perspectives*, Joseph P. Smaldone
20 *Liberia and Sierra Leone: An Essay in Comparative Politics*, Christopher Clapham
21 *Adam Kok's Griquas: A Study in the Development of Stratification in South Africa*, Robert Ross
22 *Class, Power and Ideology in Ghana: The Railwaymen of Sekondi*, Richard Jeffries
23 *West African States: Failure and Promise*, John Dunn (ed.)

24 *Afrikaners of the Kalahari: White Minority in a Black State*, Margo Russell and Martin Russell
25 *A Modern History of Tanganyika*, John Iliffe
26 *A History of African Christianity 1950–1975*, Adrian Hastings
27 *Slave, Peasants and Capitalists in Southern Angola, 1840–1926*, W. G. Clarence-Smith
28 *The Hidden Hippopotamus: Reappraised in African History: The Early Colonial Experience in Western Zambia*, Gwyn Prins
29 *Families Divided: The Impact of Migrant Labour in Lesotho*, Colin Murray
30 *Slavery, Colonialism and Economic Growth in Dahomey, 1640–1960*, Patrick Manning
31 *Kings, Commoners and Concessionaires: The Evolution and Dissolution of the Nineteenth-Century Swazi State*, Philip Bonner
32 *Oral Poetry and Somali Nationalism: The Case of Sayid Mahammad 'Abdille Hasan*, Said S. Samatar
33 *The Political Economy of Pondoland 1860–1930*, William Beinart
34 *Volkskapitalisme: Class, Capital and Ideology in the Development of Afrikaner Nationalism, 1934–1948*, Dan O'Meara
35 *The Settler Economies: Studies in the Economic History of Kenya and Rhodesia 1900–1963*, Paul Mosley
36 *Transformations in Slavery: A History of Slavery in Africa*, Paul E. Lovejoy
37 *Amilcar Cabral: Revolutionary Leadership and People's War*, Patrick Chabal
38 *Essays on the Political Economy of Rural Africa*, Robert H. Bates
39 *Ijeshas and Nigerians: The Incorporation of a Yoruba Kingdom, 1890s–1970s*, J. D. Y. Peel
40 *Black People and the South African War, 1899–1902*, Peter Warwick
41 *A History of Niger 1850–1960*, Finn Fuglestad
42 *Industrialisation and Trade Union Organization in South Africa 1924–1955*, Stephen Ellis
43 *The Rising of the Red Shawls: A Revolt in Madagascar 1895–1899*, Stephen Ellis
44 *Slavery in Dutch South Africa*, Nigel Worden
45 *Law, Custom and Social Order: The Colonial Experience in Malawi and Zambia*, Martin Chanock
46 *Salt of the Desert Sun: A History of Salt Production and Trade in the Central Sudan*, Paul E. Lovejoy
47 *Marrying Well: Marriage, Status and Social Change among the Educated Elite in Colonial Lagos*, Kristin Mann

48 *Language and Colonial Power: The Appropriation of Swahili in the Former Belgian Congo, 1880–1938*, Johannes Fabian
49 *The Shell Money of the Slave Trade*, Jan Hogendorn and Marion Johnson
50 *Political Domination in Africa*, Patrick Chabal
51 *The Southern Marches of Imperial Ethiopia: Essays in History and Social Anthropology*, Donald Donham and Wendy James
52 *Islam and Urban Labor in Northern Nigeria: The Making of a Muslim Working Class*, Paul M. Lubeck
53 *Horn and Crescent: Cultural Change and Traditional Islam on the East African Coast, 1800–1900*, Randall L. Pouwels
54 *Capital and Labour on the Kimberley Diamond Fields, 1871–1890*, Robert Vicat Turrell
55 *National and Class Conflict in the Horn of Africa*, John Markakis
56 *Democracy and Prebendal Politics in Nigeria: The Rise and Fall of the Second Republic*, Richard A. Joseph
57 *Entrepreneurs and Parasites: The Struggle for Indigenous Capitalism in Zaïre*, Janet MacGaffey
58 *The African Poor: A History*, John Iliffe
59 *Palm Oil and Protest: An Economic History of the Ngwa Region, South-Eastern Nigeria, 1800–1980*, Susan M. Martin
60 *France and Islam in West Africa, 1860–1960*, Christopher Harrison
61 *Transformation and Continuity in Revolutionary Ethiopia*, Christopher Clapham
62 *Prelude to the Mahdiyya: Peasants and Traders in the Shendi Region, 1821–1885*, Anders Bjørkelo
63 *Wa and the Wala: Islam and Polity in Northwestern Ghana*, Ivor Wilks
64 *H. C. Bankole-Bright and Politics in Colonial Sierra Leone, 1919–1958*, Akintola Wyse
65 *Contemporary West African States*, Donald Cruise O'Brien, John Dunn, and Richard Rathbone (eds.)
66 *The Oromo of Ethiopia: A History, 1570–1860*, Mohammed Hassen
67 *Slavery and African Life: Occidental, Oriental, and African Slave Trades*, Patrick Manning
68 *Abraham Esau's War: A Black South African War in the Cape, 1899–1902*, Bill Nasson
69 *The Politics of Harmony: Land Dispute Strategies in Swaziland*, Laurel L. Rose
70 *Zimbabwe's Guerrilla War: Peasant Voices*, Norma J. Kriger
71 *Ethiopia: Power and Protest: Peasant Revolts in the Twentieth Century*, Gebru Tareke

72 *White Supremacy and Black Resistance in Pre-Industrial South Africa: The Making of the Colonial Order in the Eastern Cape, 1770–1865*, Clifton C. Crais
73 *The Elusive Granary: Herder, Farmer, and State in Northern Kenya*, Peter D. Little
74 *The Kanyok of Zaire: An Institutional and Ideological History to 1895*, John C. Yoder
75 *Pragmatism in the Age of Jihad: The Precolonial State of Bundu*, Michael A. Gomez
76 *Slow Death for Slavery: The Course of Abolition in Northern Nigeria, 1897–1936*, Paul E. Lovejoy and Jan S. Hogendorn
77 *West African Slavery and Atlantic Commerce: The Senegal River Valley, 1700–1860*, James F. Searing
78 *A South African Kingdom: The Pursuit of Security in Nineteenth-Century Lesotho*, Elizabeth A. Eldredge
79 *State and Society in Pre-colonial Asante*, T. C. McCaskie
80 *Islamic Society and State Power in Senegal: Disciples and Citizens in Fatick*, Leonardo A. Villalón
81 *Ethnic Pride and Racial Prejudice in Victorian Cape Town: Group Identity and Social Practice*, Vivian Bickford-Smith
82 *The Eritrean Struggle for Independence: Domination, Resistance and Nationalism, 1941–1993*, Ruth Iyob
83 *Corruption and State Politics in Sierra Leone*, William Reno
84 *The Culture of Politics in Modern Kenya*, Angelique Haugerud
85 *Africans: The History of a Continent*, John Iliffe
86 *From Slave Trade to 'Legitimate' Commerce: The Commercial Transition in Nineteenth-Century West Africa*, Robin Law (ed.)
87 *Leisure and Society in Colonial Brazzaville*, Phyllis Martin
88 *Kingship and State: The Buganda Dynasty*, Christopher Wrigley
89 *Decolonization and African Life: The Labour Question in French and British Africa*, Frederick Cooper
90 *Misreading the African Landscape: Society and Ecology in an African Forest Savannah Mosaic*, James Fairhead and Melissa Leach
91 *Peasant Revolution in Ethiopia: The Tigray People's Liberation Front, 1975–1991*, John Young
92 *Senegambia and the Atlantic Slave Trade*, Boubacar Barry
93 *Commerce and Economic Change in West Africa: The Oil Trade in the Nineteenth Century*, Martin Lynn
94 *Slavery and French Colonial Rule in West Africa: Senegal, Guinea and Mali*, Martin A. Klein

95 *East African Doctors: A History of the Modern Profession*, John Iliffe
96 *Middlemen of the Cameroons Rivers: The Duala and Their Hinterland, c.1600–c.1960*, Ralph Derrick, Ralph A. Austen, and Jonathan Derrick
97 *Masters and Servants on the Cape Eastern Frontier, 1760–1803*, Susan Newton-King
98 *Status and Respectability in the Cape Colony, 1750–1870: A Tragedy of Manners*, Robert Ross
99 *Slaves, Freedmen and Indentured Laborers in Colonial Mauritius*, Richard B. Allen
100 *Transformations in Slavery: A History of Slavery in Africa, 2nd Edition*, Paul E. Lovejoy
101 *The Peasant Cotton Revolution in West Africa: Côte d'Ivoire, 1880–1995*, Thomas J. Bassett
102 *Re-Imagining Rwanda: Conflict, Survival and Disinformation in the Late Twentieth Century*, Johan Pottier
103 *The Politics of Evil: Magic, State Power and the Political Imagination in South Africa*, Clifton Crais
104 *Transforming Mozambique: The Politics of Privatization, 1975–2000*, M. Anne Pitcher
105 *Guerrilla Veterans in Post-war Zimbabwe: Symbolic and Violent Politics, 1980–1987*, Norma J. Kriger
106 *An Economic History of Imperial Madagascar, 1750–1895: The Rise and Fall of an Island Empire*, Gwyn Campbell
107 *Honour in African History*, John Iliffe
108 *Africans: History of a Continent, 2nd Edition*, John Iliffe
109 *Guns, Race, and Power in Colonial South Africa*, William Kelleher Storey
110 *Islam and Social Change in French West Africa: History of an Emancipatory Community*, Sean Hanretta
111 *Defeating Mau Mau, Creating Kenya: Counterinsurgency, Civil War, and Decolonization*, Daniel Branch
112 *Christianity and Genocide in Rwanda*, Timothy Longman
113 *From Africa to Brazil: Culture, Identity, and an Atlantic Slave Trade, 1600–1830*, Walter Hawthorne
114 *Africa in the Time of Cholera: A History of Pandemics from 1817 to the Present*, Myron Echenberg
115 *A History of Race in Muslim West Africa, 1600–1960*, Bruce S. Hall
116 *Witchcraft and Colonial Rule in Kenya, 1900–1955*, Katherine Luongo

For EU product safety concerns, contact us at Calle de José Abascal, 56–1°,
28003 Madrid, Spain or eugpsr@cambridge.org.

www.ingramcontent.com/pod-product-compliance
Ingram Content Group UK Ltd.
Pitfield, Milton Keynes, MK11 3LW, UK
UKHW040158230326
469255UK00012B/175